FEUDING AND WARFARE

War and Society

A series edited by S. P. Reyna and R. E. Downs

COVER: Higi boys demonstrating the use of adult-sized weapons, 1965. Photo: Keith Otterbein

This book is part of a series. The publisher will accept continuation orders which may be cancelled at any time and which provide for automatic billing and shipping of each title in the series upon publication. Please write for details.

FEUDING AND WARFARE

Selected Works of Keith F. Otterbein

Edited by

Keith F. Otterbein
State University of New York, Buffalo

Foreword by

R. Brian Ferguson
Rutgers University, Newark, New Jersey

GORDON AND BREACH
USA Switzerland Australia Belgium France Germany
Great Britain India Japan Malaysia Netherlands
Russia Singapore

Gordon and Breach Science Publishers

820 Town Center Drive
Langhorne, Pennsylvania 19047
United States of America

Christburger Str. 11
10405 Berlin
Germany

Y-Parc
Chemin de la Sallaz
1400 Yverdon, Switzerland

Post Office Box 90
Reading, Berkshire RG1 8JL
Great Britain

Private Bag 8
Camberwell, Victoria 3124
Australia

3-14-9, Okubo
Shinjuku-ku, Tokyo 169
Japan

58, rue Lhomond
75005 Paris
France

Emmaplein 5
1075 AW Amsterdam
Netherlands

Library of Congress Cataloging-in-Publication Data

Otterbein, Keith F.
    Fueding and warfare : selected works of Keith F. Otterbein /
edited by Keith F. Otterbein ; foreword by R. Brian Ferguson.
    p.   cm. -- (War and society, ISSN 1069-8043 ; v. 1)
    Includes bibliographical references and index.
    ISBN 2-88124-620-6 -- ISBN 2-88124-621-4 (pbk.)
    1. War. 2. Vendetta--Cross-cultural studies. 3. Violence--Cross
-cultural studies.   I. Title. II. Series.
GN497.O77 1993
303.6'6--dc20   93-11752
                                                         CIP

To My Wife

Contents

OVERVIEWS

INTRODUCTION TO THE SERIES

The *War and Society* book series fosters studies of organized violence and its consequences in all forms of society, from deep in the past until the present. It encourages different intellectual traditions from different disciplines. Its goal is to expand theoretical understanding of the causes and effects of war, thereby to provide intellectual tools for constructing a more peaceful world.

FOREWORD

Keith Otterbein may not have invented the anthropology of war, but he did name it, in the title of his 1973 review article (chapter 10). That article was a milestone. Previously, war had been a fringe topic within anthropology, little investigated and not important enough to merit a section in most introductory texts. That began to change in the 1960s, responding to changing theoretical concerns and the reality of war in southeast Asia. Otterbein's survey demonstrated that the anthropology of war was developing into a field of study.

Otterbein's early and sustained interest in this topic is without parallel. The articles included here span a quarter century, and he is still going strong. Even more remarkable than his persistence, however, is his breadth of interests. He is most widely known for cross-cultural statistical investigations of feuding, fraternal interest groups, and the evolution of war, but the reader will find much more than that here. His cross-cultural investigations have been complemented by case studies of Iroquois, Zulu, and Higi, the latter based on his own fieldwork. In these and other works he is concerned with strategy and tactics, an interest which connects him to military studies, and which distinguishes him from many anthropological writers who discuss war as disembodied cultural patterns. Otterbein has continued to review theoretical developments, extended fraternal interest group theory to the study of rape and capital punishment, and commented on the relevance of his findings to the problem of disarmament in the modern world. His latest topic is socialization for war, and we can expect to hear more about that in the future.

Otterbein's interests are not confined to one or a few points, but make up a structure, a house with many rooms. In his preface to this volume, we see the epistemological underpinnings of this broad interest. Most interesting to me is his 1962 "Model for Analyzing Intersocietal and Intrasocietal Relations," based in general systems theory. These days systems theory is out of vogue, unless it is to talk about "chaos." That is too bad. Otterbein's model shows how useful systems theory can be as a tool for organizing concepts and theorizing about complex phenomena, providing an abstract "blueprint" showing how to go from topic A to topic Z without

getting hopelessly lost. Systems theory also underlies two fundamental elements in Otterbein's general perspective: to look at societies and other social groups in interaction rather than as isolates,
with internal and external developments linked; and to see causal
relations as reciprocating, with aspects of war being both cause and
effect of social transformations.

For the last quarter century, anthropology's interest in war has
fluctuated, usually in response to levels of international tensions.
Thus, ironically, the Reagan years were good for the anthropology
of war. In the second half of the 1980s, new studies began to appear
at an accelerated pace, and at present it is almost impossible to keep
abreast of anthropological publications on the subject. Sadly, events
around the world seem to assure that a better understanding of war
will continue to be a pressing need. Much remains to be learned.
But given the gravity of the subject matter, it is vital that anthropologists newly come to the study of war have an understanding of
what has already been accomplished. For those who wish to come
to grips with this curse of humankind, the present volume offers
both an introduction to the anthropology of war, and a useful map
of the theoretical terrain.

R. Brian Ferguson
Rutgers University

ACKNOWLEDGEMENTS

Special thanks go to Steven P. Reyna and Richard E. Downs, series editors, for guiding the preparation of this work from initial conception to final form. Steve, a fellow anthropologist, was the primary contact person during this process. Librarian Charles D'-Aniello prepared the index. My wife, Charlotte Swanson Otterbein, has been intimately associated with every study reprinted in this work except for the two initial case studies. The book is dedicated to her.

"Why the Iroquois Won: An Analysis of Iroquois Military Tactics" originally appeared in *Ethnohistory* 11:56–63 (1964); "Huron vs. Iroquois: A Case Study in Inter-Tribal Warfare" originally appeared in *Ethnohistory* 26:141–152 (1979). They are reprinted here with permission of Duke University Press.

"The Evolution of Zulu Warfare" originally appeared in the *Kansas Journal of Sociology* 1:27–35. It is reprinted here with permission of the author.

Parts of *The Evolution of War* and *The Ultimate Coercive Sanction*, originally published by the Human Relations Area Files Press, are reprinted here with permission of HRAF Press.

"Higi Armed Combat" originally appeared in *Southwestern Journal of Anthropology* 24:195–213 (1968). It is reprinted here with permission of the *Journal of Anthropological Research*.

"Cross-Cultural Studies of Armed Combat" originally appeared in *Studies in International Armed Conflict, Research Monograph No. 1, Buffalo Studies* 4(1):91–109. It is reprinted here with permission of the author.

"A Cross-Cultural Study of Rape" originally appeared in *The Journal of Aggressive Behavior* 5:425–435 (1979). It is reprinted here with permission of Alan R. Liss, Inc.

"Feuding — Dispute Resolution or Dispute Continuation?" originally appeared in *Reviews in Anthropology* 12:73–83 (1985). It is reprinted here with permission of Gordon and Breach Science Publishers for Redgrave.

"The Anthropology of War" originally appeared in *Handbook of Social and Cultural Anthropology*, ed. John J. Honigmann, pp. 923–927

(1973). It is reprinted here with permission of Houghton Mifflin Company.

"The Dilemma of Disarming" originally appeared in *The Anthropology of War & Peace*, ed. Paul R. Turner, pp. 128–137 (1988), published by Bergin & Garvey, an imprint of Greenwood Publishing Group, Westport, CT. Reprinted with permission.

PREFACE

Although war has been one of the paramount concerns of man, its study has been largely undertaken by the warrior, rather than the social scientist. In nearly all the social sciences, including anthropology, only a handful of practitioners have devoted a substantial amount of scholarly activity to studying warfare. From 1961 to the present I have undertaken a number of studies, the purpose of which was to create a greater understanding of warfare, whether the warfare was between hunting and gathering bands or 20th-century states. To this end I have undertaken field, ethnohistorical, and cross-cultural studies. The topics considered range from weapons and tactics to strategy in the modern world. Since 1980 I have expanded my interests to include capital punishment, weapons control, and socialization for war. Theories tested, as well as developed, span the gamut from evolutionary theories to fraternal interest group theory. These diverse studies, which of course stand alone, have a relationship to each other. Thus, the intent of this collection is not only to place many of these publications in one source, but to show the relationship of the selections to one another. As described below most of the studies were conceived as part of an overall research strategy. This collection will show how each study fits into the overall design.

Among the earliest tasks I needed to perform were a literature review, the differentiation of feuding from warfare, the specification of a theoretical framework (specifically, an intergroup relations approach), and the development of a set of concepts for analyzing feuding and different types of warfare. Specific studies followed, including field research in the Mandara Mountains of Northeast Nigeria. As my research progressed I undertook several tasks. I expanded the scope of specific theories. For example, fraternal interest group theory, which was first used to explain feuding and internal warfare (1968a), was later utilized to explain rape (1979) and capital punishment in tribal societies (1986). From time to time I attempted to summarize and synthesize the growing literature on warfare. This task, while not easy, became simplified because many researchers have utilized the concepts and variables that I developed in the 1960s. That is, there is a shared vocabulary. Recently

I realized that many researchers of warfare are utilizing the same theoretical framework. This framework is described in "Convergence in the Anthropological Study of Warfare." I have applied my knowledge of warfare to international problems. In 1980 I wrote a brief essay for a newsletter. I later expanded it for a volume on war and peace (1989a). Since I believe that armed combat is learned behavior, I recently initiated studies of how this behavior is learned (1989c). Is it taught through formal instruction after conscription has occurred or is it the by-product of having learned to use weapons to kill animals (Otterbein and Otterbein n.d.)? And most recently I have related this socialization for war to weapons control (n.d.).

My intent, as stated above, has been to understand warfare. Understanding to me is both description and interpretation. Theoretical studies by myself and others have shown warfare to be related to a number of important variables, including level of sociopolitical complexity, migration history, demography, and social structure (1977b). Because I believe the topic is of great importance — theoretically as well as practically — I have been an advocate for warfare studies. Compared with other major cultural practices, such as the family or religion, the social science literature on war has been scant. Through my publications and personal contacts I have tried to encourage others to study warfare. It is difficult to know to what extent I have been successful, and I will not attempt to ascertain the extent. A major purpose in assembling this volume is to continue this propaganda effort. I would like readers to realize that warfare is an important, vastly complex topic that deserves their attention.

The relationship of the selections to each other and to an overall research strategy can be shown in two ways. Although there is great diversity to the articles and sections from books, there are a number of common threads that run through them. In the next part of this preface, five major threads or themes are identified. These themes are to be found in the earliest selections as well as in the most recent. The selections, furthermore, can be grouped by topic. Under a topic those studies most closely related are found adjacent to each other. The ordering is largely chronological. The topics under which the selections are grouped are the evolution of war, fraternal interest group theory, and overviews. In the last part of this preface, commentaries are provided for each selection; they highlight the central idea in the selection as well as indicate its relationship to the other selections in that grouping.

MAJOR THEMES IN MY STUDIES OF
FEUDING AND WARFARE

In 1961 I selected warfare and related forms of violence, such as feuding, as a topical area for specialization.[1] I developed what philosophers of science call a "research program." It was my intention to make the study of warfare one of my two major research areas. (The other area was Caribbean family organization and the Bahamas.) In the years that have followed, I have seen myself as working from a "blueprint." Other anthropologists, such as Leslie A. White and George Peter Murdock, have done the same (Otterbein 1987, p. 140). My research program has contained at least five major themes. Readers may identify more. The themes, each of which is discussed below, are as follows: (1) Intergroup relations approach; (2) Conceptual apparatus which distinguished between types of armed combat, (3) Developmental or evolutionary framework; (4) A focus on weapons and tactics, a view drawn from military analysts; (5) Methodology employing both case studies and comparative studies.

My research on feuding and warfare, since its inception, has been guided by a theoretical approach which focuses on intergroup relations. In the simplest terms this means that I do not select a single entity for study, such as a kinship group or a political unit, but rather select two or more entities and the relationships between or among them for study. This is an approach which I developed to use in the study of primitive warfare. In other words I first selected the topical area, and then I sought an approach, drawing from sociology and political science, which I thought would lead to productive results when applied to the study of warfare in primitive societies.

---

[1] The following passage describes how I, while still a graduate student, came to select warfare as a topical area for specialization (Otterbein 1977b, p. 706): "In 1960 Newcombe could write that 'few anthropologists in recent years have shown more than a passing interest in the causes underlying war.' In a footnote he continues (Newcombe 1960, p. 317): 'Since 1950 the *American Anthropologist* has published only one paper which dealt specifically with war [I would add Murphy's 1957 article to the one by Newcombe (1950)]... The first twelve volumes of the *Southwestern Journal of Anthropology* have a slightly better record, having published four articles.' It was the reading of this footnote in August 1961 which led me to first realize that my interest in military history, which dated from an early age, could be combined with my interest in cultural anthropology."

By the spring of 1962 I had completed a document titled "A Model for Analyzing Intersocietal and Intrasocietal Relations." The first and fourth sections were published as an abstract in the Spring 1984 *Society for Cross-Cultural Research Newsletter* (12(1):16). The entire document is reprinted below:

A Model for Analyzing Intersocietal and Intrasocietal Relationships

1. This model conceives of the intersocietal scene as a system composed of subsystems, between which there exist various types of relationships. The relationships within any subsystem depend in part upon the relationships that the subsystem has with other subsystems.

    1.1. Within this frame of reference, societies are considered to be subsystems.

    1.2. Intersocietal relations correspond to the relationships between subsystems.

    1.3. Internal affairs or intrasocietal relations correspond to the relationships within a given subsystem.

2. At an initial time certain types of relationships and problems exist between societies.

    2.1. Relationships can range from the type that exists between kindred peoples, that one would not think of going to war with, to the type which exists between time immemorial enemies, whom one attempts to annihilate. The various types of relationships are culturally defined and have to be ascertained through empirical investigation. The various types can be arranged along a continuum, points on which can be labeled: kindred peoples, traditional allies, potential allies, neutrals, potential enemies, mortal enemies.

    2.2. Assume two societies, each with a goal. If the goals are the same, they may be shared (in which case a relationship of cooperation exists) or not shared (in which case a relationship of competition exists). If the goals are different, they may be compatible (in which case a relationship of assistance exists) or incompatible (in which case a relationship of hindrance exists). Problems arise if societal goals are not shared or are incompatible.

2.3. The various problems which periodically arise in intersocietal relations are met with particular means (e.g., diplomacy, war) depending upon the type of relationship which exists between the societies. If there are no means for meeting the problem, new means will be devised or disturbances in intersocietal relations will arise, which may lead to a change in the relationship.

3. The relationships between societies change over time.

3.1. One or both societies may redefine goals and thereby change the problems.

3.2. The means used may consist of the societies trying to change each other's goals or of trying to change each other's society.

3.3. The means by which problems are resolved may result in changes in intersocietal relationships.

4. The response which the society makes to intersocietal problems will change certain internal relationships.

4.1. As changes in intersocietal or external relationships occur, changes occur in internal relationships.

4.2. Changes will occur in the following aspects of internal relations: shifts in power structure; changes in the allocation of resources.

4.3. Changes in internal relationships will affect the manner in which intersocietal problems are resolved.

4.4. Changes over time occur in both external and internal relationships and have an interdependent influence on each other.

The model became immediately useful for studying feuding and warfare. All that was required was to equate the subsystems of the model with political communities — the maximal politically independent territorial unit. An additional step in research was to view these subsystems/political communities as being in many instances composed of fraternal interest groups — localized groups of related males. This allowed the model to be used to study simultaneously both feuding and warfare, by defining warfare as armed combat between the political communities and feuding as armed combat between the fraternal interest groups within a political community. Thus an intergroup relations approach can be used to study feuding and warfare.

The approach includes elements drawn from several other theoretical approaches. **Social structure**: the distinguishing of social units is basic to any structural analysis, whether it be British social anthropology headed by A. R. Radcliffe-Brown or the Yale school headed by George P. Murdock. The basic unit in the intergroup relations approach is the political community, and nearly as important is the fraternal interest group. **Functionalism**: of the many functional approaches, the one embodied in the intergroup relations approach is the idea that groups and individuals struggle for survival. Carneiro's foreword to *The Evolution of War* states the approach well (1970, pp. xi–xii): "in war the test of fitness is applied, not just to military practices, but to *societies themselves*. The ultimate test of fitness, of course, is survival." **Ecological**: the superorganic environment in which a political community competes is of paramount importance. The notion that a political community's neighbors constitute as important a part of its environment as does the territory it occupies is taken from Service (1962, pp. 7, 29). This version of the ecological approach offers an opportunity to study ideas and objects which have diffused from other political communities. This builds in a time dimension and opens the way to studying short-term rapid change or long-term evolutionary change. While obvious, it should be mentioned that the physical environment provides resources and thus gives political communities, fraternal interest groups, and other social units something to fight over. (Of course, they can and often do fight for survival and for non-material things, such as status and prestige.) The two main resources are sustenance and sites for habitations.

An intergroup relations approach not only lends itself to the study of conflict between political communities, but also to cooperation between political communities. The following discussion of alliances is taken from the preface to the second edition of *The Evolution of War* (1985, pp. xx–xxi in original):

> Although information on alliance formation is often absent from ethnographic accounts, making cross-cultural research on the topic difficult, the existence of a few accounts indicates that this is a fascinating research area. Alliances are usually entered into for defensive reasons, yet alliance systems themselves generate conflict. Two types of alliance systems can be identified: an unbalanced or Yanomamö type and a balanced or Dani type. In the former, the lack

of balance or instability is created by triadic, interpolitical community relationships with the following form:

 Political community A is allied with political communities B and C, which are at war with each other. Conflict is generated when political community B attempts to get political community A to break its alliance with political community C by making a surprise attack; political community C is likely to attempt the same strategy. Alliance systems of this type, as illustrated by the Yanomamö, are composed of many sets of triadic relationships, with each political community usually being a member of several sets of triadic relationships.

Balanced alliance systems are composed of triadic relationships with the following form:

 An alliance relationship exists between each pair of members of the triad. (Such a balanced "triad" may have more than three members.) The alliances themselves are at war with each other. Thus a balance exists within and between alliances. But it is only a temporary balance. Although in balanced alliance systems, political communities usually join alliances for defensive purposes, membership in an alliance does not necessarily reduce the need for military forces. In a "world" of alliances, each major member of an alliance may believe that it must be as strong as the strongest member of an opposing alliance and preferably as strong as the entire opposing alliance. Furthermore, if it is not the strongest member of its own alliance, it may attempt to become so. If an alliance becomes militarily stronger than another alliance, it is likely to defeat it in war. The winning alliance itself may then break up, with the strongest political community within the former alliance forming alliances with the remnants of the loser. Twentieth-century European warfare has taken this form. If three or more alliances compose the system, as is the case with the Dani, the strongest alliances may briefly combine to destroy the weakest, contrary to what game theory would predict. (This is my interpretation of the Dani data.) The Dani also illustrate a second kind of situation that can end in the destruction of an alliance. A political community in one alliance secretly joins with the political communities of another alliance and assists that alliance in defeating its own former partners. Internal alliance rivalry is likely to lead to this situation (Heider 1979, pp. 103–105).

With the assistance of Alan LaFlamme I have developed a universe of neighboring societies (Otterbein and LaFlamme 1987). The universe of 736 neighboring pairs of societies is based upon the 862 societies contained in the *Ethnographic Atlas* (Murdock 1967).

The major purpose for deriving such a universe "is to obtain a universe of pairs of neighboring societies that can be used in cross-cultural studies of intersocietal relations and warfare. Several specific problems can profitably be studied with such a universe, such as the following: Under what conditions does a society expand geographically at the expense of its neighbors? When two societies are in contact, which cultural traits diffuse and which ones do not? Under what conditions do intersocietal marriages occur? What types of diplomatic negotiations occur, and with what types of pairs of societies are they found? What is the effect of different environments upon societies that were at one time the same society (i.e., neighboring societies that stem from the same ancestral society through fission)?" (Otterbein and LaFlamme 1987, p. 142).

My research on feuding and warfare employs a conceptual apparatus that distinguishes between types of armed combat. This development of a set of related concepts occurred early in my research and has been retained to the present. Thus, the conceptual apparatus remains the same over time and appears in a number of publications. Although this creates some redundancy, it has not been removed from any of the selections in this collection. (The reason for not removing the conceptual apparatus from any of the publications is so that each selection can be read singly.) The most explicit presentation of the conceptual apparatus appears in "Cross-Cultural Studies of Armed Combat" (1968a, p. 100 below). There the types of armed combat are listed in a Glossary of Terms and a Diagram of Major Concepts is presented.

My research is placed in a developmental (in the sense of change) or evolutionary framework. The case studies of the Iroquois (1964a) and Zulu (1964b) explicitly take into account changes over time, changes that in part came about due to the diffusion of military technology. The comparative studies of feuding, warfare, and capital punishment utilize evolutionary typologies. The differences in military practices among bands, tribes, chiefdoms, and states are always examined. I see changes in sociopolitical organization as occurring because of new military practices, and in turn I see the emergence of more complex sociopolitical organization as a stimulus to the acquiring or development of military technology.

Because of my early interest in military history, I have frequently focused on weapons and tactics, **or** perhaps because of my interest in weapons and tactics I became interested in military history. Battle maps have always fascinated me (for one that I created, see chapter 2, "Huron vs. Iroquois," p. 16). Military historians are often military analysts. They ask the question: Why did one side and not the other win a particular battle? Of the military histories read before 1961, probably my two favorites were by Burne (1947) and Wintringham (1943). Both deal with the above question. The following passage from Wintringham (1943, p. 18), rediscovered a few years ago, probably formed the basis for the method I used in *The Evolution of War* (Otterbein 1970, pp. 38–39 below).

> There are thousands of years of warfare which are governed by simple propositions, such as the proposition that men drilled to cooperate will beat an equal number of men not accustomed to cooperating, or men armored will beat an equal number of men unarmored, or men with weapons that can reach a long way will beat an equal number of men with weapons that reach a short way.

This passage shows one way in which military analysts have attempted to answer the question. My development of the method consisted of creating more "simple propositions" and producing an additive scale (Otterbein 1970, pp. 47–52 below).

My focus on weapons and tactics has been noted by Brian Ferguson (1984, p. 21) as being atypical of anthropologists who have studied war. I agree with his assessment, an assessment which has caused me to look at writings of other anthropologists who have written about war with this in mind. Indeed, I have found that most other anthropologists have failed to provide such descriptions, although there are notable exceptions (e.g., Kroeber and Fontana 1986, Edgerton 1988). The tendency for historians who study war not to focus on battles has been discussed by military historian John Keegan (1976, pp. 27–36). His observations seem also to apply to anthropologists.

The methodology I have employed uses both case studies (field and ethnohistorical) and cross-cultural studies. In other words, my research has been both descriptive and interpretive. In the teaching of methodology I argue that a "research progression" should be followed (Otterbein 1972; 1977a, pp. 197–211). Case studies should be conducted initially to familiarize the investigator with the topic and to suggest to him concepts, variables, and hypotheses worth testing. Refinement of concepts and variables and preliminary testing of hypotheses can be undertaken with small-scale comparative studies that use two or more political communities or longitudinal studies that use the same political community at different points in time. Explicit hypothesis testing then can take place using a large-scale cross-cultural study. Cases that deviate from the predictions of

theories can be scrutinized in a new round of case studies. The
research progression can be diagrammed as follows:

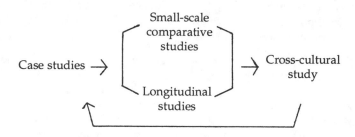

My research on warfare has followed such a research progression.
I initially undertook ethnohistorical studies (Iroquois and Zulu) and
developed expertise in cross-cultural research methodology so that
I could conduct comparative studies using the extensive ethnographic data base available on warfare. I located an area in which to
conduct field research on warfare — the Mandara Mountains of
Northeast Nigeria. The tribal group I focused on were the Higi
(1967, 1968b, 1969). Thus my research on feuding and warfare has
followed closely the research progression described above.

*   *   *

THE EVOLUTION OF WAR

1. Why the Iroquois Won

This and the next article stem from the same research. Both derive
from a study of the major primary source on the Iroquois, *The Jesuit
Relations* (Thwaites 1896–1901). This article focuses on changing tactics. The Iroquois achieved victory through the use of superior
tactics at critical times during the 17th century (p. 1 below); a discrepancy between weapons and tactics gave an advantage to the
Iroquois at three points in time (pp. 4–5 below). Anthropologists
and historians have often cited this article as support for the contention that the Iroquois had more firearms than their neighbors. Although this is true, my argument is more complex — I argue that
the Iroquois used more advanced tactics using firearms than their

neighbors and that is why they won. Five passages have been added to the footnotes. For years I have wished that I had included these passages in the text, since they are the data that, I believe, clinch the argument.

2. *Huron vs. Iroquois*

This article is a companion piece to the first. The battles described in this article were not described in the previous article; "this paper was planned at that time as a sequel to the Iroquois tactics article" (p. 21 below). This time, however, all the important passages from *The Jesuit Relations* were included. I believe they **make** the paper, with help from the battle map. An aspect of the research, not mentioned in the article, was a site visit in 1967 to Ste. Marie (a fort had been reconstructed on the site) and possible sites of Huron villages where the battles took place. Although the research and analysis were completed at this time, I did not draft the paper until the fall of 1977. (A second site visit was made in the early summer of 1975.)

The paper is written in the "decisive battle" tradition (cf. Keegan 1976, pp. 54–62) and employed a style which Keegan refers to as the "battle piece" (1976, pp. 27–54). Studies written in this style impose on troop movements a choreographic quality. Keegan is critical of this tradition and style; he believes the focus should be placed on narrative, what the participants themselves have to say about the battle. If I had read Keegan before, not soon after, the publication of my article, I might have avoided using the "decisive battle" approach and tried to imagine how the Indian participants were thinking. In my defense, I point out that I do quote extensively from the Jesuit priest who was present and that there are no Indian accounts.

3. *The Evolution of Zulu Warfare*

In this article I relate the change from one type of Zulu battle to another to changes in Zulu sociopolitical organization. I extracted from a biography of Shaka based on Zulu narratives data which were quantifiable, primarily casualty rates. Types of battles were related to casualty rates. I was not inspired to write in the decisive battle tradition or create battle pieces — E. A. Ritter, the author of *Shaka Zulu*, had already done this (Ritter 1957).

This article and the first Iroquois article provided the impetus for the research behind *The Evolution of War*. They provided the framework and the hypotheses.

4. *The Evolution of War*

This volume is the only general book on primitive war or the anthropology of war to have appeared since Turney-High published *Primitive War* (1949). Outstanding collections of original papers and first-rate ethnographies have been published, but no authored book pulls it all together. The book resulted from a broad-scale preliminary cross-cultural study of warfare. As the analysis of the data proceeded, it became clear that ecological factors and subsistence technologies had little influence, in comparison with the type of sociopolitical system, upon the warfare variables. Thus, the monograph devoted much of its space to the relationships between sociopolitical systems and various aspects of warfare. Some of these relationships were foreshadowed in the Iroquois and Zulu case studies. Just as those studies drew inspiration from military analysts, so did *The Evolution of War*. The technique of comparing similar military practices and making a judgment as to which one is more efficient derives from military analysts (pp. 38–39 below). Probably the most influential source was Tom Wintringham (1943, p. 18). I believe I learned the method from him, but had forgotten the source by the time I wrote the book. (See Wintringham quotation above, p. xxiii.)

Only a portion of *The Evolution of War* is reprinted here: the original preface, the first part of chapter 1, the first and last part of chapter 2 (chapter 2 constitutes the bulk of the book), chapter 3, and chapter 4. Footnotes have been omitted as well as sentences on pages 73, 85, and 87 (in the original). Although discussion of the various military practices has been omitted, as well as numerous hypothesis tests, the core of the book remains. The reader will learn how the military sophistication scale was constructed and how it was used to test several hypotheses central to the main argument. In brief, military sophistication leads to military success.

FRATERNAL INTEREST GROUP THEORY

5. Higi Armed Combat

This article describes five types of armed combat in Higi culture. The fieldwork was conducted after the cross-cultural studies, reported in the next article, were completed, and hence the article illustrated fraternal interest group theory rather than having played a role in its initial development. The research, however, did eventually play a role in the development of confrontation theory (see chapter 9). I sought in Higi social organization, particularly the system of "secondary marriage," the cause of the armed combat or warfare between political communities. The conclusion I reached was that since any man can attempt, by force or wit, to obtain a wife who is married to a member of another political community, a situation exists in which there is a constant state of animosity between political communities. "Armed combat may break out at any time" (p. 93 below). A Dutch ethnographer, W. E. A. van Beek, who studied the Higi in the 1970s (or Kapsiki as they are called in Cameroun, where he did his fieldwork), made the same discovery (van Beek 1978; 1987, p. 4). His analysis supports and in no way corrects any of the facts or interpretations in my article. Additional information on the Higi will be found in two other publications of mine (1967; 1969).

6. Cross-Cultural Studies of Armed Combat

This article was written in order to put the results of two studies, one on feuding (Otterbein and Otterbein 1965), the other on internal war (1968c), into the same framework. The same tripartite outline is used in all three articles: social structure, political organization, and intersocietal relations. In the article in this collection, both feuding **and** internal war are discussed under each heading. Additional tables and analyses will be found in the two original articles. Any reader with a serious interest in fraternal interest group theory should consult them. The article included here, however, includes more interpretation, and thus contributes further to the development of fraternal interest group theory.

7. A Cross-Cultural Study of Rape

This article shows an attempt to expand fraternal interest group theory to cover another realm of violence. Moderate support was found for the hypothesis that the presence of fraternal interest groups predicts rape. Now fraternal interest group theory was well supported by three studies, and a common predictor of rape, feuding, and internal war had been found. The article also shows how fraternal interest group theory can be combined with another theory — deterrence theory — to produce a better explanation for the occurrence of rape or its absence than either theory alone. The presence of a major punishment in combination with the absence of fraternal interest groups predicts that the frequency of rape is low. This article also, like "Higi Armed Combat," played a role in the development of confrontation theory.

8. Feuding — Dispute Resolution or Dispute Continuation?

This article is an extended review of Christopher Boehm's *Blood Revenge* (1984). *Reviews in Anthropology* encourages authors to not only review a book, but to provide an extensive discussion of the topic. This I did. This review provides a case study description of Montenegrin feuding and hence gives readers an opportunity to view fraternal interest groups in action. The review contrasts Boehm's functional theory of feuding with fraternal interest group theory. In overly simple terms, Boehm sees feuding as controlling conflict, while I see feuding as a process which continually generates conflict. The review provides an elaboration of fraternal interest group theory. Two types of societies are distinguished: "(1) societies with fraternal interest groups have much conflict, feuding, and little or no law, whereas (2) societies without fraternal interest groups have little conflict, no feuding, and much law" (p. 142 below). Legal anthropologists have focused on the latter type. They have also operated with a set of assumptions which, as the review shows, are refuted by fraternal interest group theory. The review also concluded with "A Unified Theory of Feuding and Warfare." This section of the review is not included. A revised version of the Unified Theory appears as the thirteenth chapter of this volume.

9. Confrontation Theory: Capital Punishment in Tribes

Chapter 7 of *The Ultimate Coercive Sanction: A Cross-Cultural Study of Capital Punishment* has been included because it sets forth confrontation theory — a major restatement of fraternal interest group theory. The last section of the chapter, as well as supporting data which appear elsewhere in the book, have been omitted.

I have always seen the study of political leadership as an important topic. A section of my cultural anthropology textbook (1977a, pp. 129–133) describes types of leaders and their degree of power. Yet in my writings on fraternal interest groups, political leaders were always in the background — they play an important role but we do not "see" them. They stop feuds in centralized political systems if their political communities are at war. They mediate in feuds in Higi society. They inflict major punishments on rapists. Confrontation theory brings political leaders forward and makes them part of fraternal interest group theory. Now three parties — the two contending fraternal interest groups and the political leader — are involved in any conflict, not just the two fraternal interest groups. Thus confrontation theory shows more clearly than fraternal interest group theory that the entire structure of society is responsible for conflict.

OVERVIEWS

10. The Anthropology of War

This article from the *Handbook of Social and Cultural Anthropology* was a response to John Honigmann's request for a comprehensive review of the literature in anthropology on warfare. The method I followed in preparing to write the article was to sort the publications in terms of the theoretical approach each employed. When I finished, I had sixteen approaches. The only consolidation I was able to perform was to group them into two major categories: (1) causes of war and (2) effects of war. A reason I wanted to write the article was to show anthropologists that here was a research area that needed much more work. Only the introductory sections of the article have been reprinted in this volume. Four years later, I wrote another review article, not included in this volume because of its highly technical review of several theories, titled "Warfare: A Hitherto Unrecognized Critical Variable" (1977b). I wanted to show that war, as a variable, should be included in research designs.

11. Convergence in the Anthropological Study of Warfare

This unpublished paper contains my intellectualizing about why theories of warfare today are so similar. Compared with 20 years ago, there are fewer theories being strongly advocated, and those that are can be fitted to three components of a theoretical model. It is also an attempt to place my approach in the context of the works of other researchers.

12. The Dilemma of Disarming

This essay puts my research on warfare and gun usage under one umbrella. Four parallels are drawn. I offer an explanation for why there is so much war and killing when most people want a world without war and violence. And I offer advice. Although written in the context of the arms race crisis of the 1980s, the deescalation of the arms race in the 1990s, first by the USSR and then by the US, shows how apropos the advice was and the soundness of the theoretical research that underlay it.

13. A Unified Theory of Warfare

An earlier version of this selection appeared as the final section of "Feuding" (chapter 8). This version, only slightly revised from the original, was an appendix to the 3rd edition of *The Evolution of War* (1989b). Minor editing has been done in order to make the piece stand alone. The main purpose I had for writing this selection was to set forth in the shortest possible space many of the basic relationships which I have discovered. I created Figure 1 because I wanted a "pretty" diagram which would illustrate these relationships.

* * *

This brief summary of each selection, along with the identification of five major themes, has prepared the reader for an in-depth look at the anthropology of feuding and warfare. I hope that the reader will gain an increased understanding of the importance of warfare in human affairs.

References

Boehm, Christopher (1984). *Blood Revenge: The Anthropology of Feuding in Montenegro and Other Tribal Societies.* Lawrence: University Press of Kansas.

Burne, Alfred H. (1947). *The Art of War on Land.* Harrisburg, PA: The Military Service Publishing Company.

Carneiro, Robert (1970). "Foreword" to Keith F. Otterbein, *The Evolution of War: A Cross-Cultural Study.* New Haven: Human Relations Area Files Press, pp. ix–xiv.

Edgerton, Robert B. (1988). *Like Lions They Fought: The Zulu Way and the Last Black Empire in South Africa.* New York: The Free Press.

Ferguson, R. Brian (1984). "Introduction: Studying War." in: *Warfare, Culture, and Environment,* ed. R. B. Ferguson. Orlando, FL: Academic Press, pp. 1–81.

Heider, Karl G. (1979). *Grand Valley Dani: Peaceful Warriors.* New York: Holt, Rinehart and Winston.

Keegan, John (1976). *The Face of Battle.* New York: The Viking Press.

Kroeber, Clifton B., and Bernard L. Fontana (1986). *Massacre on the Gila: An Account of the Last Major Battle between American Indians, with Reflections on the Origin of War.* Tucson: University of Arizona Press.

Murdock, George P. (1967). *Ethnographic Atlas: A Summary.* Pittsburgh: University of Pittsburgh Press.

Newcombe Jr., William W. (1960). "Toward an Understanding of War," in: *Essays in the Science of Culture,* eds. G. Dole and R. Carneiro. New York: Crowell, pp. 317–335.

Otterbein, Keith F. (1964a). "Why the Iroquois Won: An Analysis of Iroquois Military Tactics." *Ethnohistory* 11:56–63.

——————— (1964b). "The Evolution of Zulu Warfare." *Kansas Journal of Sociology* 1:27–35.

——————— (1967). "Mortuary Practices in Northeast Nigeria." *Bulletin of the Cultural Research Institute* 6(1/2):10–19.

——————— (1968a). "Cross-Cultural Studies of Armed Combat." *Studies in International Conflict, Research monograph No. 1, Buffalo Studies* 4(1):91–109.

——————— (1968b). "Higi Armed Combat." *Southwestern Journal of Anthropology* 24:195–213.

——————— (1968c). "Internal War: A Cross-Cultural Study." *American Anthropologist* 70:277–289.

——————— (1969). "Higi Marriage System." *Bulletin of the Cultural Research Institute* 8(1/2):16–20.

——————— (1970). *The Evolution of War.* New Haven: Human Relations Area Files Press.

——————— (1972). *Comparative Cultural Analysis: An Introduction to Anthropology.* New York: Holt, Rinehart and Winston.

——————— (1977a). *Comparative Cultural Analysis: An Introduction to Anthropology,* 2nd ed. New York: Holt, Rinehart and Winston.

——————— (1977b). "Warfare: A Hitherto Unrecognized Critical Variable." *American Behavioral Scientist* 20:693–710.

——————— (1979). "A Cross-Cultural Study of Rape." *The Journal of Aggressive Behavior* 5:425–435.

_____ (1985). *The Evolution of War*, 2nd ed. New Haven: Human Relations Area Files Press.

_____ (1986). *The Ultimate Coercive Sanction*. New Haven: Human Relations Area Files Press.

_____ (1987). "Obituary: Raoul Naroll (1920–85)." *American Anthropologist* 89:1136–1142.

_____ (1989a). "The Dilemma of Disarming." in: *Cold War and Nuclear Madness: An Anthropological Analysis*, eds. Paul R. Turner, David Pitt, and Contributors. South Hadley, MA: Bergin & Garvey Publishers, pp. 128–137.

_____ (1989b). *The Evolution of War*, 3rd ed. New Haven: Human Relations Area Files Press.

_____ (1989c). "Socialization for War." Appendix E, in: *The Evolution of War*, 3rd ed. New Haven: Human Relations Area Files Press, pp. 167–172.

_____ (n.d.). "Weapons Control, Warfare, and Socialization for War" (unpublished manuscript).

Otterbein, Keith F., and Alan LaFlamme (1987). "A Universe of Neighboring Societies Based Upon the Ethnographic Atlas." *Behavior Science Research* 21:141–159.

Otterbein, Keith F., and Charlotte Swanson Otterbein (1965). "An Eye for an Eye, a Tooth for a Tooth: A Cross-Cultural Study of Feuding." *American Anthropologist* 67:1470–1482.

_____ (n.d.). "Socialization for War: A Study of the Influence of Hunting upon Warfare." in: *New Directions in the Anthropology of War*, eds. S. P. Reyna and R. E. Downs. New York: Gordon and Breach (in press).

Ritter, E. A. (1957). *Shaka Zulu: The Rise of the Zulu Empire*. New York: G. P. Putnam's Sons.

Service, Elman (1962). *Primitive Social Organization: An Evolutionary Perspective*. New York: Random House.

Thwaites, Reuben G. (Ed.) (1896–1901). *The Jesuit Relations and Allied Documents ... 1610–1791*. 73 volumes. Cleveland: Burrows.

Turney-High, Harry H. (1949). *Primitive War: Its Practice and Concepts*. Columbia: University of South Carolina Press.

van Beek, Walter E. A. (1978). *Bierbrouwers in de Bergen*. ICAU Mededeling no. 12. Utrecht: Instituut voor Culturele Antropologie.

_____ (1987). *The Kapsiki of the Mandara Hills*. Prospect Heights, IL: Waveland Press.

Wintringham, Tom (1943). *The Story of Weapons and Tactics*. Boston: Houghton Mifflin Company.

Chapter ONE

Why the Iroquois Won: An Analysis of Iroquois Military Tactics

Iroquois military success has been attributed to several factors. These include a strategic position between the western fur supply and the eastern market, a political organization superior to those of their neighbors, access to guns and ammunition, and high morale.[1] In recognizing the importance of these factors, scholars have overlooked the fact that the Iroquois achieved victory at critical times during the 17th century through the use of superior tactics. An explanation of why the Iroquois were a military success will be provided by analyzing their tactics in terms of three variables —

This paper was delivered at the American Anthropological Association meetings in San Francisco on November 22, 1963. I am indebted to Allen W. Trelease of Wells College for critically reading an earlier draft.

weapons, armor, and mobility — which are commonly used by military analysts.

The approach used in this paper is based upon Tom Wintringham's study of the evolution of European battle tactics from ancient to modern times.[2] The development of European military methods is characterized by alternating periods of armored and unarmored warfare. The shifts from one period to another were caused by changes in either the striking power of weapons, the protection of armor, or the mobility of the armies. When weapons became so powerful that they could penetrate armor, protection was abandoned and mobility became an important element. Until armament improved or tactics based on high mobility were devised, the side with the most effective weapons would be the victor. Eventually the pendulum would swing back when armor once again could efficiently stop the firepower of weapons. Wintringham's analysis is useful in studying the military system of the Iroquois because it provides a means of determining which side had tactical superiority at a given time.

The Iroquois possessed superior weapons and tactics at various times in their intertribal conflicts, a point which has not been made by scholars of Iroquois warfare. In fact they take an opposing point of view. George T. Hunt argues that they had little superiority in firearms.[3] George S. Snyderman states that "in the formation of the war party, so in the war journey and encounter, the practices of the Iroquois were virtually identical with those of their neighbors."[4] Raymond Scheele also draws the same conclusions: "The instruments and weapons of war used by all the tribes were similar... Actual fighting tactics were the same for all the tribes"[5] If attention is focused on differences in weapons and tactics at various points in time, it will be apparent that the Iroquois did have superiority during certain periods. The following analysis pertains primarily to the Mohawk, the easternmost Iroquois nation, because the sources for the early part of the 17th century deal mainly with this tribe.

Prior to 1609 the Mohawks and their enemies wore body armor, carried shields, and fought with bows and arrows. The opposing sides formed two lines in the open and discharged arrows at each other. Champlain put an end to these tactics when he introduced the matchlock to the Algonquins in 1609.[6] For the next 25 years the Iroquois were at a great disadvantage because they possessed no firearms.[7] The Algonquins, on the other hand, were reasonably well equipped with matchlocks. This gave them such confidence that they began to increase their attacks upon the Iroquois. In order to cope with the enemy, small war parties of Mohawks would pretend to retreat and thus draw the advancing Algonquins into ambushes.[8] The dissected Allegheny Plateau and the Adirondack Mountains of upper New York State are ideally suited for hiding war parties and staging ambushes. Tactics consisted of rushing upon the enemy and engaging in hand-to-hand combat before the Algonquins could do much damage with their matchlocks and bows and arrows. In these attacks the Mohawks discarded their shields, but not their body armor; thrusting spears and war clubs replaced their bows and arrows.[9] However, shields and bows were still carried on the march, but were not used in a charge. The enemy were probably still wearing body armor and would perhaps have chosen to fight in a battle line if possible. Although the Iroquois were on the defensive during this period, they were able to maintain control of their hunting area through what is today known as guerrilla warfare.[10] Wiping out enemy raiding parties was undoubtedly a means of obtaining needed weapons.

By 1641 the Iroquois began to acquire muskets in limited quantity from the Dutch.[11] These arquebuses, flint guns with better firing mechanisms than the earlier matchlocks, were adopted to the existing tactics. In 1642 the Iroquois attacked a French fort at Quebec; their tactics consisted of charging up to the walls of the fort and firing through the loopholes.[12] In the open field the arquebuses were likewise used as assault or shock weapons. The Iroquois would charge the enemy battle line, fire their muskets at close range, and fall upon the fleeing enemy who had been dislodged from their position by the onslaught. By 1647 the Huron had developed tactics for coping with such an attack. The Huron warriors would form a crescent; just before the Iroquois would fire their guns, the Hurons would drop to the ground; after the Iroquois had discharged their weapons, they would rise, fire their own guns, and counter-charge the enemy.[13] The more effective use, however, of the arquebuses by the Iroquois was in laying ambushes along the banks of rivers for canoe convoys laden with furs.[14] Guns loaded with chain-shot could sink canoes whose crews consequently had little chance for defense and none for counter-attack.[15] The captured furs were used to purchase more arquebuses. By 1649 the Iroquois were better armed than the Indians who were allies of the French.[16]

The extensive use of firearms resulted in the abandonment of body armor and the scattered deployment of warriors. Armor was useless against bullets; and if men were close together, one discharge of a musket loaded with several balls could kill more than one warrior. When the English took over New Netherlands in 1664, they supplied the Iroquois "with still more arms in order to prevent their defection to the French."[17] By 1666 Iroquois warriors went into action only wearing a loincloth and moccasins, for in this manner greater mobility could be achieved.[18] Before the end of the 17th century, Iroquois fighting tactics had changed so much that they were no longer efficient in the use of tomahawks and clubs. Sole reliance was placed upon the sniper who fired from behind any conceivable cover. Their enemies, who were not as well armed, had to continue relying upon war clubs and in-fighting, which gave them some advantage in meadows and open fields, but left them greatly outclassed in the forests.[19] The Iroquois battle line was extended as much as possible: "They separate themselves, as far as each can hear the other's traveling signal."[20] When the battle line advanced, each wing tried to envelop the enemy forces. In order to carry out such tactics, it was necessary to put as many armed men as possible into the field.

The Iroquois were able to put into the field more and larger "armies" than many of the neighboring tribes because they were well supplied with agricultural produce. The Montagnis and certain neighboring peoples depended entirely upon hunting. Other Algonquin groups had some agriculture.[21] The Iroquois, however, were primarily an agricultural people. Each Iroquois warrior carried a bag of parched corn flour when he went on an expedition.[22] "The agricultural people prepared food to take with them on battle forays, whereas the hunters did not."[23] Not only were they well supplied when traveling in enemy territory, but when operating in Iroquoia they were able to draw upon the agricultural produce of any one of the Iroquois nations.[24] Another important factor in maintaining large bodies of warriors in the field was the practice of adopting prisoners into the tribe. Incorporation of captives replaced the casualties in the ranks of the Iroquois army and maintained its size at an average figure of 2,000 warriors for the 17th century.[25]

In summary, an analysis of Iroquois tactics as compared with those of their enemies indicates three periods in time when the discrepancy between weapons and tactics gave an advantage to the Iroquois. The first period was in the early 1630s when the Mohawks were using armor and shock weapons in conjunction with guerrilla warfare, against archers and musketeers. The second period was in the 1640s. Although the arquebus proved to be an excellent weapon for charges only for a few years, it was the decisive arm in ambushing and destroying Huron trade canoes. The third period began in the 1660s and lasted for several decades. Since nearly every Iroquois warrior had a musket by this time, tactics were adapted to the weapon.

In-fighting was abandoned and long battle lines of snipers were employed. The enemy of necessity persisted in using war clubs — a weapon which required in-fighting tactics. Thus it appears that the Iroquois were often several years more advanced in the use of weapons and tactics than their enemies. Consequently, victory was more frequently theirs, particularly in the latter half of the 17th century. The first period in which the Iroquois held an advantage was an armored phase; the second period was a transitional phase; the third period was an unarmored phase.

In conclusion, the above analysis of the evolution of Iroquois military practices has demonstrated the feasibility of using concepts, variables, and theories derived from the analysis of Western military history, for an understanding of the military success of a so-called primitive people.

NOTES

1. Trelease, "The Iroquois and the Western Fur Trade," p. 51.
2. Wintringham, *The Story of Weapons and Tactics.*
3. Hunt, *The Wars of the Iroquois*, pp. 9–10, 165–175.
4. Snyderman, *Behind the Tree of Peace*, p. 56.
5. Scheele, Warfare of the Iroquois, pp. 83 84.
6. Russell, in *Guns on the Early Frontiers*, quotes Champlain (pp. 2–3): "I saw the enemy come out of their barricade to the number of two hundred, in appearance strong, robust men. They came slowly to meet us with a gravity and calm which I admired; and at their head were three chiefs. Our Indians likewise advanced in similar order... Our Indians put me ahead some twenty yards, and I marched on until I was within thirty yards of the enemy, who as soon as they caught sight of me halted and gazed at me and I at them. When I saw them make a move to draw their bows upon us, I took aim with my arquebus and shot straight at one of the three chiefs, and with this shot two fell to the ground and one of their companions was wounded who died thereof a little later. I had put four bullets into my arquebus... The Iroquois were much astonished that two men should have been killed so quickly, although they were provided with shields made of cotton thread woven together and wood, which were proof against their arrows."
7. Hunt, *Wars of the Iroquois*, p. 167.
8. Colden, *History*, pp. 7–9.
9. Wood writes in his *New-England's Prospect*, in 1634, of the Iroquois in their wars on the Algonquians of New England (pp. 65–67): "These

Indians be more desperate in wars than the other Indians; which proceeds not only from the fierceness of their natures, but also in the fact that they know themselves to be better armed and weaponed; all of them wearing sea-horse skins and barks of trees, made by their art as impenetrable, it is thought, as steel, wearing head pieces of the same, under which they march securely and undauntedly, running and fiercely crying out..., not fearing the feathered shafts of the strong-armed bowmen, but like unruly, headstrong stallions, beat them down with their right-hand tomahawks and left-hand javelins, being all the weapons they use, counting bows a cowardly fight. Tomahawks be staves of two and a half long and a knob at the end as round and big as a football; a javelin is a short spear, headed with sharp sea-horse teeth; one blow, or thrust, with these strange weapons will not need a second to hasten death from a Mohawk's arms."

10. Scheele, *Warfare of the Iroquois*, pp. 15–17.

11. Hunt, *Wars of the Iroquois*, p. 169.

12. The attack is described in *The Jesuit Relations* (Vol. 22, pp. 277–279): "The Barbarians divided themselves into three parties, and ... they rushed upon us with so unusual fury that it seemed as if they would carry everything at the first onset... The balls from the muskets and arquebuses whistle on all sides ... but their attack was bravely repelled... One of these, who was severely wounded, threw down his arquebus and fled; another abandoned all his weapons; several dropped their shields, trusting more to their feet for safety than to their bucklers [small round shields]... Our soldiers praised their bravery, not thinking that people who are called Savages could use their arms so well ... some fired into the redout through the very loopholes."

13. According to *The Jesuit Relations* (Vol. 32, p. 181), the Hurons formed a "crescent to meet the first assault of the enemy the Iroquois, and hem them in should they come to blows and lance thrusts... When almost close enough to scorch their doublets..., they fired a volley from their arquebuses, which our Hurons received lying on the ground; after delivering their volley, they charged, not expecting to meet with so much resistance. But the Hurons rose and uttering loud yells, they received their enemies with heavy discharges from their pieces; those poor savages were taken by surprise, and fled in every direction, with the exception of one squad who tried to defend themselves with knives, but they were soon surrounded by our people. And, if the Hurons at the base of the crescent had not given away at the first report of the arquebuses, not one of the enemy would have escaped; but those cowards left open a door by which many got away."

14. Ibid., Vol. 20, pp. 269, 307.

15. Colden, *History*, p. 9.

16. Hunt, *Wars of the Iroquois*, pp. 174–175.

17. Trelease, *Indian Affairs in Colonial New York*, p. 24.
18. Snyderman, *Behind the Tree of Peace*, p. 64.
19. In La Hontan's day, a little before and after 1700, or about seven decades later than Wood, the Iroquois had lost the art of tomahawk fighting while other Indians retained it. La Hontan writes (*New Voyages to North America*, Vol. 2, pp. 497, 498, 501): "The Iroquois have this advantage over their enemies, that they are all armed with good fire-locks; whereas the others, who use these engines only for the shooting of beasts, have not above half their number provided with them... [The Iroquois] are not so spritely as most of their enemies, nor so happy in fighting with clubs; and it is for that reason that they never march but in numerous bodies, and that, by slower marches than those of the other savages... The strength of the Iroquois lies in engaging with firearms in a forest; for they shoot very dexterously; besides that they are very well-versed in making the best advantage of everything, by covering themselves with trees, behind which they stand stock-still after they have discharged, though their enemies be twice their number. But in regard that they are more clumsy and not so clever as the more southern Americans they have no dexterity in handling a club; and thus it comes to pass that they are always worsted in open field, where the clubs are the only weapons; for which reason they avoid any engagement in meadows or open fields as much as possible."
20. Snyderman, *Behind the Tree of Peace*, p. 57.
21. Hadlock, "War Among the Northeastern Woodland Indians," p. 210.
22. Snyderman, *Behind the Tree of Peace*, p. 49.
23. Scheele, *Warfare of the Iroquois*, p. 82.
24. Quain, "The Iroquois", p. 254.
25. Snyderman, *Behind the Tree of Peace*, p. 41.

REFERENCES

Colden, Cadwallader (1958). *The History of the Five Indian Nations: Depending on the Province of New York in America*. Ithaca: Cornell University Press.

Hadlock, Wendell S. (1947). "War Among the Northeastern Woodland Indians." *American Anthropologist* 49:204–221.

Hunt, George T. (1940). *The Wars of the Iroquois: A Study in Intertribal Trade Relations*. Madison: The University of Wisconsin Press.

La Hontan, Baron de (1905). *New Voyages to North America*, 2 Vols., ed. R. G. Thwaites. Chicago: Burrows.

Quain, Buell H. (1937). "The Iroquois," in: *Cooperation and Competition Among Primitive Peoples*, ed. Margaret Mead. New York: McGraw-Hill Book Company, pp. 240–281.

Russell, Carl P. (1957). *Guns on the Early Frontiers.* Berkeley: University of California Press.

Scheele, Raymond (1950). *Warfare of the Iroquois and Their Northern Neighbors.* PhD dissertation, Columbia University.

Snyderman, George S. (1948). *Behind the Tree of Peace: A Sociological Analysis of Iroquois Warfare.* Philadelphia: University of Pennsylvania Press.

Thwaites, Reuben G. (Ed.) (1896–1901). *The Jesuit Relations and Allied Documents ... 1610–1791,* 73 Vols. Cleveland: Burrows.

Trelease, Allen W. (1960). *Indian Affairs in Colonial New York: The Seventeenth Century.* Ithaca: Cornell University Press.

——————— (1962). "The Iroquois and the Western Fur Trade: A Problem in Interpretation." *The Mississippi Valley Historical Review* 49:32–51.

Wintringham, Tom (1943). *The Story of Weapons and Tactics: From Troy to Stalingrad.* Boston: Houghton Mifflin Company.

Wood, William (1865). *Wood's New-England's Prospect, 1634.* Boston: Publication of the Prince Society.

Chapter
TWO

Huron vs. Iroquois:
A Case Study in
Intertribal Warfare[1]

The final military engagement between the Iroquois and the
Huron is described and analyzed in detail. In March 1649 the
Iroquois dealt the Huron a devastating defeat and the entire
Huron nation fled Huronia. A battle-by-battle account describes
the maneuvers of each nation, and maps depict the movements of
forces on the battlefields. The analysis points out that the Huron
were vulnerable because they had isolated villages, isolated in
terms of space, communications, and military practices. Furthermore, the manner in which the Iroquois were able to use their
forces was militarily more sophisticated. But perhaps most importantly, the Hurons made the serious error of committing their
warriors piecemeal to battle. If they had been able to concentrate
their forces and thereby take advantage of a tactical error made by
the Iroquois, they might have been able to defeat the Iroquois
both in 1649 and in subsequent wars.

INTRODUCTION

In 1649 one of the most important battles ever fought on the North American continent took place near Georgian Bay. The antagonists were not European armies but the armies of two Indian nations — the Huron and the Iroquois. In March of that year the Iroquois invaded Huronland or Huronia, and launched a surprise attack upon the unprepared Huron. The battles that followed constitute the "Iroquois Campaign of 1649." This paper will describe and analyze this important military campaign which was experienced and sometimes observed by French Jesuit priests residing in Huronia. *The Jesuit Relations* contains a report by Father Paul Ragueneau (Thwaites 1899, Vol. 34, pp. 123–137), who was an eyewitness to some aspects of the campaign. His description of the battles is detailed enough to permit drawing battlefield maps of a kind found in military histories. A military analysis of the battles demonstrates why the Iroquois won and the Huron lost; the analysis also shows how the Huron might have won. The conclusions drawn have implications for the various analyses of why the Huron were defeated and dispersed by the Iroquois. I will also speculate as to what would have happened if the Huron had defeated the Iroquois in 1649.

Previous studies of the Huron and Iroquois have analyzed the background to the campaign and the aftermath, but they have not analyzed the battles and the campaign itself.[2] My own study of Iroquois warfare (1964), which focuses on weapons and tactics, omits from consideration these important battles.[3] The major works on the Huron and Iroquois give short and sometimes inaccurate treatment to the campaign. Hunt, in *The Wars of the Iroquois*, devotes only two paragraphs to the entire campaign (1940, pp. 92–93). Furthermore, the battles are inaccurately described.[4] Tooker, in a review of the causes of the Iroquois defeat of the Huron, simply states (1963, p. 116): "In March of 1649, they [the Iroquois] attacked again, destroying two more villages before being repulsed at St. Marie [the Jesuit mission]." Forbes, who reviews Iroquois warfare over a two-century period, deals with the campaign in these words (1970, p. 18): "In 1649 the inevitable happened. The Iroquois fell upon the Hurons, and the powerful, affluent Confederacy crumpled overnight." Heidenreich's comprehensive work, *Huronia*, devotes one short inaccurate paragraph to the campaign, which describes the most important battle as a "few skirmishes with a Huron force" (1971, p. 275). Trigger, in his two-volume ethnohistory of the Hurons, uses four pages to describe the campaign, providing an accurate summary of Father Ragueneau's report (1976, pp. 762–766).[5]

Since the Iroquois campaign of 1649 has apparently not been adequately described and analyzed from a military point of view, the following section provides descriptions of the battles taken from the English translation of Father Ragueneau's report; his descriptions have not been paraphrased in order to prevent the introduction into the account of slight distortions of meaning. The section begins with an outline of military activities which occurred during the previous summer. Next, each battle and the Iroquois retreat are described in detail. The schematic map is a visual rendering of each battle composing the campaign.

IROQUOIS CAMPAIGN OF 1649

Military activities during the summer of 1648 seem to occur almost entirely within the territory controlled by the Attingneenongnahac, one of the five Huron tribes. This tribe consisted of two major villages: St. Joseph (Teanaostaiae) and St. Ignace (Taenhatentaron).[6] The villages lay on a north–south line, about seven miles apart, with St. Joseph being the southernmost village. In the early spring of 1648 the Iroquois made two attacks upon hunters from St. Ignace, who were two days' journey from their village (Thwaites 1899, Vol. 33, pp. 83–89). Of far greater seriousness, however, was the attack in July upon St. Joseph (Thwaites 1899, Vol. 34, p. 87):

> Last summer, in the past year, 1648, the Iroquois, enemies of the Hurons, took from them two frontier villages, from which most of the defenders had gone forth, — some for the chase, and others for purposes of war, in which they could meet no success. These two frontier places composed the Mission which we named for St. Joseph; the principal of these villages contained about 400 families.

The second, smaller, village was probably Ekhiondastsaan. Clearly, the remaining half of this tribe was in a state of fear.

Battle 1

The initial Iroquois attack in the spring of 1649 came suddenly and without warning before dawn on March 16 at the village of St. Ignace (Thwaites 1899, Vol. 34, pp. 123–125):

The Iroquois ... to the number of about a thousand men, well furnished with weapons, — and mostly with firearms ... arrived by night at the frontier of this country, without our having had any knowledge of their approach: although they had started from their country in the Autumn, hunting in the forests throughout the Winter, and had made over the snow nearly two hundred leagues of a very difficult road, in order to come and surprise us. They reconnoitered by night the condition of the first place, upon which they had designs, — which was surrounded with a stockade of pinetrees, from fifteen to sixteen feet in height, and with a deep ditch, wherewith nature had strongly fortified this place on three sides, — there remaining only a little space which was weaker than the others.

It was at this point that the enemy made a breach at daybreak, but so secretly and promptly that he was master of the place before people had put themselves on the defensive, — all being then in a deep sleep... Thus this village was taken, almost without striking a blow, there having been only ten Iroquois killed. Part of the Hurons — men, women, and children — were massacred then and there: the others were made captives...

Three men alone escaped, almost naked, across the snows: they bore the alarm and terror to another and neighboring village, a league distant. This first village was the one which we called Saint Ignace, which had been abandoned by most of its people at the beginning of the Winter, — the most apprehensive and most clear-sighted having withdrawn from it, foreboding the danger: thus the loss of it was not so considerable, and amounted only to about four hundred souls.

Battle 2

The second attack that morning came at the Ataronchronnon village of St. Louis (Thwaites 1899, Vol. 34, pp. 125–131):

The enemy does not stop there: he follows up his victory, and before Sunrise he appears in arms to attack the village of Saint Louÿs, which was fortified with a fairly good stockade. Most of the women, and the children [more than 500 persons], had just come from it, upon hearing the news which had arrived regarding the approach of the Iroquois. The people of most courage, about eighty persons, being resolved to defend themselves well, repulse with courage the first and the second assault, having killed among the enemy some thirty of their most venturesome men, besides many wounded. But, finally, number has the advantage, — the Iroquois having undermined with blows of their hatchets the palisade of stakes, and having made a passage for themselves through considerable breaches.

Toward nine o'clock in the morning, we perceived from our house at Sainte Marie the fire which was consuming the cabins of that village, where the enemy, having entered victoriously, had reduced everything to desolation...

The Iroquois having dealt their blow, and wholly reduced to fire the village of Saint Louys, retraced their steps into that of Saint Ignace, where they had left a good garrison, that it might be for them a sure retreat in case of misfortune, and that the victuals which they had found there might serve them as refreshments and provisions for their return.

On the evening of the same day, they sent scouts to reconnoiter the condition of our house at Sainte Marie: their report having been made in the Council of war, the decision was adopted to come and attack us the next morning, — promising themselves a victory which would be more glorious to them than all the successes of their arms in the past.

Battle 3

Hostilities on the morning of the second day of battle, March 17, began between the now destroyed village of St. Louis and the French Jesuit fort of St. Marie. The Huron warriors, who were apparently attempting to defend St. Marie, were from a third tribe, the Attig-nawantan (Thwaites 1899, Vol. 34, pp. 131–135):

Meanwhile, a part of the Hurons, who are called Atinniaoenten ... having armed in haste, were at hand the next morning, the seventeenth of March, about three hundred warriors, — who, while awaiting a more powerful help, secreted themselves in the ways of approach, intending to surprise some portion of the enemy.

About two hundred Iroquois having detached themselves from the main body, in order to get the start and proceed to the attack of our house, encountered some advance-guards of that Huron troop. The latter straightway took flight after some skirmishing, and were eagerly pursued until within sight of our fort, — many having been killed while they were in disorder in the midst of the snows. But the more courageous of the Hurons, having stood firm against those who joined combat with them, had some advantage on their side, and constrained the Iroquois to take refuge within the palisades of the village of Saint Louys, — which had not been burned, but only the cabins. These Iroquois were forced into that palisade, and about thirty of them were taken captives.

The main body of the enemy, having heard of the defeat of their men, came to attack our people in the very midst of their victory. Our men were ... only about one hundred and fifty. They proceed to ...

sustain the assault of a place which, having been so recently captured and recaptured, was no longer adequate for defense. The shock was furious on both sides, — our people having made many sallies, notwithstanding their small number, and having often constrained the enemy to give way. But, — the combat having continued quite far into the night, — as not more than a score of Christians, mostly wounded, were left, the victory remained wholly in the hands of the Infidels. It had, however, cost them very dear, as their Chief had been seriously wounded, and had lost nearly a hundred men on the spot, of their best and most courageous.

Retreat

No fighting took place the next day, March 18. On March 19 the Iroquois retreated: they were pursued but not overtaken by the warriors of a fourth Huron tribe (Thwaites 1899, Vol. 34, pp. 135–137):

The whole day passed in a profound silence on both sides, — the country being in terror and in the expectation of some new misfortune. On the nineteenth, ... a sudden panic fell upon the hostile camp, — some withdrawing in disorder, and others thinking only of flight. Their Captains were constrained to yield to the terror which had seized them; they precipitated their retreat, driving forth in haste a part of their captives, who were burdened above their strength, like packhorses, with the spoils which the victorious were carrying off...

An old woman, escaped from the midst of that fire, bore the news of it to the village of Saint Michel [the only Tahontaenrat settlement, approximately seven miles to the southwest], where there were about seven hundred men in arms, who charged upon the enemy; but, not having been able to overtake him after two days' march, partly the want of provisions, partly the dread of combatting without advantage an enemy encouraged by his victories, and one who had mostly firearms, of which our Hurons have very few, — all these things obliged them to retrace their steps, without having done aught...

As for the other captives who were left to them, destined to die on the spot, they attached them to stakes fastened in the earth, which they had arranged in various cabins. To these, on leaving the village, they set fire on all sides.

ANALYSIS

The first hostilities of the Iroquois campaign of 1649 took place in the early hours of March 16 with a surprise attack upon St. Ignace. The Iroquois continued their initiative with an attack upon St. Louis.

With these two successful attacks, the Iroquois demonstrated first rate military ability both from a strategic and tactical point of view. Strategically, the decision to attack St. Ignace, the second and remaining large village of the Attingneenongnahac tribe, was seemingly deliberate, and as events turned out, a wise choice. The people of St. Ignace were already in a state of fear because of the attacks upon their hunting parties in the early spring of 1648 and because of the destruction of St. Joseph, the other large Attingneenongnahac village, that summer. The attack, thus, was upon a people already weakened by war. Furthermore, the location of St. Ignace on the eastern frontier of Huronia and approximately six miles from the Jesuit mission at St. Marie, placed them in a position to launch an attack then or in the future upon the Jesuit mission.[7] This surprise attack into the heart of Huronia bypassed the large and militarily strong village of St. Michael, which lay to the southwest. The attack upon St. Louis brought them even closer to the French fort, which appears to have been the major object of the campaign. Tactically, the ability to concentrate their entire force of 1,000 warriors for a surprise attack upon one village, and then to follow this up with an attack upon a second village, leaving behind only a garrison to secure the first village captured, meets every "principle of war" identified by great generals and military analysts (see p. 19 below).

There was probably no way the Huron could have prevented the attack upon or the destruction of St. Ignace. Even modern armies and navies with sophisticated electronic equipment are vulnerable to surprise attack. However, three refugees from St. Ignace warned the people of St. Louis of a possible impending attack: more than 500 left the village, but eighty remained to fight the Iroquois. They were so completely outnumbered that even their great courage and their well palisaded village could not prevent their defeat.[8] From a military point of view, the Hurons probably should not have tried to defend St. Louis, although it can be argued that the second battle blunted the Iroquois initiative and prevented an attack on St. Marie that day. The Huron defenders, including the two Jesuit priests who remained with them, probably did not know the size of the Iroquois force, and hence possibly believed they had a chance to repel the attack.

On the second day of battle, the Iroquois launched an attack upon St. Marie. Perhaps because of overconfidence, an advance guard of 200 warriors headed toward St. Marie while the remainder of their force apparently stayed at St. Ignace. This was a serious tactical error. By dividing their force the Iroquois created a situation which permitted a Huron army of 300 warriors to defeat their advance guard.

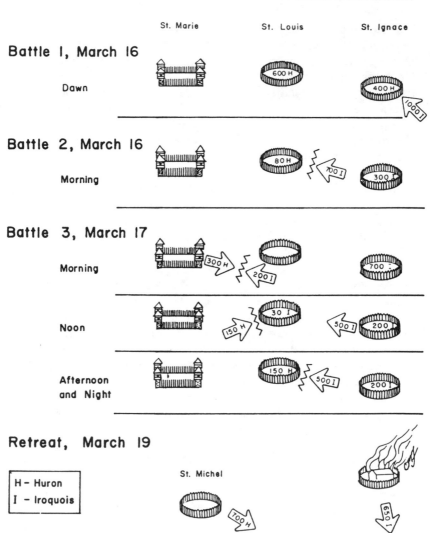

Figure 1. Iroquois campaign of 1649.

The defeat of the 200 Iroquois outside the walls of St. Marie and at St. Louis would not have occurred if the main body had been shortly behind the advance guard. (*The Jesuit Relations* imply that the "main body" was not far behind; however, at least two hours of fighting must have taken place before the main body joined the battle.) Military analysts would describe the situation as one in which the

Iroquois had divided their forces and permitted the enemy to defeat a section of their entire army. To "defeat in detail" is the classic tactic or maneuver used by great generals to defeat an enemy which greatly outnumbers them.

This division of their forces was an error which could have been fatal to the Iroquois if the Huron had not also erred. The Huron advance guard of 300 warriors, many from Ossossane (Trigger 1976, p. 764), was expecting support, presumably from other Attignawantan villages, of which there were fourteen. Although these villages all lay within fifteen miles of St. Marie, no support arrived on March 17. Thus, the Huron advance guard was left to be defeated by the main body of Iroquois, which I estimate at approximately 500 warriors. If reinforced at any time during the day by an army of approximately 300 warriors, the Huron might have won the third battle. If they had been reinforced by a larger number, say 500 warriors, they probably would have won. The Huron would then have been in an excellent position to attack and defeat the rear guard or garrison which had been left at St. Ignace. By not concentrating their forces the Huron missed an opportunity to defeat the Iroquois in detail. Indeed, what happened was that the Iroquois, who were eventually able to get the main body of their army to the battle field at St. Louis, were able to defeat a smaller Huron force, as they had done twice the previous day.

No hostilities took place on March 18. The Iroquois spent the day at St. Ignace assessing their situation. If the casualty figures given by Father Ragueneau for the Iroquois are close to being accurate, it can be concluded that approximately one-third of the invading Iroquois army had been killed by the Hurons, and many more had been wounded. (At the first battle ten were killed, twenty at the second battle, 200 in the first phase of the third battle, and 100 in the last phase of that battle; the total is 340 Iroquois killed.) Given such extensive casualties, it is not surprising that the Iroquois chose not to attempt to attack any other Huron villages. Their only realistic alternative was to retreat. Thus, on March 19 a victorious, but badly mauled, Iroquois army of approximately 650 warriors, perhaps less, hastily departed from St. Ignace. A large Huron army from St. Michael was unable to overtake them.

The Hurons had suffered immense casualties. Four hundred people were killed at St. Ignace, a figure which must include over 100 warriors. At St. Louis eighty warriors were lost. On the second day of battle an entire army of 300 warriors was destroyed. Strategically, the Huron were left in a serious position. In two summers the villages of an entire tribe had been wiped out, leaving eastern Huronia, now no longer occupied by any Huron villages, under Iroquois dominance. A second tribe had lost one of five major villages. And, the French fort of St. Marie had come under attack. It is little wonder that the remaining Huron tribes and villages viewed themselves as a defeated people. The well-armed French at St. Marie had not lifted a hand to help them on March 17, while their one army was being defeated at St. Louis. Furthermore, their geographic position on a peninsula extending into Georgian Bay excluded any easy migration that would take them beyond the reach of the Iroquois.

At least three factors seem to have contributed to the Huron defeats on March 16 and 17. First, the individual fortified villages, regardless of how large they were, were not strong enough to withstand the concentrated attack of a large army. In the 1630s the palisades appear to have been adequate for defense; that is, the palisades held small raiding parties at bay while the defenders, who outnumbered the attackers, mounted the platforms behind the walls. In the 1640s the attacking armies became much larger. Using steel axes and fire they were able to break through the palisade walls (Heidenreich 1971, pp. 142–143).

Second, there were poor communications between the villages, which were several miles apart and connected by narrow trails. *The Jesuit Relations* tell us that there was snow on the ground in March 1649. Furthermore, these trails connected only neighboring villages; routes directly connecting villages beyond their neighbors were very few (Heidenreich 1971, pp. 156–157). In other words, it was not easy for a village under attack, particularly in winter, to inform other villages which could have come to its defense. Indeed, Ossossane, the major village from which most of the warriors in the Huron advance guard had come, did not learn of the defeat on the 17th until the night of the 19th (Trigger 1976, p. 767).

Third, the Huron did not have institutionalized military or political practices, even on the tribal level, that could rally village armies to rescue besieged villages. For example, designated runners, whose messages would be heeded, appear not to have been developed. Indeed, the growing division between Christian and traditionalist Hurons (Trigger 1976, pp. 731, 744–750, 759–762) could have precluded the development of such military–political practices.

In addition to considering features of Huron society which seem to have contributed to their defeat, an examination of the quality of Huron and Iroquois military organizations must be made. In terms of utilizing efficient military practices the Huron and Iroquois appear comparable. Both score "high" on a scale which I have developed for measuring the military sophistication of so-called primitive societies. (Of the eleven efficient military practices used to build the scale, each society shares the same seven efficient practices; the precise scale score is 0.64 on a scale that ranges from 0 to 1.) In *The Evolution of War* (1970), I argue that when two societies are at war, the one with the more sophisticated military organization will win and as a consequence expand territorially at the expense of the other. Since both the Iroquois and the Huron are at the same point on the military sophistication scale, no prediction as to who would be the winner is possible, using this scale.

The military sophistication scale does not take into account the use of firearms as opposed to other projectile weapons. The Iroquois were better armed from 1641 onwards as well as during the campaign of 1649. Father Ragueneau's opening statement informs us that the Iroquois were "well furnished with weapons, — and mostly with firearms" (Thwaites 1899, Vol. 34, p. 123). Trigger estimates a maximum of 120 guns in the Huron confederacy.[9] In battles between the Iroquois and the Hurons prior to 1649, firearms — in conjunction with innovative tactics — often meant success for the Iroquois (Otterbein 1964, pp. 58–59). However, Father Ragueneau's account gives no evidence that guns were a decisive factor in the campaign of 1649. Indeed, the hand-to-hand combat that took place suggests that guns were not of major importance in any of the battles. One obtains a sense, I believe, from reading Father Ragueneau's account that the Hurons were as brave as the Iroquois and just as good fighters. Thus, in terms of quality Huron and Iroquois military organizations and practices appear comparable.

On the other hand, when the Iroquois and the Hurons are compared in terms of eight principles of war, the Iroquois appear to have been able to use their military organization in a superior manner. These eight principles, which are nearly self-defining, are as follows (Burne 1947, pp. 13–22): Maintenance of Objective, Offensive Action, Surprise, Concentration, Economy of Force, Security, Mobility, and Cooperation. (Various other similar lists varying from two to nine principles have been devised [Willoughby 1939, pp. 25–44]). In terms of these principles, the Iroquois army appears to be definitely superior to the Huron army. Indeed, on the basis of the above analysis it can be argued that the Iroquois had one army and the Huron had many armies, at least certainly during the campaign of 1649.

Why did the Iroquois win the campaign of 1649? The above analysis seems to be sufficient to answer the question. First, the Huron suffered from three weaknesses: (1) villages unable to withstand attacks by large armies, (2) poor communications between villages, and (3) absence of institutionalized practices for rallying village armies to come to the aid of villages under attack. Second, the Iroquois army, although comparable to the Huron army in terms of the use of efficient military practices, more nearly waged war in accordance with the principles of war advocated by military analysts. Third, the Huron made a serious error in not supporting their advance guard on March 17. Although the Iroquois likewise made a serious error in dividing their forces, it did not lead to disaster because the Huron failed to concentrate their forces for a decisive counter-attack.

To summarize in a different fashion: Given the existence of isolated villages with inadequate fortifications — a condition that also existed in Iroquoia — the army that struck hard first was likely to win, provided no serious military errors were made. The Iroquois in March of 1649 were able to concentrate their forces and audaciously carry out a surprise attack upon two Huron villages they had chosen for destruction. If they had been able to maintain the concentration of their forces, they might have been able to destroy St. Marie on the following day. (If that had occurred, we would not have a report from Father Ragueneau describing the battles.)

CONCLUSION

Why did the Iroquois win? The answer is that they won the last battle, the campaign of 1649. However, the more important question, of course, is why did they win the campaign as well as many of the previous battles. Of the several explanations which have been offered (Hunt 1940; Tooker 1963; Otterbein 1964) I find the most convincing to be that the Iroquois (1) had access to guns and ammunition, (2) had a strategic position between the western fur supply and the eastern market, and (3) used superior tactics at critical times during the 17th century. The 1649 victory is another example of the use of superior tactics. In these battles, as well as earlier in the 17th century, the Iroquois show a military ability greater than that possessed by their enemies. It appears that, in the case of the Huron and Iroquois, a military analysis of the wars they fought provides evidence that superior military ability was a major factor in "Why the Iroquois Won" (Otterbein 1964). Such an analysis does not deny, of course, that social, political, and economic factors underlie military organizations. Quite the contrary — such factors are of extreme importance. Nevertheless, the manner in which a military organization fights and its fortunes in war do play an important role in determining whether that nation or people will survive, or whether it will vanish from the earth.

In conclusion, speculation concerning the battles of March 17 leads to an interesting scenario. If other Atinniaoenten villages had sent their armies to St. Marie and St. Louis at any time on March 17, the main body of the Iroquois army that lay siege to St. Louis would have perished. The remainder of the Iroquois army at St. Ignace could have easily been defeated that night or the next day by the victorious Huron army. Even if the garrison at St. Ignace had escaped, the large Huron army at St. Michel would have been able to effectively pursue the retreating Iroquois. Thus, an Iroquois army of 1,000 warriors would have been annihilated. Since this was early spring, the Huron would have had the entire summer to raid and besiege Iroquois villages. The Iroquois might then have panicked, as did the Huron, and abandoned Iroquoia. If the Huron had won, then the history of the North American continent would have been different. This is why I regard these battles of 1649 as being among the most important fought on this continent.

NOTES

1. This paper was read at the 1977 Conference on Iroquois Research held in Rensselaerville, New York, on October 7–9. I am indebted to Charlotte Swanson Otterbein, James F. Pendergast, A. T. Steegmann, and Bruce G. Trigger for helpful comments and criticisms on this article. Carol McMillan-Feuille drew the map.

2. The extensive bibliographic search was conducted during the summer of 1976 by a professional librarian, Albert Riess.

3. This paper was planned at that time as a sequel to the Iroquois tactics article.

4. For example, in regard to the most important battle Hunt states that "a small Huron contingent of about a hundred and fifty warriors kept the whole Iroquois army engaged until far into the night, retiring only when all but a mere score had been killed" (1940, p. 92). Father Ragueneau's report leaves little doubt that the wounded survivors were taken captive and later killed.

5. Four excellent maps in Trigger show the location of the Huron villages and the direction from which came the "major Iroquois raids" (1976, pp. 768–769).

6. For a discussion of the location of the villages shown on the map see Heidenreich (1974, pp. 42–48). The location of St. Louis can be fixed with a fair amount of certainty one league (1 league = 2½ miles) east of St. Marie, but the location of St. Ignace, one league southeast of St. Louis, has not been definitely determined. Although Heidenreich believes that St. Ignace was Attingneenongnahac, Bruce Trigger has been unable to determine if the village was either Attingneenongnahac or Arendarhonon but suspects it was Arendarhonon (personal communication dated 2/9/78).

7. In a letter to me dated 9/61/78, Bruce Trigger writes: "As I have already written, it seems to me that the aims of this campaign were to get booty and disperse the Huron. The capture of St. Ignace and nearby villages would have contributed to both these objectives. The capture of Ste. Marie would further have yielded more furs and French goods, priests as hostages to be bargained with the French, and a crippling blow to Huron security. Thus, it seems ... that the Iroquois set out with the aims of (a) destroying St. Ignace and surrounding villages (an objective they felt they could likely achieve) and (b) *if possible* to capture Ste. Marie. The archaeology of Ste. Marie suggests to me that in 1649 the transformation of the original wooden defenses into stone ones was still in progress and the eastern defenses in particular were not finished. Hence it was a good time for an attack as parts of walls had been torn down and not rebuilt ... in stone."

8. The French may have had a hand in fortifying both villages that fell to the Iroquois on March 16 (Heidenreich 1971, p. 143; Trigger 1976, p. 743).

9. Personal communication from Bruce Trigger dated 2/9/78.

REFERENCES

Burne, Alfred H. (1947). *The Art of War on Land*. Harrisburg, PA: The Military Service Publishing Company.

Forbes Jr., Allan (1970). "Two and a Half Centuries of Conflict: The Iroquois and the Laurentian Wars." *Pennsylvania Archaeologist* 40(3/4):1–20.

Heidenreich, Conrad (1971). *Huronia*. Toronto: McClelland and Stewart Ltd.

Hunt, George T. (1940). *The Wars of the Iroquois*. Madison: The University of Wisconsin Press.

Otterbein, Keith F. (1964). "Why the Iroquois Won: An Analysis of Iroquois Military Tactics." *Ethnohistory* 11:56–63.

_____ (1970). *The Evolution of War*. New Haven: Human Relations Area Files Press.

Thwaites, Reuben G. (Ed.) (1896–1901). *The Jesuit Relations and Allied Documents ... 1610–1791*. 73 volumes. Cleveland: Burrows.

Tooker, Elisabeth (1963). "The Iroquois Defeat of the Huron. A Review of Causes." *Pennsylvania Archaeologist* 33:115–123.

Trigger, Bruce G. (1976). *The Children of Aataentsic: A History of the Huron People to 1600.* Montreal & London: McGill-Queen's University Press.

Willoughby, Charles A. (1939). *Maneuver in War.* Harrisburg, PA: The Military Service Publishing Company.

Chapter THREE

The Evolution of Zulu Warfare[1]

Although anthropological literature is replete with references to Zulu warfare and to Shaka, the famous Zulu warrior-king, there is no brief analytic treatment of the development of Zulu warfare prior to and during Shaka's reign. This study uses both qualitative and quantitative data on Zulu wars to graphically show the trends and changes which occurred during this thirty-year period (1798–1828). In particular, this study focuses on the factors which produced changes in the casualty rates of Zulu wars. The following factors are selected for treatment as independent variables: type of weapons, type of formations or tactics, type of military organization, and goals or reasons for war. Changes in one or more of these variables led to changes in casualty rates.

This paper was read at the November 1964 American Anthropological Association meetings in Detroit.

For approximately 300 years prior to 1800, Nguni tribes had been migrating into southeast Africa, now Zululand and Natal, from the northwest. Rivalry between the sons of the tribal leader frequently led to fission of the royal patrilineage. Such splitting kept the tribes small and scattered. The economy, which was based on shifting cultivation and cattle raising, also contributed to this dispersion by requiring tribes to constantly seek better land (Gluckman 1958, pp. 28–29). When conflict arose between tribes, a day and a place were arranged for settling the dispute by combat. On that day the rival tribes marched to battle, the warriors drawing up in lines at a distance of about 100 yards apart. Behind the lines stood the remaining members of each tribe, who during the battle cheered their kinsmen on to greater efforts. The warriors carried five-foot tall, oval shields and two or three light javelins. These rawhide shields, when hardened by dipping in water, could not be penetrated by the missiles. Chosen warriors, who would advance to within 50 yards of each other and shout insults, opened the combat by hurling their spears. Eventually more and more warriors would be drawn into the battle until one side ceased fighting and fled, "whereupon a rush would follow for male and female prisoners and enemy cattle, the former to be subsequently ransomed [for cattle], the latter to be permanently retained" (Ritter 1957, p. 10). If the pursued dropped their spears, it was a sign of surrender and no more blood would be shed. Since wounds were seldom fatal, the number of casualties was low.

By 1800 the increase in population and the dwindling of unoccupied land created a situation in which fission could no longer solve the problem of dynastic disputes. According to Gluckman (1958, p. 31):

> As far as one can understand the process from the almost contemporary records, under the distribution of population then prevailing it became more difficult for tribes to divide and dissident sections to escape to independence; as the Nguni cultural stress on seniority of descent and the relatively great inheritance of the main heir caused strong tensions in the tribes, chiefs began to press their dominion not only on their subordinate tribal sections, but also on their neighbors. The development of this trend was possibly facilitated by the unequal strength of the tribes.

There emerged from this situation a leader of the Mtetwa tribe called Dingiswayo, who was able to achieve military success by organizing the age grades of young warriors into regiments of soldiers (Bryant 1929, p. 98). Without altering weapons or tactics, but simply by increasing organizational efficiency and hence the discipline and size of his forces, he was able from 1806 to 1809 to defeat over 30 tribes and establish for himself a chiefdom. "After subduing a tribe with as little slaughter as possible, he left it under its own chiefly family, perhaps choosing from it a favorite of his own to rule, though the young men of the tribe had to serve in his army" (Gluckman 1960, p. 162).

Shaka, the illegitimate son of a Zulu chief, while he was an officer in Dingiswayo's army, invented in approximately 1810 a new technique of fighting. He replaced his javelins with a short, broad-bladed stabbing spear; he retained his shield, but discarded his sandals in order to gain greater mobility. By rushing upon his opponent he was able to use his shield to hook away his enemy's shield, thus exposing the warrior's left side to a spear thrust. Shaka also changed military tactics by arranging the soldiers in his command — a company of about 100 men — into "a close-order, shield-to-shield formation with two 'horns' designed to encircle the enemy or to feint at his flanks, the main body of troops at the center and the reserves in the rear ready to exploit the opportunities of battle" (Gluckman 1960, p. 162). Dingiswayo, however, always refused to use the formation and to adopt the short spear because it meant high casualties for both sides.

In 1816, when Shaka's father died, Dingiswayo helped him to become chief of the Zulu. Shaka immediately outfitted his army of 500 soldiers with the short spear and taught them the new tactics. Although he remained within Dingiswayo's chiefdom, he began to conquer tribes on his own. Early in 1818 Shaka prepared to join with Dingiswayo in a campaign against the Ndwandwe tribe ruled by Zwide. Dingiswayo foolishly left the army without an escort and was captured and killed by Zwide before the regiments of Shaka and Dingiswayo could join forces. Shaka was forced to retreat and establish a defensive position on Qokli Hill, from which he defeated Zwide. After the battle the Mtetwa and several small tribes joined Shaka. The following year (1819) the Ndwandwe again invaded Shaka's domain and were defeated at the Battle of Umhlatuze. Statistical data on these and other battles are listed in Table 1.[2]

Following the consolidation of his kingdom, Shaka launched forth on a series of wars for the next three years which resulted in expanding the kingdom into an empire of 80,000 square miles. Table 2 shows the increase in the size of territory, in the number of tribes in the kingdom, and in the size of the army for the period 1816 to 1822. However, once the empire was secure the army — which by then totaled 30,000 men — had few military duties. Shaka's answer to the question of what a nation does with a large army that is only neces-

Table 1. Six Zulu Battles

	Year and name of battle	Tribes involved	Size of armies	Number killed	Average number killed	Average % killed
1.	1810	Butelezi	600	50	35	3
		Mtetwa	1,800	20		
2.	1813 Um Mona	Ndwandwe	2,500	500	325	15
		Mtetwa	1,800	150		
3.	1816	Butelezi	600	550	300	44
		Zulu	750	50		
4.	1818 Qokli Hill	Ndwandwe	11,000	7,500	4,550	60
		Zulu	4,300	1,600		
5.	1819 Umhlatuze	Ndwandwe	18,000	17,000	11,000	80
		Zulu	10,000	5,000		
6.	1826 Ndololwane	Ndwandwe	20,000	19,000	12,000(?)	42(?)
		Zulu	40,000	6,000(?)		

Table 2. Expansion of the Zulu Empire

Year	Size of territory in square miles	Number of tribes in the kingdom	Size of army
1822	80,000	300	20,000
1819[a]	11,500	46	10,000
1818[b]	7,000	30	8,000
1817[c]	400	6	2,000
1816[d]	200	2	1,000
1816	100	1	500

[a]After battle of Umhlatuze.
[b]After battle of Qokli Hill.
[c]After second battle with Butelezi.
[c]After incorporation of one tribe.

sary for defensive purposes (although the soldiers herded Shaka's cattle and worked his fields) was to send it on long-range campaigns; usually the army returned with plunder which consisted primarily of cattle. These campaigns occurred during the last four years of Shaka's reign, until he was assassinated by his brothers in 1828.

The idea of organizing armies into regiments and the use of new weapons and tactics diffused rapidly to neighboring tribes. In 1817 and 1818 Dingiswayo faced tribes that had organized their armies around age-grade regiments. In 1818 the Ndwandwes seemed to be familiar with enveloping tactics; they certainly were in 1819 (Ritter 1957, pp. 175–176). In 1818 the invading Ndwandwes carried javelins; in 1819 they carried one heavy spear and two throwing spears, but still wore sandals (Ritter 1957, p. 167). Thus it took only three years from the time Shaka became the Zulu chieftain for the innovations in weapons and tactics to diffuse to enemy tribes.

The evolution of Zulu warfare can be analyzed in terms of a progression of types of wars, the types being named for the goals of war (see Table 3). The first type can be characterized as "dueling battles" between small tribes whose warriors agreed upon the time and place of the battle and who fought for cattle. Since spears were only used as projectile weapons, casualties were slight. The nature of war changed when Dingiswayo created — for the purpose of conquering other tribes — a more efficient military force by organizing his warriors into age-grade regiments. Thus he created a new concept of war by using his newly formed army as an instrument of political expansion. These "battles of subjugation," in which there were still few casualties, constitute the second type of wars. Shortly after the establishment of Dingiswayo's chiefdom, Shaka invented a short stabbing spear and enveloping tactics which he had no opportunity to use until he became leader of the Zulu. Upon the death of Dingiswayo and the breakup of his domain, Shaka was forced to defend Zululand from invasion. The use of these new weapons and tactics and new motives for fighting resulted in a third type of war in which casualties were very high. The defense of Zululand was followed by a series of successful offensive battles in which casualty rates remained high; these "battles of conquest" resulted in the creation of an empire. The fourth type of war was the long-range "campaigns" into enemy territory, the aim of which was to keep the army busy rather than conquering new peoples. Casualty rates became low again as they had been prior to 1816. It should be noted that each of these four types of war corresponds to a different level of sociopolitical development. In terms of Service's taxonomy (1962), "dueling battles" occurred on the tribal level, "battles of subjugation" led to the development of chiefdoms, "battles of conquest" brought about the emergence of the state, and with the eventual development

Table 3. Types of Zulu Wars

	2.		3.			4.	
1	2	3	4 5			6	
B B B	B B	B	B B	B B B	B	C C	C C C
1806 1808 1810	1812 1814	1816	1818 1820	1822 1824		1826	1828

1. = Dueling battles (not shown), 2. = Battles of subjugation, 3. = Battles of conquest, 4. = Campaigns.
B = battle, C = campaign. Arabic numerals above battles identify the battle as one of the six in Table 1.

Categories of comparison	Dueling battles	Battles of subjugation	Battles of conquest	Campaigns
1. Type of weapon	projectile	projectile	shock	shock
2. Type of formation	lines	lines	envelopment	envelopment
3. Type of military organization	patrilineage	age-grade regiment	age-grade regiment	age-grade regiment
4. Goals of war	settling disputes	subjugation	conquest	plunder
5. Casualty rate	very low	low	high	low
6. Sociopolitical system	tribe	chiefdom	state	empire

of empires long-range "campaigns" became the dominant form of war.

In conclusion, the development of a new type of military organization (age-grade regiments) and a change in the goals of war from settling disputes to subjugation of other tribes led to a slight increase in casualty rates. This is described as a change from "dueling battles" to "battles of subjugation." The introduction of shock weapons and enveloping tactics combined with new reasons for war — namely conquest, rather than subjugation, of neighboring peoples — greatly accelerated casualty rates. This has been described as a shift from "battles of subjugation" to "battles of conquest." With a change in the goals of war from conquest to plunder, casualty rates once again became low. This was a shift from "battles of conquest" to "campaigns."

NOTES

1. I am indebted to Arthur Harkins for his helpful comments and criticisms.

2. The major source drawn upon for quantitative data is Ritter (1957). It should be noted that Ritter, who was born in 1890, grew up among the Zulu. This account contains information on military affairs not found in the basic sources on the Zulu, such as Bryant (1927), Gibson (1911), or Krige (1936). This information was gathered by an army officer who campaigned in South Africa in the latter half of the nineteenth century: "The tactical and strategical details of the principal battle descriptions were supplied by the author's father, Captain C. L. A. Ritter" (p. 377). [For a favorable assessment of the Ritter volume published after this article was written, see Gluckman (1974, p. 117).]

REFERENCES

Bryant, Alfred T. (1929). *Olden Times in Zululand and Natal, Containing Earlier History of the Eastern-Nguni Clans*. London: Longmans, Green and Co.

Gibson, James Young (1911). *The Story of the Zulus*. London: Longmans, Green and Co.

Gluckman, Max (1958). *Analysis of a Social Situation in Modern Zululand*. The Rhodes-Livingstone Papers 28. Manchester: Manchester University Press.

_____ (1960). "The Rise of a Zulu Empire." *Scientific American* 202(April):157–168.

_____ (1974). "The Individual in a Social Framework: The Rise of King Shaka of Zululand." *Journal of African Studies* 1(2):113–144.

Krige, Eileen J. (1936). *The Social System of the Zulus*. London: Longmans, Green and Co.

Ritter, E. A. (1957). *Shaka Zulu: The Rise of the Zulu Empire*. New York: G. P. Putnam's Sons.

Service, Elman R. (1962) *Primitive Social Organization*. New York: Random House.

Chapter
FOUR

The Evolution of War:
A Cross-Cultural Study

PREFACE

In the fall of 1964 I initiated a cross-cultural study of primitive war, the objective of which was to devise and test a series of hypotheses as to the causes of war and the conditions under which wars occur. The hypotheses I wished to test derived in part from two case studies, one dealing with Iroquois (1964) and the other with Zulu warfare (1967), and a cross-cultural study of feuding which my wife-to-be and I (Otterbein and Otterbein 1965) conducted at the Summer Institute of Cross-Cultural Research held at the University of Pittsburgh during the summer of 1964. Hypotheses were also taken from the theoretical literature dealing with war. These hypotheses were primarily concerned with the influence of ecological, economic, and sociopolitical factors on warfare. More specifically, I wished to examine the relationship between terrain, mode of subsistence, and type of sociopolitical system, treated as independent variables, and military organization, tactics, and goals of war, treated as dependent variables. In conducting the research, I collected data during the spring of 1965 on 26 variables for 50 societies and did preliminary analyses of the data with a high-speed computer. The research was delayed while I initiated a study of tribal warfare in Northeastern Nigeria during the summer of 1965. The results of this field research were analyzed and written up during the 1965–66 academic year (Otterbein 1968c). During the summer and fall of 1966, I returned to the analysis of the cross-cultural data. Two articles dealing with types of warfare were produced during the spring of 1967 (Otterbein 1968a, 1968b). *The Evolution of War*, which reports the major results of the cross-cultural study of primitive war, was written during the summer and fall of 1967.

As the analysis of the data proceeded, it became clear that ecological and economic factors had little influence, in comparison with the type of sociopolitical system, upon the warfare variables. (For example, the empirical relationship between mode of subsistence and fortified villages is not significant; whereas the correlation between type of sociopolitical system and fortified villages is significant.) Initially it was planned to organize the results of the study into three major sections, each section dealing with the influence of one of the three independent variables upon the warfare variables. Since ecological and economic variables had little influence upon the warfare variables, the monograph in its present form consists of one major section, entitled "The Waging of War," which deals largely with the relationships between types of sociopolitical systems and various aspects of warfare. The military sophistication scale, which is employed as an independent variable in the chapter entitled "The Outcomes of War," was developed as the writing on "The Waging of War" chapter progressed. The development of such a scale grew out of the need for a composite, independent variable which would predict certain outcomes of war — outcomes which were not correlated with the ecological, economic, and sociopolitical variables.

I am indebted to a number of individuals who have assisted me at various stages in the research and preparation of this manuscript. I received my training in cross-cultural research from George P. Murdock, Frank W. Young, and Melvin Ember. My wife, Charlotte Swanson Otterbein, and Raoul Naroll provided advice on sampling procedures in the initial stage of research. Support for the summer of 1967 was provided by a Faculty Research Fellowship from the Research Foundation of the State University of New York. My wife, who assisted in the development of the military sophistication scale, has provided a methodological appendix describing the rationale behind the scale, and Robert L. Carneiro, who provided critical comments on the manuscript, has kindly consented to write a foreword to the monograph. My wife and the editorial staff of the Human Relations Area Files Press have spent many hours editing the manuscript.

Chapter 1: INTRODUCTION

From the time that evolutionary theory developed in the mid-nineteenth century, scientists have proposed theories of social evolution which relate the evolution of war to various levels of political centralization. The following review of some of these theories is not meant to be exhaustive, but is intended to provide a basis for deriving a general outline of their underlying theoretical structure. Spencer (1896) argued that leadership and subordination developed first in the military and were then transferred to political society. Thus an increase in military efficiency preceded the development of centralized political systems. Sumner (1911), who saw warfare as playing a less creative role in the evolution of society, contended that war and peace developed side by side as social institutions from the lowest to the most advanced levels of society. Another social evolutionist, Keller (1916), set forth the theory that only the customs of those societies which prevailed in intersocietal conflicts would be found widely distributed among human groups. A student of his, Davie (1929), traced the course of the development of warfare from the earliest evidence of its existence. Hobhouse, Wheeler, and Ginsberg (1930), in a cross-cultural study, showed that with increasing technological levels the killing of captives taken in war declined. Using four levels of political centralization, Wright (1942) demonstrated cross-culturally that with increasing political centralization the type of warfare waged by societies changes. His types of warfare included defensive, social, economic, and political war. According to Malinowski (1941), warfare only slowly evolved as a mechanism of organized force for the pursuit of national policies. He described six types of armed contest, each of which "presents an entirely different cultural phase in the development of organized fighting." Only two of these types Malinowski considered to be war. Turney-High (1949) argued that few nonliterate tribes have reached the "military horizon," by which he meant military efficiency. Such societies are unable to wage true war; it is only the advanced societies which have reached the "military horizon." White (1949), a cultural evolutionist, contended that as man's cultural heritage increases, economic and political goals become the basis for war. Another cultural evolutionist, Steward (1955), has shown that with the emergence of states, warfare comes to play a major role in intersocietal relations. More recently, Service (1962) applied an evolutionary perspective to the study of social organization. Warfare, which he describes as being frequent and intense at all levels of sociopolitical development, selects societies for social and political integration. When two societies engage in war, the more highly integrated society will be the winner.

All the above theories have in common the notion that societies become socially and politically more developed through time. As societies evolve, they come to wage war in more efficient ways. Sometimes war is seen as producing the evolution of societies; sometimes it is the political level of the societies which is seen as being responsible for the type of war waged. In either instance, the level of political centralization and degree of military efficiency are viewed as being functionally related. This study tests a series of hypotheses which relate level of political centralization to various aspects of warfare. In most instances it will be shown that more efficient military practices are associated with centralized political systems. Support is also provided for the general hypothesis that as societies become politically more centralized, they wage war in a more efficient manner. The study also demonstrates that societies which wage war efficiently are likely to be militarily successful.

Concepts and Approach

Warfare is a vital activity performed for a political community by its military organization. A political community is a "group of people whose membership is defined in terms of occupancy of a common territory and who have an official with the special function of announcing group decisions — a function exercised at least once a year" (Naroll 1964, p. 286). Each political community has a political structure which is the administrative center or organization of the political community. This structure can vary in its degree of centralization. The more centralized the structure of a political community, the higher its level of political centralization.

Contiguous political communities which are culturally similar comprise a cultural unit. In most instances, the cultural unit is the same as a society, which is the unit used in the universe from which the sample was drawn. Although a single political community may be coterminous with a cultural unit, a cultural unit usually consists of more than one political community.

Warfare is defined as armed combat between political communities. Armed combat, which is fighting with weapons, is performed by military organizations. When political communities within the same cultural unit engage in warfare, this is considered to be internal war. When warfare occurs between political communities which are not culturally similar, this is referred to as external war. If there is more than one military organization within a political community, and these military organizations engage in armed combat, this is considered feuding or civil war, depending upon the scope of the conflict. This study restricts itself to warfare between political communities.

The concepts of political community, cultural unit, and level of political centralization will be used throughout this study whenever theoretical issues are being considered. When the discussion deals with political communities with different degrees of centralization, the political communities will be said to be either centralized or uncentralized. On the other hand, whenever empirical data are being discussed, the corresponding concepts of political system, society, and type of political system will be employed. Political systems are of two types, centralized and uncentralized. Thus on the empirical level, societies are said to be composed of political systems; while on a theoretical level, cultural units are said to be composed of political communities. There are two reasons for maintaining the two sets of terminology. First, the only universes available from which a sample could be drawn are composed of societies, not cultural units. Second, it is a methodologically correct procedure to keep separate the theoretical realm from the empirical realm, for the application of such a procedure makes it possible for a reader to distinguish between data and interpretation. The distinction should, therefore, make it easier for a reader to evaluate the results of this monograph.

The approach employed in this study focuses upon military organizations, their structure, the activities they perform, why they perform them, and the results of their actions. More specifically, military organizations engage in armed combat in order to obtain certain goals. In the attempt to obtain these goals through armed combat, certain consequences occur. These include the effect of the armed combat upon both the military organizations themselves and the political communities which host them. Military organizations thus are viewed as a particular type of social organization. Like any organization, they have a social structure, consisting of a charter and

norms. The personnel of the organization pursue objectives or functions by engaging in activities with the material apparatus at their
disposal (Malinowski 1960, pp. 43–53). Organizations, including military organizations, since they are articulated with the larger social
system of the political community, have an influence upon and in
turn are influenced by the larger social system. However, military
organizations differ from many organizations in that the goals or
objectives they pursue are directed at political communities other
than the political communities from which they derive. The goals of
war include subjugation and tribute, land, plunder, trophies and
honors, defense, and revenge. All of these objectives are carried out
at the expense of other political communities. The military organization that is the winner of the armed combat is more likely to achieve
its goals than is the defeated military organization.

The outcome of an armed combat between two military organizations depends upon the efficiency of their military practices. These
practices include the structure of the military organization, its activities, its material apparatus, and its goals. A military organization
which employs an efficient military practice will defeat in armed
combat a military organization which does not employ the practice
or employs a similar but less efficient military practice, if the two
military organizations are otherwise equally matched. Such an efficient military practice is said to confer a survival advantage upon a
society by increasing the likelihood that its military organization will
defeat other military organizations. A victorious military organization makes a political community militarily successful and increases
its likelihood of survival in intersocietal conflicts. If two military
organizations are pitted against each other, the one that employs the
greater number of efficient practices will defeat the other. A political
community with a military organization which employs one or more
efficient practices will be militarily successful when in conflict with a
political community with a military organization employing fewer
efficient practices. The more efficient the military organization of a
political community (measured in terms of the number of efficient
practices employed), the more likely is the political community to be
militarily successful and hence to survive in intersocietal struggles.

Methodology

The approach outlined above utilizes the following procedures: First
I make an informed judgment as to which of two paired alternative
military practices is the more efficient (i.e., which one increases the

likelihood that the military organization employing it will defeat other military organizations, all other things being equal). I may argue, for example, that shock weapons are more efficient than projectile weapons and that a high degree of subordination is more efficient than a low degree of subordination. Sometimes the prevalence of societies employing a particular military practice can be used as an indication of the efficiency of the practice. If over half of the societies in this study employ the practice, this fact in itself may indicate that the practice is efficient, since a less efficient practice would have been abandoned by a military organization, or else the military organization would have been defeated, and hence fewer than half of the societies would employ the practice. Although it may seem obvious that a high degree of subordination is more efficient than a low degree of subordination, it is useful to observe that 75 percent of the societies in this study for which there are data have a high degree of subordination in their military organizations. The pairs of military practices are used to develop a military sophistication scale which permits the comparison of military organizations in terms of their degree of military efficiency. To obtain an overall measure of the efficiency of a military organization, the number of efficient military practices employed by the military organization is used to compute a military sophistication score. It is later shown that the higher the degree of military sophistication of the military organizations of the political communities of a cultural unit, the more likely it is that the cultural unit will be militarily successful and will survive in intersocietal conflicts.

The cross-cultural research method consists of testing hypotheses, which are stated in such a way that they are applicable to a wide range of societies. Usually a sample of societies drawn from a larger universe or population is used to test the hypotheses. If the hypotheses are confirmed, using acceptable statistical procedures, the results are considered to be applicable to the larger universe. The method is thus well suited for testing hypotheses which are derived from general theories. There are two major reasons why the methodology of cross-cultural research should be used for studying warfare. First, there are a few recent case studies of primitive warfare which present hypotheses. Some of these hypotheses are evolutionary in nature, and thus can be considered within this larger theoretical framework. These case studies, like any case study, merely provide the hypotheses; they do not test them beyond the single society from which they are derived. Hence, this cross-cultural study of war brings together a series of hypotheses and tests them within the same theoretical framework and with the same body of data. Second, it is becoming more difficult to conduct case studies of primitive warfare, unless they are ethnohistorical. Field sites where primitive war can still be studied firsthand are rare. Perhaps only in isolated regions of highland New Guinea, the Orinoco River Basin of South America, and the Mandara Mountains of Nigeria can one find tribal peoples who still engage in armed combat. Thus it is nearly impossible to test in a field situation hypotheses which have been derived from other case studies. Furthermore, it is obvious that experimentation in the realm of warfare is virtually out of the question.

The type of analysis employed in this study requires that hypotheses be stated such that one of the two variables is presumed to be causal; this is because each hypothesis is phrased in terms of two variables, one of which is considered independent, one dependent. Moreover, most social scientists have become accustomed to interpreting the variable to the left of the contingency table as the independent variable. The 2 × 2 contingency table, which will be used to present data throughout this study, gives the distribution of cases for each point on each variable. A hypothesis is tentatively confirmed if there are a greater number of cases in the lower left and upper right cells than in the upper left and lower right cells. In Table 1, the majority of cases (30 out of 46) conform to the hypothesis. In other words, if a society has a centralized political system, there is a greater likelihood that it will be characterized by a military organization composed of professionals than if the society has an uncentralized political system. The relationship shown in such a table can also be described more formally by using two simple statistical procedures: the phi coefficient (ϕ), which indicates the strength of the relationship and varies from +1.00 to −1.00, with zero representing the point of no relationship; and the related chi-square statistic (χ^2), which can be used to determine the probability (p) that the distribution of cases in the contingency table could have occurred through chance factors, rather than through some meaningful relationship between the two variables. When the probability that the relationship could have occurred by chance is greater than one in ten, the relationship is said to be not significant (ns). However, a relationship not strong enough to be considered significant by these standards can still indicate a valid relationship. In Table 1, the phi coefficient is +0.31, and the probability that a relationship this strong, either positive or negative, could have occurred by chance alone is less than one in twenty ($0.02 < p < 0.05$). Therefore the relationship is considered to be significant.

Table 1. Composition of Military Organization

Political systems	Nonprofessionals		Professionals		Total
	No.	Society	No.	Society	
Centralized	5	Lau Marshallese Monachi Mutair Sema	11	Ambo Aymara Aztec Egyptians Hawaiians Japanese Javanese Mende Mossi Saramacca Thai	16
Uncentralized	19	Amba Andamanese Comox Fox Gisu Ila Jivaro Kurtatchi Motilon Mundurucu Orokaiva Papago Tehuelche Tiv Tiwi Tibetans Toradja Trumai Wishram	11	Abipon Albanians Cherokee Ingassana Kazak Nandi Plains Cree Santa Ana Somali Timbira Yukaghir	30
Total	24		22		46

$$\phi = 0.31, \chi^2 = 4.30, 0.02 < p < 0.05$$

Chapter 2: THE WAGING OF WAR

As political communities evolve in terms of centralization, there are corresponding changes in the manner in which they wage war. The procedure followed in demonstrating this relationship consists of testing a series of 13 hypotheses, each of which relates a different aspect of warfare to the degree of centralization of the political communities. The cultural units are classified as having either centralized or uncentralized political communities. The 13 aspects of warfare are military organization, subordination, initiating party, initiation of war, diplomatic negotiations, tactical systems, weapons, armor, field fortifications, cavalry, fortified villages, siege operations, and causes of war. Each of these aspects can be dichotomized into two alternative military practices, one of which is more efficient than the other. The 13 hypotheses are derived from the theoretical literature dealing with warfare. Each hypothesis, with one exception, predicts that the more efficient military practice will be associated with centralized political communities and the less efficient military practice will be associated with uncentralized political communities. The more efficient practices are used to construct a scale of military sophistication, which is highly correlated with the level of political centralization.

Political Communities

Political communities vary from one cultural unit to the next in their degree of centralization. Among many hunting and gathering peoples, the largest political unit is the band, with a leader who is often chosen by consent and who has little authority over band members. At the other extreme is the large despotic state, whose leader has almost unlimited power over the members of his political community. Between these two extremes lies a variety of tribal peoples and chiefdoms. It is possible to rank these different types of political communities in terms of increasing levels of political centralization.

A taxonomy which can be used for classifying types of political communities has been developed by Service (1962) in his book *Primitive Social Organization: An Evolutionary Perspective*. In this book are delineated four types of social organizations, each of which is structurally more developed than the preceding type (Service 1962, p. 181). Although Service's types or levels pertain to cultural units as defined in this study (1962, p. 167–168), the traits that he uses to define his types can be used to classify political communities. These types are *bands, tribes* (which are characterized by pan-tribal sodalities), *chiefdoms* (which have chiefs with redistributive functions), and *states* (which possess governments with the legitimate use of force). Bands, as political communities, do not extend beyond the residential group. On the other hand, tribes, as political communities, are composed usually of several local groups which are politically united by nonresidential organizations (pan-tribal sodalities) whose memberships include individuals from the several local groups. More centralized are the political communities classified as chiefdoms; at this level, local groups are united politically by a redistributing agent. And states achieve their political centralization through a bureaucracy employing legal force. The traits which define these types are cumulative in that with each successive level of centralization a new trait is added; i.e., bands are defined by an absence of any of the three traits, tribes by the presence of sodalities, chiefdoms by the presence of sodalities and redistribution, and states by the presence of sodalities, redistribution, and a government.

Using these traits, each society in the study was coded for one of the four types. Although it would appear inadmissible to code descriptions of the political systems of 50 societies as if they were political communities, there is in fact an empirical reason for employing such a procedure. Most ethnographic accounts purport to describe a society, a people, a nation, or a tribe, when in actuality most accounts are of a local community or group (Young 1965, p. 43–44). Thus most descriptions available to the comparativist are accounts not of the cultural and social systems of the entire society or cultural unit, but of a specific local group. This local group may well be a political community. In any case, it is unlikely that the accounts describe units larger than political communities. Therefore we are justified in coding societies as if they were political communities. After the coding was completed, bands and tribes were grouped together and considered to be uncentralized political systems; chiefdoms and states were considered to be centralized political systems. Such a dichotomization is justified in that chiefdoms and states are both characterized by a central administrative agency (although it may be only one individual) which collects and redistributes goods, even though a government which can use force is not present; bands and tribes, on the other hand, are characterized by an absence of a central authority with redistributive or governmental functions.

Military Organization

The type of military organization employed by a political community is one of the most important aspects of warfare. Military organizations can range in size from small raiding parties composed of
several warriors to large standing armies composed of hundreds of
thousands of men (Mead 1964, p. 270). Four logical types of military
organizations were constructed from two dichotomous variables:
presence or absence of professional military personnel and presence
or absence of nonprofessional military personnel. When both professionals and nonprofessionals are absent, there is, of course, no military organization. When either professionals or nonprofessionals are
present, and the others are absent, the military organization is composed solely of one type of personnel. When both professionals and
nonprofessionals are present, the military organization is composed
of both professionals and nonprofessionals.

Professionals, in contrast to nonprofessionals, devote a substantial
part of their time during their early adulthood to intensive training,
which may include not only practice in the use of weapons but also
practice in performing maneuvers. They may belong to age-grades,
military societies, or standing armies, or they may serve as mercenaries. Societies with age-grades, military societies, and standing
armies are considered to have military organizations composed solely of professionals; societies which employ mercenaries to lead, train,
or assist untrained warriors are classified as having both professionals and nonprofessionals in their military organizations.

The political systems of only four societies used in this study —
Copper Eskimo, Dorobo, Tikopia, and Toda — do not have any kind
of military organization. Isolation from other societies seems to be
chiefly responsible for the absence of military organizations. The
Copper Eskimo live in small isolated communities along the northern coast of North America. They are occasionally attacked by Indian
groups from the south (Stefánsson 1914, p. 70), and although they
will fight to defend themselves on an individual basis, there is no
evidence that they form military organizations. The Dorobo live in a
forest on a mountaintop in East Africa. They apparently once lived
on the plains below, but they were driven into their forest retreat by
such warlike peoples as the Nandi. Non-Dorobo who enter their
forest are killed (Huntingford 1954, p. 134). The Tikopians are a
Polynesian people who live on a small isolated island in Melanesia.
Their only neighbors, with whom they intermarry, live on Anuta, a
smaller island about 70 miles away (Firth 1963, p. 312). Although

Firth (1963, p. 374) discusses conflicts in which the losers are forced to flee Tikopia, and heads this discussion "War," there is no evidence of a military organization. The Toda live on a plateau in South India in a symbiotic relationship with two neighboring tribal groups, the Kota and Badaga. They apparently have lived for several centuries on this plateau, which is surrounded by a tropical forest infested with malaria-bearing mosquitoes. In the past, the Toda apparently had a military organization, for both shock and projectile weapons are used in ceremonies (Rivers 1906, p. 586).

There are indications that the members of all four of these societies were driven from other areas and forced to seek refuge in isolated locations, such as islands, Arctic wastelands, or mountaintops. Protected by their isolation, they have found it unnecessary to maintain military organizations. The other 46 societies in the sample do have military organizations. Thus it appears from this study that for cultural units and their constituent political communities to remain social entities, they must have the means, through capable military organizations, to defend themselves from attack. A cultural unit composed of political communities whose military organizations are unable to defend them will either be annihilated and absorbed into the political communities of other cultural units or will flee and seek safety, not by arms, but by hiding in an isolated area.

Of the three types of military organization, the most common is composed solely of nonprofessionals. Societies possessing military organizations of this type are listed in the first column of Table 1, which contrasts these societies with those whose military organizations are composed in part or entirely of professionals. The second column of Table 1 thus groups together societies which have the other two types of military organizations; together, these add up to two fewer societies than the number of societies with nonprofessional military organizations.

Redistribution and/or a government would seem to be almost a necessity for a political community if full-time military personnel are to constitute the backbone of its military organization. Such a relationship is described by Rosenfeld in his study of "The Social Composition of the Military in the Process of State Formation in the Arabian Desert" (1965). Ruling groups gained power over rival lineages by conquering towns and converting them into tribute states and trade centers; this was achieved by organizing a military composed of slaves, mercenaries, and townsmen, which was supported by tribute and taxes. Thus Rosenfeld's case analysis provides support for the argument that a political community, in order to have a professional military organization, must have the social, economic, and political development to support such a military. This argument can be formulated into the following hypothesis: *The higher the level of political centralization, the more likely that the military organization is composed of professionals.* The relationship between political centralization and the composition of the military organization is shown in Table 1. The data confirm the hypothesis. The phi coefficient is +0.31, and it is significant at the 0.05 level. Of the 11 uncentralized political systems which have military organizations composed of professionals, seven are of the type in which there are nonprofessionals as well as professionals. Only the Cherokee, Nandi, Plains Cree, and Timbira have military organizations composed solely of professionals; these militaries are professional in the sense that either age-grades or military societies are present. Since military societies, age-grades, and military organizations composed of a nucleus of professional warriors can be maintained without extensive economic support, it is understandable why some uncentralized political systems do not conform to the hypothesis.

Confirmation of the hypothesis, although it provides support for the argument that a certain degree of political centralization is necessary for the emergence of a professional military, does not answer the more basic question of why any political community will make the effort to produce and maintain a professional military organization. The answer seemingly lies in the fact that men who devote themselves full-time to war for at least part of their lives are more efficient in warfare than nonprofessional warriors. This increase in the efficiency of military personnel confers a survival advantage upon the political communities composing the cultural unit, in that the chances of such political communities surviving in intersocietal struggles will increase. Political communities which do not have a military which can defend them from attacks will be destroyed by other political communities and can survive only if they take refuge in isolated regions. Moreover, the need for an efficient defense is as important for uncentralized as for centralized political communities. For an uncentralized political community to survive when engaged in armed combat with more centralized political communities, an efficient military is needed. A military can become more efficient by professionalizing, i.e., by having its personnel devote a substantial part of their time during their early adulthood to intensive training in the art of war. Thus it appears that one reason for the occurrence of a number of uncentralized political systems which have military organizations composed of professionals is that such political systems are more viable in intersocietal struggles with centralized political systems as well as with other uncentralized political systems.

Military Sophistication Scale

Thirteen variables dealing with warfare have been described in this chapter. For each variable a theoretical argument was derived, based wherever possible on the existing literature dealing with warfare, which related it to level of political centralization. The hypothesis stemming from each theoretical argument was tested, using level of political centralization as the independent variable and the variable dealing with warfare as the dependent variable. In developing the arguments basic to several of the hypotheses, assumptions were made which were tested with data available in this study. For six variables an alternative hypothesis was tested, namely that the type of military organization was the major factor influencing the dependent variable. The results of testing the hypotheses are summarized in Table 15. [Tables 2–14 are included in text not reproduced here.] Each table, except Table 12, was interpreted in terms of the phi coefficient and the chi-square test of probability. Since each variable dealing with warfare was dichotomized, the dependent variable consisted of two military practices. For each variable, an argument was made as to which of the two practices was the more efficient in terms of potential survival advantage to the political community: that is, an attempt was made to ascertain which of the two practices was more efficient in the sense that a political community following the more efficient practice would be more likely to defeat its enemies and thereby be the survivor in intersocietal struggles. As is shown in Table 15, all 13 variables dealing with warfare are correlated with level of political centralization. For only two of the variables are the correlations not significant. Thus the evidence clearly indicates that the level of centralization characteristic of a political community is an important determinant of the manner in which warfare is waged.

Shown in Table 16 are the two contrasting manifestations of each variable, and the level of political centralization associated with each practice. From the point of view of an individual political community, the more military practices it has from the right-hand column of Table 16, the greater the number of efficient military practices it has at its disposal for waging war. A scale of military sophistication was constructed from the military practices listed in Table 16. For a practice to be included in the scale, two conditions had to be met: First, the practice had to be independent of any of the other practices

Table 15. Summary of Results

| | Independent variables | | | |
| | Level of political centralization | | Military organization | |
Dependent variables	ϕ	p	ϕ	p
1. Military organization	0.31	$0.02 < p < 0.05$	*	*
2. Subordination	0.23	ns	0.40	$0.01 < p < 0.02$
3. Initiating party	0.48	$p < 0.01$	*	*
4. Means of initiation	0.29	$0.05 < p < 0.10$	*	*
5. Diplomatic negotiations	0.30	$0.05 < p < 0.10$	*	*
6. Tactical systems	0.26	$0.05 < p < 0.10$	0.03	ns
7. Weapons	0.26	$0.05 < p < 0.10$	0.40	$p < 0.01$
8. Protection	0.36	$0.02 < p < 0.05$	0.44	$p < 0.01$
9. Field fortifications	0.41	$0.02 < p < 0.05$	0.13	ns
10. Cavalry	0.16	ns	0.38	$0.01 < p < 0.02$
11. Fortified villages	0.46	$p < 0.01$	*	*
12. Siege operations	*	$p < 0.05$	*	*
13. Causes of war	0.68	$p < 0.001$	*	*

*Not computed.

— i.e., a practice was not included if it depended logically rather than empirically for its existence upon the presence of another military practice. Thus, the practice of siege operations, which is dependent upon the existence of fortified villages, was not included in the scale (only fortified villages are included in Table 12). Second, the practice had both to be associated with centralized political systems and to confer a survival advantage upon those political communities which followed the practice. Although all the military practices in the right-hand column of Table 16 are associated with centralized political systems, one of these practices — the initiation of war by announcement or arrangement — does not confer a survival advantage, in comparison with initiating war by surprise. Thus the initiation of war by announcement or arrangement was not included in the scale. A scale of military sophistication can therefore be constructed, using 11 of the 13 military practices listed in Table 16. Each of the 11 practices is an independent measure, is associated with centralized political systems, and confers a survival advantage.

Table 16. Distribution of Military Practices by Level
of Political Centralization

Dependent variables	Political level	
	Uncentralized political systems	Centralized political systems
1. Military organization	nonprofessionals	professionals
2. Subordination	low	high
3. Initiating party	anyone	official
4. Means of initiation	surprise	announcement or arrangement
5. Diplomatic negotiations	absent	present
6. Tactical systems	ambushes or lines	lines and ambushes
7. Weapons	projectile	shock
8. Protection	absent	present
9. Field fortifications	absent	present
10. Cavalry	absent	present
11. Fortified villages	absent	present
12. Siege operations	absent	present
13. Causes of war	defense, plunder, or prestige	political control

The degree of military sophistication of any society can be computed by totaling the number of military practices listed in the right-hand column of Table 16 and then dividing this total by the total number of military practices which are reported for that society. If there are no data for a given variable, the variable is not included in the calculation. For example, the Sema follow six practices which are listed in the right-hand column and four which are listed in the left-hand column; there are no data on field fortifications. The total of both columns, ten, is divided into six, which produces a quotient of 0.60. Using this procedure, the degree of military sophistication was computed for each society in this study except the four societies without military organizations. The military sophistication score for each society is listed in Table 17; the higher the score, the higher the degree of military sophistication.

From a series of 11 dependent variables, a sophistication scale has been derived which can be used as an independent variable in testing hypotheses. In order to construct 2 × 2 contingency tables and to test the hypotheses with phi coefficients and chi-square tests, it is necessary to dichotomize the scale. The scale was dichotomized at 0.50 for two reasons. First, dichotomizing at the midpoint of the scale separates the 46 societies into those which have a majority of military practices which are deemed efficient and those which have only a minority of military practices which are deemed efficient. Second, since there are no societies falling between scores 0.45 and 0.55, there is an appreciable gap which separates the societies into two groups. The midpoint of this gap would be a scale score of 0.50.

Since each of the military practices used to construct the scale is associated with centralized political systems, it is to be expected that societies with high scale scores will be centralized political systems and that societies with low scale scores will be uncentralized political systems. This expectation can be formulated into a testable hypothesis: *The higher the level of political centralization, the higher the degree of military sophistication.* The relationship between political centralization and degree of military sophistication is shown in Table 17. The phi coefficient is +0.59, and it is significant at the 0.001 level. The point biserial correlation is +0.64, and it is significant at the 0.001 level. Thus, the hypothesis is strongly supported. Since the military sophistication scale measures the proportion of efficient military practices utilized by political communities in the waging of warfare, it can be concluded that as political communities evolve in terms of increasing centralization, the manner in which they wage war becomes more sophisticated. Only nine societies do not confirm the hypothesis, as measured by the fourfold table and the phi coefficient. Of the three centralized political systems with low scale scores, two are chiefdoms (Monachi and Marshallese) and one is a state (Aymara) which was conquered by the Inca. Nevertheless, this state has a scale score (0.44) which is close to the midpoint of the scale (0.50), the point at which the scale was dichotomized. All six of the uncentralized political systems with high scale scores have scores which are close to the midpoint and which rank them low among those societies with high scale scores. In terms of the point biserial correlation, which treats the scale of military sophistication as a continuous variable, it is questionable as to whether one should even consider these nine societies as deviant cases.

This chapter has demonstrated that as the political communities of a cultural unit evolve in terms of centralization, they wage war in a

Table 17. Military Sophistication

Political systems	Low			High			Total
	No.	Score	Society	No.	Score	Society	
Centralized	3	0.22	Monachi	13	0.55	Lau	16
		0.36	Marshallese		0.60	Sema	
		0.44	Aymara		0.64	Ambo	
					0.64	Mende	
					0.64	Mutair	
					0.78	Mossi	
					0.80	Saramacca	
					0.82	Aztec	
					0.89	Hawaiians	
					0.90	Japanese	
					0.90	Javanese	
					0.91	Egyptians	
					1.00	Thai	
Uncentralized	24	0.00	Tiwi	6	0.60	Abipon	30
		0.00	Trumai		0.60	Ingassana	
		0.09	Gisu		0.60	Plains Cree	
		0.10	Andamanese		0.60	Timbira	
		0.14	Motilon		0.67	Somali	
		0.20	Ila		0.67	Wishram	
		0.20	Tehuelche				
		0.22	Amba				
		0.27	Kurtatchi				
		0.27	Orokaiva				
		0.30	Jivaro				
		0.30	Mundurucu				
		0.33	Albanians				
		0.33	Tiv				
		0.36	Fox				
		0.36	Tibetans				
		0.36	Toradja				
		0.40	Comox				
		0.40	Papago				
		0.43	Kazak				
		0.44	Cherokee				
		0.44	Yukaghir				
		0.45	Nandi				
		0.45	Santa Ana				
Total	27			19			46

$$\phi = 0.59, \; \chi^2 = 16.15, p < 0.001$$
$$r_{pb} = 0.64, \; t = 5.53,, p < 0.001$$

more sophisticated manner. An important question, however, remains: Does a cultural unit whose political communities wage war in a sophisticated manner have an increased advantage in intersocietal struggles in comparison with cultural units whose political communities do not wage war in a sophisticated manner? The answer to this question will be explored in the next chapter.

Chapter 3: THE OUTCOMES OF WAR

As political communities develop more efficient means of waging war, the outcomes of war change. The procedure followed in demonstrating the influence of war upon its outcomes consists of testing five hypotheses, each of which relates the military sophistication scale to a different outcome of war. These outcomes include casualty rates, the frequency of different types of war, and military success.

Casualty Rates

Casualty rates, by which is meant the proportion of deaths upon the battlefield, cannot be measured precisely for most primitive societies, just as they cannot be accurately determined for most historical and modern wars (Richardson 1960, pp. 4–12). It was, however, possible to estimate casualty rates as either high or low; if over one-third of the combatants are usually killed while the military organization is employing its most efficient type of military formation, the society was classified as having high casualty rates; if under one-third are usually killed, the society was classified as having low casualty rates. These casualty rates pertain only to the societies in the sample and not to the neighboring societies with whom they war. Thus it is not possible with the present data to investigate the effect which an efficient military organization has upon enemy casualty rates. It is, however, possible to investigate the relationship between the degree of sophistication with which war is waged and the casualty rates which are incurred by the military organization.

Most of the military practices which contribute to high military sophistication scale scores are ones which bring the military organization into direct and prolonged contact with the enemy. Such military practices are efficient because they make it possible for the military organization to inflict heavy casualties upon the enemy by fighting at close quarters for an extended period of time. But the enemy in turn has the same opportunity to inflict heavy casualty rates. A case study of Zulu warfare shows that as the Zulu developed more efficient means of waging war (i.e., as shock weapons replaced projectile weapons, the double envelopment replaced the line, age-grade regiments replaced the patrilineage as the military organization, and wars were fought for conquest and incorporation rather than for subjugation and tribute or for settling disputes), the casualty rates for the Zulu, in addition to those of their enemies, rapidly increased. In one battle, for which there are quantitative data, the combined casualty rate went as high as 80 percent (Otterbein 1967, pp. 356–357). For the Zulu, at least, the high casualty rates were a consequence of the new modes of waging war, which brought the personnel of the military organization into hand-to-hand combat with the enemy for prolonged periods of time. This conclusion, drawn from a case study, can be tested cross-culturally by formulating it into the following hypothesis: *The higher the degree of military sophistication, the higher the casualty rates.* The relationship between degree of military sophistication and casualty rates is shown in Table 18. Although the phi coefficient is +0.26, it is not significant; however, the point biserial correlation of +0.48 is nearly double that of the phi coefficient, and it is significant at the 0.01 level. Thus the hypothesis is strongly confirmed. Although this hypothesis pertains only to the casualty rates of the societies in the sample, it is in all probability correct to assume that the enemy's casualty rates are as high, if not higher. This assumption is supported by the fact that societies with high military sophistication scores not only have high casualty rates but are militarily successful in terms of expanding boundaries (cf. "Military Success", below). As victors, their casualty rates should be lower, or at least should not be higher, than those of the defeated.

Frequency of War

Two major types of warfare can be distinguished: (1) internal war, which is warfare between political communities within the same cultural unit, and (2) external war, which is warfare between political communities which are in different cultural units. Contiguous political communities which are culturally similar comprise a cultural unit. Thus with internal war, the warring political communities are culturally similar; while with external war, the political communities are culturally different. There are two aspects of external war which can be measured separately: political communities of a cultural unit can either attack (offensive external war) or be attacked by (defensive

Table 18. Casualty Rates

Military sophis-tication	Low			High			Total
	No.	Score	Society	No.	Score	Society	
High	7	0.55	Lau	8	0.60	Timbira	15
		0.60	Abipon		0.78	Mossi	
		0.60	Sema		0.80	Saramacca	
		0.64	Mutair		0.80	Hawaiians	
		0.67	Somali		0.90	Japanese	
		0.67	Wishram		0.90	Javanese	
		0.82	Aztec		0.91	Egyptians	
					1.00	Thai	
Low	13	0.00	Tiwi	5	0.30	Jivaro	18
		0.09	Gisu		0.30	Mundurucu	
		0.10	Andamanese		0.36	Fox	
		0.14	Motilon		0.40	Comox	
		0.20	Ila		0.40	Papago	
		0.22	Amba				
		0.22	Monachi				
		0.33	Tiv				
		0.36	Marshallese				
		0.36	Tibetans				
		0.36	Toradja				
		0.43	Kazak				
		0.45	Nandi				
Total	20			13			33

$$\phi = 0.26, \chi^2 = 2.24, \text{ns}$$
$$r_{pb} = 0.48, t = 3.04, p < 0.01$$

external war) culturally different political communities. On the other hand, it is not possible to differentiate these two aspects for internal war, since the unit of analysis is the cultural unit and its member political communities; the focus would have to be upon a single political community in order to make this differentiation.

A society which scores high on the military sophistication scale is composed of political systems whose military organizations employ a large number of efficient military practices. A theory which can be tested is that the military organizations have come to employ the more efficient practices through a process of trial and error, i.e., those military practices which were observed to have a tactical value were retained by the military organizations and those which did not were replaced by more efficient modes of waging war. For this process of trial and error to bring about military sophistication, the military organizations must engage in warfare frequently. If this is the case, then those political communities which frequently engage in warfare are more likely to have military organizations which employ a large number of efficient military practices; while those political communities which have learned to wage war efficiently are more likely to frequently engage in warfare. (Although it has been argued in the previous chapter that the more efficient military practices are associated with centralized political systems, it is nevertheless true, as is shown in Table 17, that uncentralized political systems also may have military organizations which wage war in a sophisticated fashion.) This supposition can be formulated into a testable hypothesis: *The higher the degree of military sophistication, the more likely that the political communities of a cultural unit will engage in frequent or continual internal war.* The relationship between degree of military sophistication and internal war is shown in Table 19. Neither the phi coefficient of +0.06 nor the point biserial correlation of –0.05 is significant. Thus the degree of military sophistication of the political communities within a cultural unit has no influence upon the frequency with which they wage war upon each other. Therefore, the trial-and-error theory outlined above cannot be accepted.

Although the frequency of internal war is not related to the degree of military sophistication of the warring political communities, it has been shown in a cross-cultural study of internal war reported elsewhere that a high frequency of internal war is characteristic of political communities which have fraternal interest groups (Otterbein 1968a).

This study of internal war also shows that internal war is not related to level of political centralization nor to frequency of external war. Thus it is the presence of fraternal interest groups rather than a high military sophistication score which accounts for high frequencies of internal war. It will be demonstrated in the next section (cf. "Military Success") that societies with high military sophistication scores usually expand at the expense of neighboring societies. This expansion occurs primarily through warfare. [A full discussion of why societies with high military sophistication attack neighboring societies is found on p. 183 below.] The attacking of a cultural unit by the political communities of a neighboring cultural unit is one of two aspects of external war, as noted above. Thus societies with high military sophistication scores engage in external war, which involves frequent attacks upon neighboring cultural units. This argument can be formulated into the following hypothesis: *The higher the degree of*

Table 19. Internal War

Military sophis-tication	Infrequent			Continual or frequent			Total
	No.	Score	Society	No.	Score	Society	
High	4	0.60	Ingassana	11	0.55	Lau	15
		0.60	Plains Cree		0.60	Abipon	
		0.78	Mossi		0.60	Sema	
		0.80	Saramacca		0.60	Timbira	
					0.64	Ambo	
					0.64	Mende	
					0.64	Mutair	
					0.67	Somali	
					0.89	Hawaiians	
					0.90	Japanese	
					0.90	Javanese	
Low	8	0.00	Trumai	17	0.00	Tiwi	25
		0.22	Monachi		0.09	Gisu	
		0.30	Mundurucu		0.10	Andamanese	
		0.40	Papago		0.14	Motilon	
		0.44	Cherokee		0.20	Ila	
		0.44	Yukaghir		0.20	Tehuelche	
		0.45	Nandi		0.22	Amba	
		0.45	Santa Ana		0.27	Kurtatchi	
					0.27	Orokaiva	
					0.30	Jivaro	
					0.33	Albanians	
					0.33	Tiv	
					0.36	Marshallese	
					0.36	Tibetans	
					0.40	Comox	
					0.43	Kazak	
					0.44	Aymara	
Total	12			28			40

$$\phi = 0.06, \chi^2 = 0.13, \text{ns}$$
$$r_{pb} = -0.05, t = 0.305, \text{ns}$$

military sophistication, the more likely that the political communities of a cultural unit will engage in frequent or continual offensive external war. The relationship between the degree of military sophistication and offensive external war is shown in Table 20. Although the phi coefficient of +0.17 is not significant, the point biserial correlation of +0.32 is significant at the 0.05 level. Thus the hypothesis is mildly confirmed. Inspection of Table 20 shows that a substantial number of societies which engage in continual or frequent attacks upon other

Table 20. External War: Attacking

Military sophis-tication	Infrequent			Continual or frequent			Total
	No.	Score	Society	No.	Score	Society	
High	5	0.55	Lau	13	0.60	Abipon	18
		0.64	Ambo		0.60	Ingassana	
		0.64	Mutair		0.60	Plains Cree	
		0.89	Hawaiians		0.60	Sema	
		0.90	Japanese		0.60	Timbira	
					0.67	Somali	
					0.67	Wishram	
					0.78	Mossi	
					0.80	Saramacca	
					0.82	Aztec	
					0.90	Javanese	
					0.91	Egyptians	
					1.00	Thai	
Low	11	0.00	Tiwi	14	0.20	Ila	25
		0.00	Trumai		0.20	Tehuelche	
		0.09	Gisu		0.27	Kurtatchi	
		0.10	Andamanese		0.30	Jivaro	
		0.14	Motilon		0.30	Mundurucu	
		0.22	Amba		0.33	Tiv	
		0.22	Monachi		0.36	Fox	
		0.27	Orokaiva		0.36	Tibetans	
		0.33	Albanians		0.40	Comox	
		0.36	Marshallese		0.40	Papago	
		0.45	Santa Ana		0.44	Aymara	
					0.44	Cherokee	
					0.44	Yukaghir	
					0.45	Nandi	
Total	16			27			43

$$\phi = 0.17, \chi^2 = 1.18, \text{ns}$$
$$r_{pb} = 0.32, t = 2.17, p < 0.05$$

societies have low military sophistication scores. One possible reason for this is that many societies, in spite of the inefficiency of their military organizations, may be forced to attack other societies which are attacking them in order to defend their territorial boundaries. In the cross-cultural study of internal war, a strong relationship was found between frequency of being attacked and frequency of attacking; the phi coefficient was +0.41 and it was significant at the 0.01 level (Otterbein 1968a). In other words, those societies which are frequently attacked by their neighbors are also those societies which frequently attack their neighbors. Retaliation for the purposes of defense seemingly accounts for the 14 societies with low military sophistication scores which continually or frequently attack other societies, since 11 of these 14 societies are frequently attacked by other societies.

Although an efficient military organization can be developed in order to attack and defeat enemies, it is perhaps more likely to be developed in order to defend the political community in case of attack. Most peoples and their leaders probably justify the development of their military in terms of presumed defensive needs. In many political communities there probably have been advocates of what has come to be called the deterrence theory: the theory that an efficient military organization will deter would-be aggressors from attacking the political community. This theory can be tested with data from this study if it is formulated into the following hypothesis: *The higher the degree of military sophistication, the less likely that the political communities of a cultural unit will be attacked.* The relationship between degree of military sophistication and defensive external war is shown in Table 21. Neither the phi coefficient of +0.15 nor the point biserial correlation of +0.04 is significant. The deterrence hypothesis is not confirmed. Similar results have been obtained by Naroll (1966, p. 18). Although he did not distinguish between different types of warfare nor construct a scale of military sophistication, his cross-cultural study provides no evidence of an inverse relationship between any of his measures of military orientation and the frequency of war. One possible reason for the lack of correlation between the degree of military sophistication and the frequency of attacks upon the society is that political communities with efficient military organizations employ them in attacking culturally different political communities, an action which evokes retaliation. The high correlation between attacking and being attacked provides evidence that such retaliation does in fact occur. Since it is societies with high military sophistication scores which frequently attack other societies, and since societies which frequently attack other societies are in turn attacked themselves, there is no reason to expect that societies with high military sophistication scores will be relatively free from attack because their military efficiency deters would-be attackers. The attackers may well have been attacked first by the militarily efficient societies. In fact, it is surprising that there is not an association between a high degree of military sophistication and continual or frequent defensive external war and an association between a low degree of military sophistication and infrequent defensive external war.

Table 21. External War: Being Attacked

Military sophis-tication	Continual or frequent			Infrequent			Total
	No.	Score	Society	No.	Score	Society	
High	8	0.60	Abipon	10	0.55	Lau	18
		0.60	Plains Cree		0.60	Ingassana	
		0.60	Timbira		0.60	Sema	
		0.64	Mutair		0.64	Ambo	
		0.67	Wishram		0.67	Somali	
		0.80	Saramacca		0.78	Mossi	
		0.91	Egyptians		0.82	Aztec	
		1.00	Thai		0.89	Hawaiians	
					0.90	Japanese	
					0.90	Javanese	
Low	15	0.00	Trumai	10	0.00	Tiwi	25
		0.09	Gisu		0.10	Andamanese	
		0.20	Ila		0.14	Motilon	
		0.20	Tehuelche		0.22	Amba	
		0.27	Kurtatchi		0.22	Monachi	
		0.30	Jivaro		0.27	Orokaiva	
		0.33	Albanians		0.30	Mundurucu	
		0.36	Fox		0.33	Tiv	
		0.40	Comox		0.36	Marshallese	
		0.40	Papago		0.36	Tibetans	
		0.44	Aymara				
		0.44	Cherokee				
		0.44	Yukaghir				
		0.45	Nandi				
		0.45	Santa Ana				
Total	23			20			43

$$\phi = 0.15, \chi^2 = 1.02, \text{ns}$$
$$r_{pb} = 0.04, t = 0.27, \text{ns}$$

In summary, this section has shown that neither internal war nor defensive external war are related to the degree of military sophistication of a society. On the other hand, military sophistication and offensive external war are correlated. Thus societies with high military sophistication scores are no more likely to be characterized by frequent internal war than are societies with low scores, but they are likely to attack other societies frequently. Furthermore, it has been shown that the possession of an efficient military organization does not deter the attacks of other societies.

Military Success

One of the great difficulties in making a study of warfare is determining which party is militarily successful. Is it the political community which wins the most battles? Wins the most campaigns? Inflicts heavy casualties upon other political communities? Obtains the objectives which it set for itself prior to battle? If victory in battle is used as a measure of military success, several problems arise. Casualty rates in battle need not reflect the extent of the losses to a political community; the side with the lower casualties may be the smaller political community and hence may have lost a larger proportion of its adult male population than the political community with the greater population. The dislodging of one side from its positions need not constitute a victory, if those retreating are withdrawing in order to regroup for another battle. The side that attacks and flees has not necessarily been defeated if the objective of the attack was simply to loot or to kill one person. A campaign, by definition, consists of a series of battles, the last battle of the campaign usually being considered the most important. Since the campaign is a military practice that is found, presumably, only among highly centralized political communities, the success of a campaign cannot be used to measure victory in war among peoples with uncentralized political communities. Heavy casualties may he offset by a high birth rate; it appears from societies in this study that many political communities which frequently engage in warfare have populations which are on the increase. And finally, from most ethnographic reports it is impossible to determine what the objectives of war were prior to battle or whether the political community believes that it obtained its objectives after the war. Studies of Iroquois warfare in the eighteenth century provide an example of this difficulty; in spite of the ample historical data on the Iroquois of this period, much controversy has occurred concerning the political and military motivations of the Iroquois (Hunt 1940; Otterbein 1964; Trelease 1962).

One method of solving this problem, which has been followed in this study, is to measure military success in terms of the expansion or contraction of territorial boundaries. In spite of the number of battles won or lost, casualty rates, or whether the objectives of war are obtained, a political community which is expanding territorially is achieving a measure of success over neighboring political communities, whether the neighboring groups are being driven from their territory or are simply failing to occupy uninhabited territory which is being occupied by the expanding political community. Naroll

(1966, p. 19), who has developed a similar measure of success, argues that this success is usually accomplished by force of arms. It is difficult to imagine that a political community which is being defeated by its neighbors could he expanding territorially, unless it is being driven into marginal, uninhabited land (Vayda, 1961). The four societies in this study which do not have military organizations — Copper Eskimo, Dorobo, Tikopia, and Toda — were apparently driven from more desirable lands. However, there is no evidence that they now occupy more extensive territories than they did prior to their migrations. For any cultural unit and its constituent political communities, four types of territorial change can occur: their boundaries can expand, they can contract, they can remain relatively stationary, or the total amount of territory can remain approximately the same while the boundaries shift due to displacement caused by wars. Of the societies in the sample employed in this study for which there are data available, 13 have boundaries which are expanding, 24 have boundaries which are relatively stationary, 3 have boundaries which are contracting, and 3 have shifting boundaries. Such a distribution of societies indicates that it is the militarily successful societies which are best described, presumably because they are the ones which have survived or, in the ethnographic present, were surviving in intersocietal conflicts. Societies which are characterized by the latter three types of territorial change can be combined into one category and contrasted with those societies whose boundaries are expanding, thus creating a dichotomous variable which can he used as a dependent variable in the hypothesis tested below. Those societies which are expanding territorially are assumed to be militarily more successful than those societies whose territory remains constant or is contracting.

In the previous chapter, a military sophistication scale was developed from 11 military practices which were thought to confer military advantages upon those societies following the practices. A society with a high scale score should have a military advantage over a society with a low scale score. Although it would be desirable to examine pairs of neighboring societies in order to ascertain whether that society with the higher scale score was in fact the society which was expanding at the expense of the other society, the data do not permit such a comparison. For each of the societies in this study it can be assumed, because of the unbiased procedure followed in choosing this sample of societies, that the higher the scale score the higher the probability that neighboring societies will have a lower scale score. With this assumption, it is possible to test the following

Table 22. Military Success — I

Military sophis-tication	Territory constant or contracting			Territory expanding			Total
	No.	Score	Society	No.	Score	Society	
High	9	0.55	Lau	10	0.60	Abipon	19
		0.60	Ingassana		0.60	Plains Cree	
		0.64	Ambo		0.60	Sema	
		0.64	Mende		0.60	Timbira	
		0.64	Mutair		0.67	Somali	
		0.67	Wishram		0.82	Aztec	
		0.78	Mossi		0.90	Japanese	
		0.80	Saramacca		0.90	Javanese	
		0.89	Hawaiians		0.91	Egyptians	
					1.00	Thai	
Low	17	0.00	Tiwi	3	0.30	Jivaro	20
		0.00	Trumai		0.30	Mundurucu	
		0.09	Gisu		0.33	Tiv	
		0.10	Andamanese				
		0.14	Motilon				
		0.20	Ila				
		0.22	Amba				
		0.22	Monachi				
		0.27	Orokaiva				
		0.33	Albanians				
		0.36	Fox				
		0.36	Marshallese				
		0.36	Tibetans				
		0.40	Papago				
		0.44	Aymara				
		0.45	Nandi				
		0.45	Santa Ana				
Total	26			13			39

$$\phi = 0.40, \chi^2 = 6.21, 0.01 < p < 0.02$$
$$r_{pb} = 0.44, t = 2.96, p < 0.01$$

hypothesis: *The higher the degree of military sophistication, the more likely that the political communities of a cultural unit will be militarily successful.* The relationship between degree of military sophistication and military success is shown in Table 22. The phi coefficient of +0.40 is significant at the 0.02 level; the point biserial correlation is +0.44, and it is significant at the 0.01 level. Thus the hypothesis is strongly confirmed.

The distribution of cases in Table 22 can be interpreted in light of the above assumption. Societies with low scale scores are likely to be surrounded by societies with higher scale scores; therefore, a society ranking low in military sophistication has little likelihood of expanding territorially. This prediction is supported by the data in Table 22. Only 15 percent (3 out of 20) of the societies with low scale scores are expanding territorially. On the other hand, societies with high scale scores are likely to be surrounded by societies with lower scale scores; therefore, only societies ranking high in military sophistication are likely to expand territorially. Once again the prediction is supported by the data in Table 22. Over 75 percent (10 out of 13) of the societies which are expanding territorially have high scale scores, and over 50 percent (10 out of 19) of the societies with high scale scores are expanding territorially. Of the deviant cases, 75 percent (9 out of 12) are societies with high scale scores; all 9 of these societies have boundaries which are relatively stationary. In other words, although these societies are not expanding, none of them can be considered militarily unsuccessful in terms of contracting boundaries. In fact, several of the societies could expand further only with difficulty because of the effect of physical boundaries which cannot readily he transcended. For example, for the island states of Hawaii and Lau, there are no nearby lands to conquer.

Confirmation of the hypothesis provides clear evidence that the military sophistication scale does in fact measure military efficiency. The military practices composing the scale were selected on logical grounds as being more efficient than the military practices with which they were paired (see Table 16). Those practices so selected were combined to produce an overall measure of military efficiency. If expansion of territorial boundaries is accepted as an index of military success, then confirmation of the hypothesis supports the contention that the military sophistication scale does measure military efficiency. It does not prove, of course, that each practice is militarily efficient or that the practices are of equal efficiency. It does, however, provide support for the argument that most of the practices selected for military efficiency do contribute to military success. If nearly half of the military practices selected as efficient were less efficient than the practices with which they were compared, the military sophistication scale would not measure military efficiency, and hence, the scale would not correlate with military success.

It has been shown in this section that military sophistication and military success are highly correlated, thereby supporting the hypothesis that the higher the degree of military sophistication, the more likely it is that the political communities of a cultural unit will be militarily successful. An alternative hypothesis, however, is available; namely, that it is the degree of centralization of the political communities, rather than their military sophistication that explains the military success of the cultural unit as measured by expanding territorial boundaries. It is a widely held view in social science that centralized political communities, because of the coercive nature of their administrative structure, are characterized by an inherent tendency to expand. Service (1962, p. 151) has argued that "other things being equal," politically developed societies, including chiefdoms, will prevail in intersocietal struggles when pitted against tribes or bands. This hypothesis can be formulated for testing as follows: *The higher the level of political centralization, the more likely that the political communities of a cultural unit will be militarily successful.* The relationship between political centralization and military success is shown in Table 23. Even though the phi coefficient is in a positive direction, it is not significant. Thus the hypothesis is not confirmed.

This conclusion is surprising. Since it has been shown in Chapter 2 (cf. "Military Sophistication Scale") that level of political centralization and degree of military sophistication are highly correlated (see Table 17), and that degree of military sophistication and military success are also correlated (see Table 22), one could predict on logical grounds alone that level of political centralization will be correlated with military success. But this has been shown not to be the case (see Table 23). Thus one is left with the conclusions, on the one hand, that level of political centralization does not predict the military success of a society, as measured by territorial change, and, on the other hand, that the degree of military sophistication of a society predicts its military success. Since there are important conclusions which can be drawn from these results (cf. Chapter 4), it is appropriate to examine the combined effect which the two independent variables — political centralization and military sophistication — have upon the dependent variable — military success. In order to examine this effect, it is necessary to deal at one time with three rather than two variables. The technique followed is to control one variable while the relationship between the other two variables is examined; level of political centralization is used as the control variable. This is accomplished in Table 24 by placing all uncentralized political systems into a contingency table, which appears as the left half of the larger table, and by placing all centralized political systems into a contingency table, which appears as the right half of the larger table. In other words, this more complex table is simply composed of two

Table 23. Military Success — II

Political system	Territory constant or contracting		Territory expanding		Total
	No.	Society	No.	Society	
Centralized	10	Ambo Aymara Hawaiians Lau Marshallese Mende Monachi Mossi Mutair Saramacca	6	Aztec Egyptians Japanese Javanese Sema Thai	16
Uncentralized	20	Albanians Amba Andamanese Copper Eskimo Dorobo Fox Gisu Ila Ingassana Motilon Nandi Orokaiva Papago Santa Ana Tibetans Tikopia Tiwi Toda Trumai Wishram	7	Abipon Jivaro Mundurucu Plains Cree Somali Timbira Tiv	27
Total	30		13		43

$$\phi = 0.12, \chi^2 = 0.64, \text{ns}$$

four-cell contingency tables; they are interpreted by examining the differences between the phi coefficients of each contingency table. The greater the difference between the phi coefficients, taking into

Table 24. Centralized Political Systems and Military Success

Uncentralized political systems

Military success

Military sophistication	Territory constant or contracting			Territory expanding		
	No.	Score	Society	No.	Score	Society
High	2	0.60	Ingassana	4	0.60	Abipon
		0.67	Wishram		0.60	Plains Cree
					0.60	Timbira
					0.67	Somali
Low	14	0.00	Tiwi	3	0.30	Jivaro
		0.00	Trumai		0.30	Mundurucu
		0.09	Gisu		0.33	Tiv
		0.10	Andamanese			
		0.14	Motilon			
		0.20	Ila			
		0.22	Amba			
		0.27	Orokaiva			
		0.33	Albanians			
		0.36	Fox			
		0.36	Tibetans			
		0.40	Papago			
		0.45	Nandi			
		0.45	Santa Ana			
Total	16			7		

$\phi = 0.47, \chi^2 = 5.03, p < 0.05$

Centralized political systems

Military success

Military sophistication	Territory constant or contracting			Territory expanding		
	No.	Score	Society	No.	Score	Society
High	7	0.55	Lau	6	0.60	Sema
		0.64	Ambo		0.82	Aztec
		0.64	Mende		0.90	Japanese
		0.64	Mutair		0.90	Javanese
		0.78	Mossi		0.91	Egyptians
		0.80	Saramacca		1.00	Thai
Low	3	0.22	Monachi	0		
		0.36	Marshallese			
		0.44	Aymara			
Total	10			6		

$\phi = 0.37, \chi^2 = 2.22,$ ns

Table 25. Military Sophistication and Military Success

Military sophistication low

Military success

Political systems	Territory constant or contracting			Territory expanding		
	No.	Score	Society	No.	Score	Society
Centralized	3	0.22	Monachi	0			3
		0.36	Marshallese			
		0.44	Aymara			
Uncentralized	14	0.00	Tiwi	3	0.30	Jivaro	17
		0.00	Trumai		0.30	Mundurucu
		0.09	Gisu		0.33	Tiv
		0.10	Andamanese			
		0.14	Motilon			
		0.20	Ila			
		0.22	Amba			
		0.27	Orokaiva			
		0.33	Albanians			
		0.36	Fox			
		0.36	Tibetans			
		0.40	Papago			
		0.45	Nandi			
		0.45	Santa Ana			
Total	17			3			20

φ = −0.18, χ² = 0.62, ns

Military sophistication high

Military success

Political systems	Territory constant or contracting			Territory expanding		
	No.	Score	Society	No.	Score	Society
Centralized	7	0.55	Lau	6	0.60	Sema	13
		0.64	Ambo		0.82	Aztec
		0.64	Mende		0.90	Japanese
		0.64	Mutair		0.90	Javanese
		0.78	Mossi		0.91	Egyptians
		0.80	Saramacca		1.00	Thai
		0.89	Hawaiians			
Uncentralized	2	0.60	Ingassana	4	0.60	Abipon	6
		0.67	Wishram		0.60	Plains Cree
					0.60	Timbira
					0.67	Somali
Total	9			10			19

φ = −0.19, χ² = 0.69, ns

account positive and negative relationships, the greater is the influence of level of political centralization upon the relationship between the other two variables. As is shown in Table 24, the relationship between the two variables is not altered by controlling for level of political centralization. The phi coefficients remain essentially the same in both contingency tables. It is also possible to use military sophistication as the control variable and examine the relationship between the other two variables. The procedure followed is the same as that employed in Table 24. As is shown in Table 25, controlling for military sophistication does not create a relationship between political centralization and military success in either of the contingency tables. Thus the evidence seems conclusive that it is the degree of military sophistication rather than the degree of political centralization of a society which explains its military success as measured by expanding territorial boundaries.

This chapter has demonstrated that the political communities of a cultural unit which wage war in a sophisticated manner are likely to have high casualty rates, to frequently attack the political communities of neighboring cultural units, and to be militarily successful. Even though the possession of an efficient military organization does not deter the attacks of political communities of neighboring cultural units, it confers an advantage in intersocietal struggles by increasing the territory controlled by the cultural unit. This expansion should be explained in terms of military efficiency, not the degree of centralization of the political communities within the cultural unit. Thus the question posed at the end of the previous chapter can be answered in the affirmative. A cultural unit whose political communities wage war in a sophisticated manner has an increased advantage in intersocietal struggles in comparison with cultural units whose political communities do not wage war in a sophisticated manner.

Chapter 4: CONCLUSION

This cross-cultural study of the evolution of war has accomplished two major purposes. First, a series of hypotheses was tested, relating different types of political systems to each of 13 warfare variables. It was demonstrated that centralized political systems consistently tend to utilize those military practices which are more efficient than the military practices employed by uncentralized political systems. These warfare variables were used to develop a scale of military sophistication, which made it possible to evaluate the relative efficiency of the warfare waged by each society; this scale was found to be highly correlated with level of political centralization. Thus it was concluded that as political communities evolve in terms of increasing centralization, the manner in which they wage war becomes more sophisticated. Second, a series of hypotheses was tested which related the military sophistication scale to five different outcomes of war. It was shown that societies which ranked high on this scale were more likely to be militarily successful, as measured by expanding territorial boundaries, than societies which ranked low. However, high ranking societies had high casualty rates and frequently engaged in warfare with neighboring societies. It was also shown that societies which ranked high on the scale were just as likely to be attacked by neighboring societies as societies which ranked low; thus no evidence was found to support the theory that a well-developed military system will deter the attacks of enemies.

It can be argued that this study provides evidence for the evolution of war, if the following assumption is made: namely that for any pair of alternative military practices, the more efficient practice is more evolved than the less efficient practice. The basis for making this assumption is that the more efficient military practice confers a survival advantage upon a political community by increasing the likelihood that its military organization will defeat the military organizations of other political communities, thus also increasing the likelihood that the political community will be the survivor in intersocietal struggles. By equating efficient with evolved, the following argument can be derived: The greater the number of efficient or evolved military practices which are employed by the military organization of a political community, the more efficient or evolved is the manner in which it wages war. Since the military sophistication scale is a measure of the degree to which the political systems of a society employ efficient or evolved military practices, the military sophistication scale measures the extent to which the manner of waging war has evolved in that society. Thus a society which has a high scale score can be said to wage war in a manner which is more evolved than that of a society which has a low scale score. Therefore, it can be concluded that warfare has evolved to a greater extent in some societies than in others.

If the conclusion is accepted that warfare has evolved, as measured in terms of military sophistication, then two hypotheses can be derived from it: (1) If it is granted that centralized political communities are more developed in an evolutionary sense than uncentralized political communities (cf. "Political Communities"), a hypothesis which has been confirmed earlier — *"the higher the level of political centralization, the higher the degree of military sophistication"* (see Table 17) — can be rephrased as follows: *As a political community evolves in terms of increasing centralization, the more evolved the manner of waging war.* (2) Another hypothesis confirmed earlier — *"the higher the degree of military sophistication, the more likely that the political communities of a cultural unit will be militarily successful"* (see Table 22) — can also be rephrased: *The more evolved the manner of waging war, the more likely that the political communities of a cultural unit will be militarily successful.* These two hypotheses can be considered to be substantiated, since the hypotheses upon which they are based have been confirmed.

This study has also demonstrated that great variability in the use of military practices occurs among both uncentralized and centralized political systems. Both types of political systems were found to be characterized by both of the alternative military practices composing each variable. Examination of the lower two cells of the 13 tables used to test the hypotheses shows that for nearly every warfare variable a substantial proportion of the uncentralized political systems employed the more efficient of the two military practices composing the variable. In fact, for four variables — subordination, initiation of war, diplomatic negotiations, and weapons — a majority of the uncentralized political systems employed the more efficient practice. Furthermore, 20 percent (6 out of 30) of the uncentralized political systems had high scores (over 0.50) on the military sophistication scale. For centralized political systems, examination of the upper two cells of the tables reveals that for nearly every warfare variable a substantial proportion of the centralized political systems employed the less efficient military practice. In fact, for two variables — means of initiation and cavalry — a majority of the centralized political systems employed the less efficient practice. Moreover, 19 percent (3 out of 16) of the centralized political systems had low scores (under 0.50) on the military sophistication scale. This great variability in the use of military practices by both uncentralized and centralized political systems indicates that some uncentralized political systems wage war in a more sophisticated manner than some centralized political systems. If it is true that a political community will probably defeat any political community which wages war in a manner less sophisticated than its own, then it is to be expected that some uncentralized political communities will be able to defeat some centralized political communities.

Although this study, because of the method used in drawing the sample, does not provide direct evidence that there are uncentralized political communities with high military sophistication scale scores which have defeated centralized political communities with low military sophistication scale scores, it does provide indirect evidence that this may occur. The fact that a cultural unit is composed of centralized political communities does not ensure it of military success. As was shown in Table 23, the correlation between level of political centralization and military success is not significant. On the other hand, a cultural unit whose political communities wage war in a sophisticated manner is likely to be militarily successful. As was shown in Table 22, there is a significant correlation between military sophistication and military success. Of the 19 societies with high military sophistication scale scores, over half (10 out of 19) are militarily successful, in the sense that their territory is expanding. Not one of the societies with a high military sophistication scale score has contracting boundaries. Six of these societies have uncentralized political systems. The evidence appears conclusive: it is the military ability of a cultural unit's political communities, not simply the level of their political centralization, that determines military success. This supports the contention that if an uncentralized political community wages war in a more sophisticated manner than neighboring centralized political communities, it will on average defeat them by expanding territorially at their expense. Therefore, this cross-cultural study of war has demonstrated that although military sophistication increases with an increase in political centralization, an increase in political centralization is not a necessity in order for a political community to develop a sophisticated military system and to become militarily successful. Moreover, the development of an efficient military organization appears to be a necessary condition for a political community to remain viable in intersocietal conflicts; whereas the development of a centralized political community which is not supported by an efficient military organization will not prevent a political community from being engulfed by militarily more efficient neighbors. This relationship between military efficiency and territorial expansion at the expense of other political communities has been eloquently stated by Quincy Wright:

> Out of the warlike peoples arose civilization, while the peaceful collectors and hunters were driven to the ends of the earth, where they are gradually being exterminated or absorbed, with only the dubious

satisfaction of observing the nations which had wielded war so effectively to destroy them and to become great, now victimized by their own instrument [Wright 1942, p. 100].

REFERENCES

Davie, Maurice R. (1929). *The Evolution of War*. New Haven: Yale University Press.

Firth, Raymond (1963). *We, the Tikopia*, 2d ed. Boston: Beacon Press.

Hobhouse, Leonard T., Gerald C. Wheeler, and Morris Ginsberg (1930). *The Material Culture and Social Institutions of the Simpler Peoples*. London: Chapman and Hall.

Hunt, George T. (1940). *The Wars of the Iroquois*. Madison: The University of Wisconsin Press.

Huntingford, George W. B. (1954). "The Political Organization of the Dorobo." *Anthropos* 49:123–148.

Keller, Albert G. (1916). *Societal Evolution*. New York: Macmillan.

Malinowski, Bronislaw (1941). "An Anthropological Analysis of War." *American Journal of Sociology* 46:521–550.

_____ (1960). *A Scientific Theory of Culture, and Other Essays*. New York: Oxford University Press.

Mead, Margaret (1964). "Warfare is Only an Invention — Not a Biological Necessity." in: *War: Studies from Psychology, Sociology, Anthropology*, eds. Leon Bramson and George W. Goethals. New York: Basic Books, pp. 269–274.

Naroll, Raoul (1964). "On Ethnic Unit Classification." *Current Anthropology* 5:283–312.

_____ (1966). "Does Military Deterrence Deter?" *Trans-Action* 3(2): 14–20.

Otterbein, Keith F. (1964). "Why the Iroquois Won: An Analysis of Iroquois Military Tactics." *Ethnohistory* 11:56–63.

_____ (1967). "The Evolution of Zulu Warfare." in: *Law and Warfare*, ed. Paul Bohannan. Garden City: Natural History Press, pp. 351–357.

_____ (1968a). "Internal War: A Cross-Cultural Study." *American Anthropologist* 70:277–289.

_____ (1968b). "Cross-Cultural Studies of Armed Combat." *Buffalo Studies* 4(1):91–109.

_____ (1968c). "Higi Armed Combat." *Southwestern Journal of Anthropology* 24:195–213.

Otterbein, Keith F., and Charlotte S. Otterbein (1965). "An Eye for an Eye, A Tooth for a Tooth: A Cross-Cultural Study of Feuding," *American Anthropologist* 67:1470–1482.

Richardson, Lewis F. (1960). *Statistics of Deadly Quarrels.* Pittsburgh: Boxwood Press.

Rivers, William H. R. (1906). *The Todas.* New York: Macmillan.

Rosenfeld, Henry (1965). "The Social Composition of the Military in the Process of State Formation in the Arabian Desert." *Royal Anthropological Institute, Journal* 95:76–86, 174–194.

Service, Elman (1962). *Primitive Social Organization: An Evolutionary Perspective.* New York: Random House.

Spencer, Herbert (1896). *The Principles of Sociology,* Vol. 2. New York: D. Appleton.

Stefánsson, Vilhjálmur (1914). "The Stefánsson–Anderson Arctic Expedition of the American Museum: Preliminary Ethnological Report." *American Museum of Natural History, Anthropological Papers* 14(1).

Steward, Julian H. (1955). *Theory of Culture Change.* Urbana: University of Illinois Press.

Sumner, William G. (1911). *War, and Other Essays.* New Haven: Yale University Press.

Trelease, Allen W. (1962). "The Iroquois and the Western Fur Trade: A Problem in Interpretation." *The Mississippi Valley Historical Review* 49:32–51.

Turney-High, Harry H. (1949). *Primitive War: Its Practice and Concepts.* Columbia: University of South Carolina Press.

Vayda, Andrew P. (1961). "Expansion and Warfare Among Swidden Agriculturalists." *American Anthropologist* 63:346–358.

White, Leslie A. (1949). *The Science of Culture.* New York: Farrar, Straus and Cudahy.

Wright, Quincy (1942). *A Study of War,* Vol. 1. Chicago: University of Chicago Press.

Young, Frank W. (1965). *Initiation Ceremonies: A Cross-Cultural Study of Status Dramatization.* Indianapolis: Bobbs-Merrill.

Chapter
FIVE

Higi
Armed
Combat[1]

One approach to the study of the warfare of a tribal people is to analyze the total range of types of armed combat in the society. Any fight involving weapons, whether it be between individuals, an individual and a group, or between groups, is considered armed combat. A perusal of the anthropological literature dealing with warfare reveals only two studies which have employed such an approach. Nearly 40 years ago W. Lloyd Warner, in his classic study of Murngin warfare (1931), described six types of engagements in which these Australian aborigines used weaponry. These types included fights, killings, night raids, planned battles, pitched battles between regions, and peace-making fights. Recently, Napoleon A. Chagnon studied the Yanomamö of Venezuela (1967) and examined five forms of violence through which these Indians express their fierceness. This "graded system of violence" includes duels, club fights, spear fights, raids, and the assassination of visitors.

The following analysis of Higi armed combat describes five types of conflict in this society: duels, staff fights, feuds, raids, and battles. The social and political context of each type of combat is discussed, and the causes and outcomes of the conflicts are analyzed. The present study differs from those of Warner and Chagnon in that the three types of armed combat — duels, staff fights, and feuds — which occurred within the Higi political community[2] focused upon are classified as internal conflict; and the two types of armed combat — raids and battles — which occurred between this political community and other Higi political communities are classified as external conflict. Such a distinction is useful because it separates those types of armed combat which can be properly classified as warfare from other types which arise out of disputes generated within the political community.[3]

MWECIKA HIGI

The Higi, a tribal people numbering perhaps 120,000, inhabit the western flanks of the Mandaras, a rugged mountain range which separates Nigeria from Cameroun. Their territory, totaling approximately 500 square miles, lies predominantly to the east of the Madagali-Uba road, a section of the highway linking Maiduguri with Yola (Fig. 1). Traditions of the Higi relate that their ancestors migrated westward into what is now Nigeria from Gudur[4] in Cameroun and established settlements from which other settlements later derived. These migrations brought the Higi into conflict with the Marghi, whom they eventually drove from the mountain slopes (Kirk-Greene 1958, pp. 18–19); even today the Higi are peacefully expanding at the expense of their Marghi neighbors. Linguistically the Higi are related to other tribes in the area, such as the Bura, Chibuk, Fali, Kilba, and Marghi (Meek 1931, pp. 252, 253). Greenberg (1955, p. 48) has placed the language in the Bata-Marghi group of the Chad division of his Afroasiatic stock. There are considerable differences in customs and dialects among the clusters of Higi villages which form political communities.

The Higi described in this paper live in three villages (Tamwe, Wamari, and Lughui) east of the town of Michika, which was established by Fulani invaders in the 19th century (Vaughan 1964, p. 1086); these villages form a political community whose members

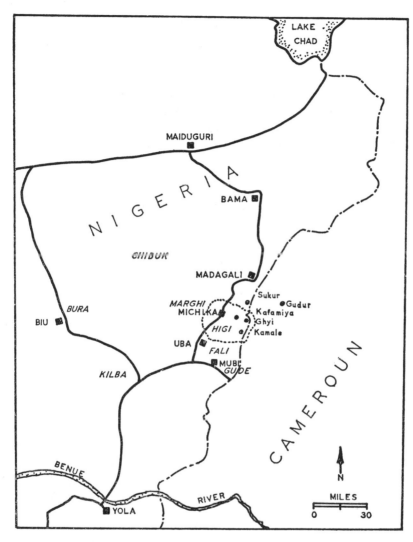

Figure 1. Sketch map of Northeastern Nigeria showing location of the Higi. The dotted line encloses Higi tribal area.

refer to themselves as Mwecika Higi.[5] The armed combat described below pertains to a period approximately thirty years ago. Fighting, however, has continued in some Higi areas until the present time; in

1964 there was a battle between a Higi and a Fali village in which several men were wounded and two were killed.

The ancestor of the Mwecika Higi came from Gudur to Ghyi and then to Kafamiya (Fig. 1). His first son went to Mwecika, but returned to Kafamiya, bringing his two brothers with him. The first son founded the Kwacha lineage, the second son the Kwaga lineage, and the third son the Kwaba lineage. During the period when warfare prevailed, the male members of a lineage resided in the same village; by virtue of lineage exogamy and patrilocal residence married women lived in their husband's villages.[6] The three Mwecika Higi villages, from north to south, are listed below, with the lineage occupying each, the approximate number of constituent compounds, and the name by which the inhabitants are called:

Village	Lineage	No. of compounds	Name of people
Tamwe	Kwacha	40	Mekurahai
Wamari	Kwaga	80	Gapa
Lughui	Kwaba	60	Lughui

The compounds, occupied by polygynous, patrilocal extended families, and built in relatively inaccessible places in the hills, are surrounded by stone walls approximately 5 feet in height.[7] Outside the compound walls are labyrinths of tall, almost impenetrable euphorbia hedges; these cacti have been grown only since the coming of the Fulani. Fields of guinea corn lie to the west of the villages; each village has a strip of land, stretching for several miles, upon which shifting cultivation is practiced.

A political community composed of the villages of Dlaka, Hidziku, and Kafamiya is located east of Mwecika; slightly north of this is a community comprising Ghijwa, Brazhewe, Lidle, and Mikisi. To the south lies the community of Miziku. The same dialect is spoken in these villages, and their founders reputedly were related to the Mwecika ancestor. South of Miziku is the political community of Bazza, with the village of Kandai to the southeast (Fig. 2). The Mwecika Higi fought with all these political communities.

Since hostile relationships between political communities rendered negotiations concerned with bride-price, bride-service, and

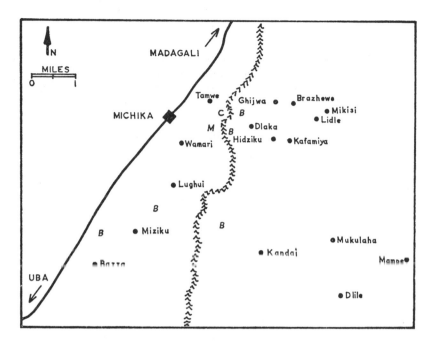

Figure 2. Sketch map locating the Mwecika Higi and their neighbors. B indicates a battlefield, M the meeting place, and C the ceremonial center.

dowry difficult, a man was not likely to marry as his first wife a girl from outside of Mwecika, although there was no rule against this. Additional wives, however, were often acquired by marrying women who were already married to members of other political communities (cf. section on "Secondary Marriage," below). This practice led to disputes over (1) women, (2) the custody of children, and (3) bride-price; these quarrels often erupted into armed combat between Higi political communities.

Mwecika Higi political organization comprises several officials and council members who play important roles in the procedures surrounding the five types of armed conflict. The chief (*mbage*) is the major political and religious figure of the political community. He is an elder of the village of Tamwe, chosen by his peers in the political community. Each village has several elders (the number depends on village size); these are men too old for active warfare, who have achieved prominence in their lineages. Together with the chief, they constitute an informal council. The council frequently convenes outside the chief's compound, but it may meet wherever quarrels take place.

The chief is usually accompanied by the *thlfa*, the official who installs him in office; if the chief cannot keep an engagement, the *thlfa* will act for him. The *thlfa* is from the village of Wamari, and a descendant of the man who anointed the first chief. Another important assistant of the chief, the priest (*zakure*), is a resident of Tamwe; he has charge of the ceremonial center in a cave east of Tamwe. Only the priest and the chief may enter the cave, which the chief often visits alone. However, the priest is primarily responsible for interpreting signs from the ancestors, which make it possible for him to foresee future events such as smallpox, death and, most importantly, the outcome of war.

INTERNAL CONFLICT

Four primary causes of conflict within the political community are likely to lead to armed combat: quarrels over land, jealousy over women, accusations of theft, and homicide. These conflicts are resolved by various types of armed combat, depending upon the parties to the dispute (see Table 1).

Duel

Two men who have quarreled may attempt to resolve their conflict by fighting with knobbed clubs in the presence of the elders and villagers. The club (*buthli*) is carved from one piece of wood; it is approximately two feet long, and has a ball at the end of the handle. This weapon is not used in war, but is sometimes carried for protection. A fight is initiated when one of the men touches the other man or the ground, a rock, or a tree close to him. The elders attempt to prevent serious injury to either man.

There are, however, two ways in which men can resolve a conflict without resorting to armed combat. One possibility involves the mediation of the chief, who sends the disputants (with the *thlfa* and a witness) to the priest at Kamale, a ceremonial center on the border between Nigeria and Cameroun. The chief does not initiate the proceedings, nor does he have the authority to force the men to go to Kamale. (Accusations of theft and quarrels over land are the most common disputes taken to the Kamale shrine for settlement.) So that their peaceful intentions will be communicated to the peoples whose territory they must pass through, the men do not carry weapons. A chicken or goat is given to the priest in charge of the proceedings. Each man brings with him a fighting cock which he places before the pot symbolizing the Kamale spirit (Meek 1931, p. 261). If the cocks fight, the owner of the winner is deemed to have justice on his side. If they do not fight, the owner of the cock that does not crow is the loser of the quarrel.

Another method of conflict resolution is for the accused to swear innocence, and then step over a *shafa*, made from three kinds of leaves, placed on the ground. If a man swears falsely, it is thought that he will be beset with misfortune: perhaps a child may die; his goats may be decimated; or sickness may strike him or his wife. If calamities occur and the guilty party makes reparation, well-being will be restored.

Staff Fight

If a disagreement occurs between two men from different villages within the same political community, it is possible that many men will be drawn into the quarrel before the elders and chief can intercede. When this happens a staff fight is likely to occur. Men from one village line up side-by-side, facing those from the other village; not all men in the villages are necessarily included. Each man fights with a pole as tall as himself and as thick as his wrist; the knobbed club is never used. The pole is held in both hands, and is used to beat a man in the opposing line. When a man is knocked down, his friends pull him away. Many men are usually felled before the fight is over; the side receiving the worst beating is the loser. If a man is killed accidentally no one is held responsible; in these circumstances compensation need not be paid.

The most common reason for staff fights is a dispute over land, with two men asserting rights to the same plot by virtue of ownership by their forefathers. If the elders have knowledge of the facts of the case, they intercede and settle the issue; if they do not, a staff fight may result to determine ownership. Jealousy also may lead to staff fights. A young man will harbor animosity if he has lost the girl to whom he was engaged to another man. When the opportunity arises he will commence a fight; since a man's extended family and his lineage are parties to the marriage arrangements, they are likely to come to his assistance. Fights over married women or the custody of children do not occur, since men do not take the wives of members of their political community.[8]

Table 1. Paradigm for the Analysis of Armed Combat

Levels	Parties	Causes	Institution	Tactics	Weapons	Outcomes	Mediators
Within political communities	individuals	1. accusations of theft	duel	hand-to-hand combat	clubs	1. loser is in wrong	elders
		2. quarreling over land				2. winner takes land	
	villages	1. quarreling over land	staff fight	lines	poles	1. winner takes land	none
		2. jealousy over women				2. revenge	
		3. selection of new chief				3. winner selects chief	
	lineages	1. homicide	feud	ambush	arrows	1. revenge or compensation paid	chief and elders

cont'd

Levels	Parties	Causes	Institution	Tactics	Weapons	Outcomes	Mediators
Between political communities	raiding party and individual	1. abduction and rape 2. show bravery 3. grief killings 4. trespassing	raid	ambush	arrows	1. wives and sexual exploits 2. increase in status for warriors 3. relief of grief 4. retain control of fields	none
	political communities	1. disputes over women and children 2. revenge for raid 3. stealing	battle	lines	arrows spears	1. revenge and captives that can be ransomed 2. revenge and captives that can be ransomed 3. revenge and captives that can be ransomed	none

Disputes over succession to the chieftainship may result in staff fighting. Although the eldest son of the deceased chief normally succeeds, the appointment occasionally is contested by Lughui, and the two villages may resort to a staff fight to resolve the issue. Lughui, with a larger male population, usually emerges as the winner of the contest. (Of the 17 chiefs of Mwecika, more than half were from Tamwe, and the remainder from Lughui.) When a Lughui chief dies, the chieftainship reverts to Tamwe.

Feud

Blood feuds occur between patrilineages: if a man of one lineage kills a man of another, the dead man's lineage will try to kill the assailant or one of his relatives. Revenge is usually taken by shooting an arrow from ambush, or into a compound. Children and male in-laws are immune from attack; women are not. When a homicide occurs the chief and elders intervene, and attempt to persuade the victim's relatives to accept compensation. The council meets outside the chief's compound and confers with the relatives of both the killer and the deceased, after which the amount of compensation, usually in sheep and goats, is determined by the council. If the killing was an accident, the deceased's relatives are less likely to demand revenge, and they may accept a smaller amount of compensation. Successful negotiations sometimes are difficult to achieve because many of the elders belong to the feuding lineages and may not want to accept compensation. If a homicide occurs within a lineage, the dead man's brothers will attempt to take the life of the killer; however, the elders of the lineage will intercede, and insist that compensation be paid.

SECONDARY MARRIAGE

The system of "secondary marriage" is the major cause of armed combat between Higi political communities.[9] Such marriages permit a man to marry a woman who is already married, provided she is not living in his political community and does not have a former husband living there. The man arranges through the woman's father to have her transferred to him, unknown to her husband, in exchange for a bride-price. A man may learn about a possibly available woman in another political community from her relatives in his village or from a friend who knows her and her family. Before attempting to make arrangements with the father, he seeks out the woman in a market or on a path, and informs her of his intentions. If she is interested, he sends one of her female relatives to inquire whether the father is willing to arrange a new marriage for his daughter. If the father agrees, the female relative leads several armed friends of the man to the father's compound at night; they take guinea corn beer with them and discuss the bride-price. Unless the woman happens to be at her parents' home at the time, the man does not accompany the party, as he is in grave danger of being ambushed and killed by the present husband if the latter discovers what is happening. The woman's father is also in danger if the husband suspects his connivance.

The transfer cannot be completed until the woman visits her father's compound. A woman usually is permitted to visit her parents, but a husband who suspects his wife's father of wishing to arrange a new marriage for her may refuse permission except on occasions of serious illness or death. The wife is likely to be angered by continued refusal, however, and may desert her husband and return to her parents.

A wife can be taken from her husband if the bride-price has not been paid in full. A father who wishes to arrange a new marriage for his daughter may try to force her to return by accusing her husband of not fulfilling the contract, thus starting a quarrel with him. When the woman has returned to her father's compound, he attempts to persuade her to accept a new husband. If he is successful, he requests the prospective husband to send his friends with the bride-price, which has a value approximately one-fourth that of the original bride-price, and like it consists of iron bars, goats, gowns, and blocks of salt. The woman accompanies these friends to her new husband. If the bride-price is not transferred at this time, and the new husband refuses to pay it, the girl's father sends her mother to claim it. Should the husband be foolish enough to quarrel with his mother-in-law, his wife supports her and leaves him. After he has paid the bride-price and the woman has lived with him a while, he cannot reclaim any of the bride-price if she leaves.

When a woman quits her first husband before any children have been born, his parents are entitled to the return of most of the bride-price (which, in fact, would be more correctly termed a child-price). If she has borne two children — even if they die — before she leaves her husband, no portion of the bride-price may be reclaimed. If she has had one child, approximately half of the bride-price should be returned. Since very young children remain with their mother, the first husband should, in theory, regain about half of the bride-price for each child whose custody he loses. The greed of many fathers-in-law, however, often makes recovery difficult, and in any case they have the right to deduct the items given to a daughter as part of her dowry. The more friends and relatives a man has to support his cause the better are his chances of recovering a portion of the bride price, but he would not visit the new husband's village to attempt to reclaim his children or the bride-price, as he could be killed. Some of the gifts received from the second husband may be used to repay the first husband. However, since the bride-price for a secondary marriage is lower than for a primary marriage, a father-in-law makes no profit if he returns the amount society prescribes as correct.

A man is most in danger of losing his wife after the birth of her third child; the first two children have canceled the bride-price, and the presence of a third child who will accompany the woman makes her desirable in the eyes of other men. Moreover, the father-in-law can demand a larger bride-price than usual from the second husband. A man gives only a male goat to his wife's father after a third child has been born, and nothing after the birth of a fourth child. Since the value of a goat is small compared with the bride-price obtainable from a second husband, the father-in-law is tempted to enter into negotiations with a suitor from another political community.

If a man desperately wants his wife to return and is willing to risk his life, he may go at night to the compound of her new husband. If he is caught, he may be killed, particularly if a member of the new husband's lineage has been slain by a member of his lineage and the death is still unavenged. Even if he is released, his captors may torture him by driving a thorn under each fingernail and toenail. When a woman still loves her first husband and does not want to have him killed or tortured, she will leave quietly with him.

A woman frequently returns to her first husband, perhaps because he treated her better or because she has children living in his compound and has none by her second husband. A woman may marry innumerable times, but she will not marry a member of a political community into which she has previously married as long as her former husband is alive and resident there.

MILITARY ORGANIZATION AND EQUIPMENT

As background to the analysis of armed combat between political communities, a description of Higi military organization and of the equipment carried by warriors is in order. The military organization has three types of personnel: warriors, *katsala*, and the war leader (*medala*). A young man becomes a *katsala* when he distinguishes himself through bravery and skill in archery. Each village has several *katsala*; since all able-bodied men (including blacksmiths) go to war, every man has the opportunity to achieve this status. A *katsala* slain in battle is not buried until vengeance is taken; an ordinary warrior will be buried first. A man who distinguishes himself as a *katsala* by killing many enemies is eligible to become war leader. The war leader is chosen by the elders, but if many of his men are killed while he is in command, he is removed from office.

Bows and arrows are carried by all warriors. Arrows, and all iron weapons, must be made by blacksmiths. Warriors, however, often make their own bows, quivers, and shields. The iron point of the arrow, which has a single barb, is fitted into a reed shaft approximately 1½ feet long; there are no feathers at the notched end, but the ends of the shaft are wrapped with thin tendons. Poison, made by blacksmiths and warriors, is smeared on the tip and shank of the iron point. The poison is composed of parts of two different trees, a root, a wild grain, and a fruit; these are cooked together until a sticky mass forms. Poisoned arrows are used both for hunting and for war. Bows about 5 feet in length are preferred for fighting because they are stronger, and arrows can be shot faster and farther. Short bows (about 3 feet long) are chosen for hunting, since they are less likely to become caught in bushes. Bows are manufactured from bamboo, and bow strings from the skin of the duiker, a small antelope. Two types of arrow releases are used: (1) the arrow is pulled back with the thumb and middle joint of the first finger; (2) it is drawn with the first finger above and the second finger below the shaft, while the thumb rests on the notch. Although both methods are used by warriors, the latter is preferred because the string can be drawn further and deliver greater force to the arrow. Since the bow is shot from a crouched position, it is held at an acute angle to the ground. The bow also is used to strike an enemy in hand-to-hand combat.

Shields, made from the hide of a wild buffalo or a domestic cow, are carried in battle by many warriors. They are constructed as follows: the shape of the shield — straight at the bottom and pointed at the top — is cut from the hide, moistened, and placed face down on a concave indentation in the earth.

The hide, which is approximately 2 feet wide and 4 feet long, is pounded with a blunt instrument so that there are indentations in the back and protrusions in the front. After several days, when the hide has dried, it is removed from the ground. The front is painted with stripes of brown and red ocher; either a metal handle wrapped with leather or a braided leather handle is attached to the inside of the concave back. Shields are light in weight and can be carried in one hand.

A warrior usually carries a double-edged knife, approximately a foot long, which resembles a short stabbing sword rather than a cutting knife. Some warriors also carry light axes for hand-to-hand combat, and throwing spears, 5 feet long, for fighting at close range. These spears have four-inch iron points with many small barbs. (Today one sees men carrying spears with long, broad blades; these are of Fulani origin.) The *nggalewai*, a slashing weapon, is carried at night for protection. It is made entirely from iron in the shape of a lower-case "f"; the back of the neck of the "f" is sharpened for several inches. The crossbar, which extends in the direction opposite to the cutting edge, makes it possible for a man to rest the weapon on his shoulder with the blade up while he holds it by one hand. The *nggalewai* is not used in war.

Warriors wear cloth caps, breechcloths made from animal skins and, if they are *katsala*, sheep skins. The breechcloth is put on by tying the skin from the hind legs around the waist so that it hangs down over the man's buttocks; then the skin is brought forward between the legs and tucked into the belt thus formed. In front of the breechcloth is hung a cloth which is made by Higi men. A knife sheath and two quivers hang at the left side from cords looped over the left shoulder; this enables the warrior to draw his knife and arrows with his right hand. Each quiver holds 20 to 30 arrows. Attached to one of the quivers is a leather bag containing medicines to prevent wounds, tamarind beans for drawing poison, an extra bow string, and medicines which foster accurate shooting. The tips of the arrows are touched against the medicines before they are placed in the quiver.

A young man about to become a warrior drinks medicine, obtained from a blacksmith, to prevent wounds. Since the medicine may become weak, a leather cord is worn around the waist for protection during combat. If the medicines a warrior carries, the medicines he has drunk, and the leather cord he wears around his waist are efficacious, enemy arrows will miss him and any knife used to stab him will bend.

EXTERNAL CONFLICT

Seven potential conflict situations may lead the Mwecika Higi to engage in armed combat with neighboring political communities: disputes over women and children, abduction and rape, trespassing, stealing, revenge, display of bravery, and alleviation of grief. Two types of armed combat — raids and battles — are employed in these engagements.

Raid

Since a husband usually accompanies his wives to the fields, attackers must kill or drive him away before taking his wives. Abductors attempt to persuade the women to marry them; if they succeed, bride-prices will be paid. Sometimes the attackers rape the women rather than attempt to acquire them as wives, since they realize that it will be difficult to persuade women to marry them if the latter have children living in another political community. Abduction and rape lead to war, even in cases in which the husband is not killed in the attack.

Young men may organize a raiding party in order to demonstrate their bravery. Several warriors, perhaps intoxicated by guinea corn beer, will enter the territory of another political community by stealth and either ambush someone coming along a trail or creep up to a compound at night and shoot arrows at someone sitting near the fire. The victim will shout to attract the attention of fellow villagers, who pursue the fleeing attackers into the hills. When the raiding party is safe, the warrior responsible for the wounding announces his name by shouting from a hilltop.

A raid may be the occasion for a grief killing after the death of an important man. Although no one is held responsible for the death, the mourners apparently believe that they can alleviate their grief by killing someone in another political community. Several relatives of the deceased organize a raiding party to carry out the attack.[10]

A final purpose for a raid is to prevent a neighboring political community from using one's fields. When people suspected of this intention trespass, they are attacked. Some villages are short of land; for example, Dlaka, whose inhabitants attempt to use territory belonging to Tamwe. Thus, Dlaka people are attacked whenever they are discovered on Tamwe land. The Mwecika Higi rationalize their attacks on the ground that the people in neighboring political communities grow a red guinea corn which makes their excrement red; they detest having these people defecate on their land.

Battle

Higi wars are instigated most commonly by disputes over women, bride-prices, and the custody of children (cf. "Secondary Marriage," above), but another reason is revenge for an attack by a raiding party. A third cause of war is the stealing of animals from a neighboring political community. If the chiefs of two political communities are on amicable terms, they may enter into secret negotiation to resolve conflicts engendered by disputes over women or stealing. Such friendships may result from marriage connections; however, friendship between chiefs does not necessarily establish amicable relations between their political communities.

The Mwecika Higi do not fight with neighboring tribes, such as the Marghi, Fali, and Gude, because they are separated from them by other Higi political communities; however, other Higi groups fight with the Marghi. The closer the Mwecika Higi are to neighboring political communities, the more frequently they fight with them. In descending order of frequency of raids and wars, their enemies can be ranked as follows: Miziku; Dlaka-Hidziku-Kafamiya; Bazza; Ghijwa-Brazhewe-Lidle-Mikisi; Kandai. The reasons for raids vary slightly for each of the five political communities. The two adjacent communities, Miziku and Dlaka-Hidziku-Kafamiya, are more likely than distant ones to be subject to raids to relieve grief and demonstrate bravery. Dlaka-Hidziku-Kafamiya and Ghijwa-Brazhewe-Lidle-Mikisi are attacked to prevent trespassing and to abduct women. On the other hand, disputes over women and children are the primary reasons for warfare with all of the communities except Kandai. The Mwecika Higi rarely attack Kandai, but Kandai raiders sometimes shoot Mwecika people as they sit around their fires at night. Vengeance for raids is the second common ground for war, although with Miziku wars arising from stealing are more frequent than those related to raids.

Higi warfare may occur at any time during the year, but hostilities are less likely to occur during the rainy season (May through September) when people are busy in agricultural pursuits. War is never declared, nor is peace ever arranged. The chief and the priest consult the idols to determine whether it is an auspicious time to wage war. The chief may call a council of war by sending a messenger (usually the *thlfa*) to summon the elders to his compound. If the chief is opposed to war, he instructs the elders to warn the warriors that fighting is not advisable. In the event the council favors warfare, the war leader blows a horn to call the warriors together.[11] They gather outside their compounds with their weapons, and then go to the central meeting ground near Tamwe to meet with the council. If a village does not send men, the men of other villages call them women, the most derogatory epithet that can be addressed to a man. Any man guilty of wrong-doing — such as stealing goats or grain from a member of the political community, practicing sorcery or poisoning people, fighting or quarreling, or having an affair with another man's wife — must confess it to the elders or he is likely to be killed or seriously wounded in battle. When the confessions are finished, the chief performs a rite to give the warriors strength and protect them from being killed. He dips an ox tail in a pot of water containing medicines and with one sweep sprinkles the warriors; he tells them to go to battle, to win, and to capture enemies. The fighters sing of war and shout as they separate into columns by village and converge on the battlefield. Every pair of political communities has its traditional battleground, which is a level, almost barren site, located approximately halfway between them.

The war leader precedes the columns, but waits until all the warriors have arrived on the battlefield before he initiates the battle by shooting the first arrow. If one of his own warriors shoots first, the action will not be punished later. The warriors scatter over the battlefield, forming long irregular lines arranged so that the men in the rear line are able to shoot between the men in the front line. Archers stand at least 10 yards apart. Men who carry shields protect the archers by standing in front of them, although some archers prefer to dodge arrows, rather than depend upon their fellows' shields. Since trees and rocks are sparse on the battleground, warriors have little natural protection. The archer's basic strategy is to pretend to shoot at one man, and then turn quickly to shoot at another. When a warrior exhausts his own supply of arrows, he will use those of the enemy; however, he must exercise caution lest he be shot while stooping to pick them up.

Children, who sometimes do not remain in the villages, may retrieve arrows and give them to the archers or take them home. Combatants avoid shooting children, as Higi believe that a man who kills a child will be unable to beget children.

The war leader takes a position behind the lines from which he can survey the course of the battle. He and several warriors who stay with him during the battle move to the sections of the lines which seem to be faltering and provide encouragement; they also recover enemy arrows for the archers. When a warrior is hit by an arrow, the war leader's attendants carry the wounded man behind the lines. The arrow is cut out, and the masticated outer covering of the tamarind bean placed on the wound to help draw the poison; to achieve further cleansing the injured area is sucked. The wound is bandaged with leaves and cord, and the man is carried to his compound where hot water is poured over his head to purify him. The latter procedure is supposed to make men bald. The chief and elders watch the battle from a hill behind the lines. Women stand far back from the lines and encourage the warriors; some of the bravest ones approach close enough to throw stones at the enemy.

In battle, a man does not shoot at in-laws and certain relatives of in-laws; this is achieved by changing places in the battle lines, so as not to be opposite these kinsmen. This rule applies to the wife's father and brothers; the sister's husband, his brothers, and father; the sister's children and their father (who may no longer be the sister's husband); first cousins and the children of first cousins. The rule is observed because men are afraid of losing their wives or of being assassinated if they shoot an in-law.

A battle may last all day and continue the next day if the side with the greater losses wishes to prolong the engagement in order to even the score. In a hard-fought battle, five to ten men on a side may be killed. When the opposing lines draw close together, and spears and axes are used, many more warriors are killed. The side with the greater losses will eventually flee to their villages and compounds. Pursuers attempt to kill or capture as many of the retreating enemy as possible. However, they do not enter the compounds, for it would be easy for the defeated foe to rally behind their hedges and stone walls for a counter-attack; furthermore, those who remained in the villages will help in the defense of the compounds.

The victors return home singing. If they have a captive, they go to the chief's compound. The prisoner is degraded; leaves are placed on him, front and back, like a woman, and he is forced to grind grain. His feet are locked in a log stock, he is beaten with a stick, and children tease him. A warrior who has been on night raids or is a *katsala* receives more abuse than an ordinary warrior. He is required to sing the praises of his captors and to relate stories derogatory to his own people. If he refuses, he will be killed. But he may be killed in any case if his captors hate him, or if his political community owes a life for someone previously killed. However, the desire for ransom (shared equally between the chief and the captor), restrains people from killing most prisoners. The ransom, consisting of goats, a small cow, and garments, is taken by relatives of the prisoner to the chief. However, they may fear capture themselves and request representatives in another village to deliver the ransom. If a warrior is captured a second time, his relatives must pay twice as much to have him returned.

CONCLUSION

For the Higi, three types of armed combat — duels, staff fights, and feuds — occur within the political community while two types — raids and battles — take place between political communities. From a conceptual point of view, any type of armed combat within the political community can be considered internal conflict. This case study has described the social and political factors which lead to conflicts between individuals, villages, and the lineages which compose the Mwecika Higi political community.

The study has also described the outcome of such violent conflict, and the roles which political leaders play as mediators. Hostile encounters between political communities are categorized as external conflict or warfare. The analysis has shown that the social and political factors which lead to warfare differ from those involved in internal conflicts: the practice of "secondary marriage" is primarily responsible for the conflict between Higi political communities. Since it is possible for almost any man to attempt to obtain a wife who is married to another man, a situation is created in which a constant state of enmity and hostility exists between political communities. Armed combat may break out at any time.

NOTES

1. The research upon which this paper is based was conducted in Northeast Nigeria during the summer of 1965. It was made possible by a grant-in-aid from the Wenner–Gren Foundation for Anthropological Research and by an Elizabeth M. Watkins Summer Fellowship from the University of Kansas. My wife, Charlotte Swanson Otterbein, and Gerald A. Neher have provided helpful comments and criticisms on the paper. The maps were drawn by Gordon S. Schmahl.
2. "By a 'political community' I mean a group of people organized into a single unit managing its affairs independently of external control (except that exercised nowadays by European governments)" (Schapera

1956, p. 8) A more precise formulation of this concept is the definition of a "territorial team" by Naroll (1964, p. 286): "A group of people whose membership is defined in terms of occupancy of a common territory and who have an official with the special function of announcing group decisions — a function exercised at least once a year." Garland (1962) has provided an extensive review and analysis of the concept of political community.

3. A recent cross-cultural study of feuding has shown the theoretical importance of this distinction. Otterbein and Otterbein (1965; see also Otterbein 1968) demonstrate that feuding, a type of armed combat which is found within a political community, does not occur as an institution in societies with a high level of political integration if frequent warfare is present. This same study indicates that both feuding and warfare are present in societies with a low level of political integration (the Higi would be classified as such); in a society with a low level of political integration there is apparently no authority which can prevent feuding when the society is engaged in warfare.

4. Gudur is also known as Shakiri (Meek 1931, p. 252), Cheklri (Baker and Yola 1955, p. 213), Mpsakali, Cskiri (Kirk-Greene 1960, p. 70), and Nekeli (John Guli, informant).

5. In order to differentiate the Fulani town from the Higi who live in the vicinity, two different spellings have been used — one for the town (Michika), the other for the people (Mwecika).

6. Meek's description of Higi social organization (1931) is difficult to understand because he does not make it clear that a village consists of a localized patrilineage. Villages are said to belong to the "same clan" (p. 254), to be the "political unit" (p. 262), and to regard all other villages, except those that use the same water supplies and market, as enemies (p. 254). On the other hand, the lineages — "kindreds are patrilineal and each kindred is exogamous" (p. 262) — are the "unit of government" (p. 254), are the "social unit" (p. 262), form "local groups" under the "spiritual authority of the local chief priest" (p. 254), and fought each other only with clubs (p. 262). Meek's description only becomes clear, to me at least, if village and kindred (lineage) are equated. The "local group" is apparently a political community. Meek (1931, p. 254) states that "the Higi never had ... any system of secular chieftainship... Though the chief priest had no executive power, he served as a unifying agent and exercised considerable control." Contrary to Meek, I found that the chief performed many executive functions.

7. There are photographs of the hills at Michika and of a wall of a Higi compound in Meek (1931, pp. 254, 268). Kirk-Greene (1960, p. 74), in discussing the stone architecture at Sukur (a mountain kingdom approximately 15 miles from Michika), states that "such architecture is rare in Nigeria, and in Adamawa the only other place where I have

seen it is in the Higi villages tucked away high above Michika, rarely visited by Government officials."

8. A different pattern of marriage and staff fights holds for the political community of Mampe-Mukulaha-Dlile. The villagers of Dlile and Mampe came from the same place, while the people of Mukulaha came from Mampe. Staff fights do not occur between Mampe and Mukulaha or Mampe and Dlile, but they do occur between Mukulaha and Dlile. Both primary and secondary marriages occur between Mampe and Dlile, but only primary marriages between Mampe and Mukulaha; presumably primary and secondary marriages take place between Mukulaha and Dlile.

9. Although Meek (1931, p. 267) states "that disputes over women and the custody of children are endless and the main cause of the inter-village hostility which is so pronounced among the Higi," and provides a description (1931, pp. 265–268) of secondary marriage which is essentially the same as mine, he fails to describe the manner in which the transactions connected with secondary marriage lead to war. In fact, he is probably in error — although I realize he may be referring to a political community which has this practice — when he notes (1931, p. 263) "that among the Higi there is no prohibition against eloping with the wife of a member of any kindred [lineage] of the local group [political community?] (other than of one's own kindred), provided the woman is not a member of one's own kindred." He adds in a footnote that "it is unusual to elope with the wives of neighbours who use the same water supplies and roads."

10. I was not able to confirm Meek's assertion that "When the chief died his sons immediately seized their arms and proceeded to the confines of some neighbouring hostile village where they slew a grown-up male member of that village. For it was considered necessary that when the chief died one of his enemies should also die" (1931, p. 256).

11. If the council is opposed to war, and some of the warriors disregard the advice, any fatality that results will be given special treatment. The dead warrior is carried to the central meeting site and placed on the ground, with the arrow that killed him laid across his abdomen. The chief again visits the ceremonial center and consults with the ancestral spirits. If the signs are auspicious, the elders are summoned again, and the warriors called together. Confessions are heard and the chief performs the important rites. The man is buried, drums are beaten, and the people mourn.

REFERENCES

Baker, R. I., and M. Zubeiru Yola (1955). "The Higi of Blazza Clan." *Nigeria* 47:213–222.

Chagnon, Napoleon A. (1967). "Yanomamö — The Fierce People." *Natural History* 76:22–31.

Garland, William (1962). *The Nature and Determinants of the Political Community: An Inquiry into the Concepts and Hypotheses of Political Anthropology.* PhD Dissertation, University of Minnesota, Minneapolis.

Greenberg, Joseph H. (1955). *Studies in African Linguistic Classification.* New Haven: Compass Publishing Company.

Kirk-Greene, A. .M. (1956). "Tax and Travel among the Hill-Tribes of Northern Adamawa." *Africa* 26:369–378.

_____ (1958). *Adamawa: Past and Present.* London: Oxford University Press.

_____ (1960). "The Kingdom of Sukur: A Northern Nigerian Ichabod." *The Nigerian Field* 25:67–96.

Meek, C. K. (1931). *Tribal Studies in Northern Nigeria,* Vol. 1. London: Kegan Paul, Trench, Trubner & Co.

Naroll, Raoul (1964). "On Ethnic Unit Classification." *Current Anthropology* 5:283–312.

Otterbein, Keith F. (1968). "Cross-Cultural Studies of Armed Combat," in *Buffalo Studies,* ed. Glenn H. Snyder. Buffalo: State University of New York, Vol. 4, No. 1, pp. 91–109.

Otterbein, Keith F., and Charlotte S. Otterbein (1965). "An Eye for an Eye, A Tooth for a Tooth: A Cross-Cultural Study of Feuding." *American Anthropologist* 67:1470–1482.

Schapera, Isaac (1956). *Government and Politics in Tribal Societies.* London: Watts.

Vaughan Jr., James H. (1964). "Culture, History, and Grass-Roots Politics in a Northern Cameroons Kingdom." *American Anthropologist* 66:1078–1095.

Warner, W. Lloyd (1931). "Murngin Warfare." *Oceania* 1:457–494.

Chapter
SIX

Cross-Cultural Studies of Armed Combat[1]

Armed combat between culturally similar peoples is a widespread social phenomenon; it has been found in both primitive groups and historical nations and continues in some modern nations. Two types of armed combat involving culturally similar peoples can be distinguished: feuding, or blood revenge following homicide, which occurs within a political community; and internal war which occurs between political communities. Three aspects of society can be examined for factors which may influence the occurrence of feuding and internal war: social structure, political organization, and intersocietal relations. First, within the social structure of many societies are fraternal interest groups, which are localized groups of related males, who can engage in feuding or war by making attacks upon members of their own or neighboring political communities. Second, the political organization of highly developed political sys-

97

tems contains officials who not only can intervene to bring about settlements in cases of homicide, but can also prevent fraternal interest groups from making unauthorized attacks. And third, intersocietal relations, when they result in warfare, should produce cohesiveness and thereby eliminate feuding and internal war.

This paper reports a synthesis of the results of two cross-cultural studies — one dealing with feuding, the other with internal war; in each study three hypotheses, each stemming from one of the above three aspects of society, were tested using samples of 50 societies. The corresponding hypotheses in each study are combined into single hypotheses which contain the same independent variable or predictive factor. Each hypothesis is tested with data from the two studies;[2] the results of each test are discussed in terms of the influence of the factors upon feuding and internal war. Where the factors have a differential effect upon the two types of armed combat, an attempt is made to explain the difference in the light of the fundamental distinction between feuding and internal war — namely, that feuding occurs within a political community, while internal war occurs between political communities.

The methodology employed in both studies being synthesized in this paper consisted of drawing probability samples of 50 societies from universes of so-called primitive or tribal societies. The societies included in these samples are given in Table 1. The exact sampling and coding procedures are described elsewhere (Otterbein and Otterbein 1965; Otterbein 1968). A glossary of terms or concepts used in the studies is given in Table 2. Figure 1 is included as a graphic illustration of the relationships between the major concepts; concepts dealing with aspects of social and political organization are represented by circles, and types of armed combat between social and political organizations are shown by double-headed arrows.

RESULTS

The independent variables which have been hypothesized as the factors influencing the occurrence of feuding and internal war can be grouped under three aspects of society: social structure, political organization, and intersocietal relations.

Social Structure

Fraternal interest groups are localized groups of related males who can resort to aggressive measures when the interests of their mem-

Table 1. Samples Employed in Cross-Cultural
Studies of Armed Combat

Feuding study	Internal war study
1. Abipon	1. Abipon
2. Andamans	2. Albanians, 1900 AD
3. Aymara	3. Amba
4. Bemba	4. Ambo
5. Carib	5. Andmanese
6. Chuckchee	6. Aymara
7. Creek	7. Aztec
8. Delaware	8. Cherokee
9. Iban	9. Comox
10. Ifugao	10. Copper Eskimo
11. Jivaro	11. Dorobo
12. Kapauku	12. Egyptians, 1250 BC
13. Kazak	13. Fox
14. Lepcha	14. Gisu
15. Lesu	15. Hawaiians, 1800 AD
16. Luo	16. Ila
17. Mandan	17. Ingassana
18. Maricopa	18. Japanese, 1200 AD
19. Marshalls	19. Javanese, 1300 AD
20. Mataco	20. Jivaro
21. Miao	21. Kazak
22. Micmac	22. Kurtatchi
23. Montagnais	23. Lau
24. Mosquito	24. Marshallese
25. Mundurucu	25. Mende
26. Murngin	26. Monachi
27. Navaho	27. Mossi
28. Nyakyusa	28. Motilon
29. Nootka	29. Mundurucu
30. Nuer	30. Mutair
31. Omaha	31. Nandi
32. Orokaiva	32. Orokaiva
33. Papago	33. Papago
34. Pomo	34. Plains Cree
35. Rundi	35. Santa Ana
36. Samoa	36. Saramacca
37. Siriono	37. Sema
38. Siwans	38. Somali
39. Tallensi	39. Tehuelche
40. Thonga	40. Tibetans, 1920 AD
41. Tikopia	41. Thai, 1600 AD
42. Timbira	42. Tikopia
43. Tiwi	43. Timbira
44. Tlingit	44. Tiv
45. Tupinamba	45. Tiwi
46. Vedda	46. Toda
47. Woleai	47. Toraja
48. Wolof	48. Trumai
49. Yakuts	49. Wishram
50. Yao	50. Yukaghir

Table 2. Glossary of Terms

CENTRALIZED POLITICAL SYSTEM. A political community in which there is at least one jurisdictional level beyond the local community (this was the measure used in the feuding study) or which possesses a government with the legitimate use of force and/or an official with economic redistributive functions (this was the measure used in the internal war study). Such political communities are politically more complex than uncentralized political systems.

CULTURAL UNIT. An ethnic unit composed of contiguous political communities which are culturally similar. In most instances the cultural unit is the same as a society, which is the unit used in the universes sampled from.

EXTERNAL WAR. Warfare between culturally different political communities, i.e., political communities which are not members of the same cultural unit. There are two aspects of external war which can be measured separately: political communities of a cultural unit can either attack or be attacked by culturally different political communities.

FEUDING. A type of armed combat occurring within a political community in which, if a homicide occurs, the kin of the deceased take revenge through killing the offender or any member of his kin group.

FRATERNAL INTEREST GROUPS. Localized groups of related males who can resort to aggressive measures when the interests of their members are threatened.

INTERNAL WAR. Warfare between political communities within the same cultural unit.

PATRILOCAL RESIDENCE. Requires the bride to reside with the groom either nearby or in the home of the groom's parents.

POLITICAL COMMUNITY. A group of people whose membership is defined in terms of occupancy of a common territory and who have an official with the special function of announcing group decisions — a function exercised at least once a year.[3] There is usually more than one political community in a cultural unit.

POLYGYNY. The marriage of one man to two or more women at the same time.

UNCENTRALIZED POLITICAL SYSTEM. A political community which is coterminous with the local community (this was the measure used in the feuding study) or which lacks a government with the legitimate use of force and/or an official with economic redistributive functions (this was the measure used in the internal war study). Such political communities are politically less complex than centralized political systems.

WARFARE. Armed combat between political communities.

---

bers are threatened (Thoden van Velzen and van Wetering 1960). Such groups can come into existence either through the operation of a patrilocal residence rule, since patrilocal residence produces a settlement pattern in which related males live near each other, or through the practice of polygyny, since polygyny usually produces a situation in which men will have a number of unmarried sons living

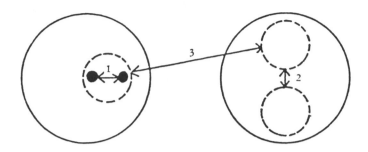

KEY:
Circles   Double-headed arrows
Solid circles represent fraternal interest groups   1 feuding
Broken-line circles represent political communities   2 internal war
Solid-line circles represent cultural units   3 external war

Figure 1. Diagram of major concepts.

with them. Thus both patrilocal residence and polygyny can be used as indices of fraternal interest groups.

One way in which fraternal interest groups can resort to aggression is to form small-scale military organizations which attack enemies who are members of either the same or a neighboring political community. Such armed combats are usually initiated by a small group of men who lie in ambush and attack the unsuspecting victim, who is often alone and has little chance of escape. The ambushers are of necessity sufficiently armed and organized that the group which they form can be referred to as a military organization; that is, a sufficient degree of organization must prevail if the warriors are to arrange the ambush in secret, to remain silently in hiding, and to spring the attack at the appropriate moment. If the members of such a military organization make an attack upon someone who is a member of their own political community, it is feuding or the initiation of a feud; if the next day these warriors ambush a member of another political community, it is war. Thus, fraternal interest groups, employing ambushing tactics, can be responsible for both feuding and warfare.

The first hypothesis tested in this study can be stated as follows: *societies with fraternal interest groups are more likely to have both feuding and internal war than societies without fraternal interest groups.* Using

Table 3.

	Feuding		
	Frequent or infrequent	Absent	
Other	7	18	25
Patrilocal	15	10	25
	22	28	50

$\phi = 0.32$, $\chi^2 = 5.20$, $p < 0.05$.

patrilocal residence as an index of fraternal interest groups, the relationship between patrilocal residence and feuding is shown in Table 3.

The 2×2 contingency table, which will be used to present data throughout this paper, gives the distribution of cases for each point on each variable. A hypothesis is tentatively confirmed if there are a greater number of cases in the lower left and upper right cells than in the upper left and lower right cells. In Table 3 the majority of cases (33 out of 50) conform to the hypothesis. In other words, if a society practices patrilocal residence there is a greater likelihood that it will be characterized by feuding than if patrilocal residence is absent. The relationship shown in such a table can also be described more formally using two simple statistical procedures: the phi coefficient (ϕ), which indicates the strength of the relationship, and varies from +1.00 to −1.00, with zero representing the point of no relationship; and the related chi-square statistic (χ^2), which can be used to determine the probability (p) that the distribution of cases in the contingency table could have occurred through chance factors, rather than through some meaningful relationship between the two variables. When the probability that the relationship could have occurred by chance is greater than one in ten, the relationship is said to be not significant (ns). However, a relationship not strong enough to be considered significant by these standards can still indicate a valid relationship. In Table 3 the phi coefficient is +0.32 and the probability that the relationship could have occurred by chance alone is less than one in twenty ($p < 0.05$), and therefore it is considered to be significant.

Table 4.

	Feuding		
	Frequent or infrequent	Absent	
Polygyny absent	9	20	29
Polygyny present	13	8	21
	22	28	50

$\phi = 0.31$, $\chi^2 = 4.71$, $p < 0.05$.

Using polygyny as an index of fraternal interest groups, the relationship between polygyny and feuding is shown in Table 4. The distribution of cases is almost identical to that of Table 3. Thus if a society practices polygyny, there is a greater likelihood that it will be characterized by feuding than if polygyny is absent. In more formal terms, the phi coefficient is +0.31 and the probability that the relationship could have occurred by chance is less than one in twenty ($p < 0.05$). Thus Tables 3 and 4, by demonstrating that there is a significant relationship between fraternal interest groups (as indexed by patrilocal residence and polygyny) and feuding, confirm one part of the hypothesis being tested.

Using patrilocal residence as an index of fraternal interest groups, the relationship between patrilocal residence and internal war is shown in Table 5. Although the number of cases in the lower left and upper right cells exceed the number of cases in the upper left and lower right cells by 26 to 16, yielding a phi coefficient of +0.14, the relationship is not significant.[4]

Using polygyny as an index of fraternal interest groups, the relationship between polygyny and internal war is shown in Table 6. The distribution of cases is similar to that of Table 5: 26 cases conform to the hypothesis and 16 do not. However, due to the properties of the formulae, the phi coefficient is higher (0+.31) and the relationship is significant ($p < 0.05$). Thus Tables 5 and 6, by demonstrating that there is a relationship (which is significant in Table 6) between fraternal interest groups and internal war, confirm the second part of the hypothesis being tested.

Therefore, since both parts of the first hypothesis being tested in this study have been confirmed by Tables 3 through 6, it can be

Table 5.

	Internal war		
	Continual or frequent	Infrequent	
Other	8	6	14
Patrilocal	20	8	28
	28	14	42

$\phi = 0.14, \chi^2 = 0.86$, ns.

Table 6.

	Internal war		
	Continual or frequent	Infrequent	
Polygyny absent	13	11	24
Polygyny present	15	3	18
	28	14	42

$\phi = 0.31, \chi^2 = 3.93, p < 0.05$.

concluded that societies with fraternal interest groups are more likely to have both feuding and internal war than societies without fraternal interest groups. (Although the tabulations are not presented in this study, there is no relationship between fraternal interest groups and external war.)

Political Organization

It has been argued that, as society becomes politically more complex, officials and courts gain the authority and power to intervene and prevent the relatives of a homicide victim from taking revenge (Hoebel 1954, p. 330) and to prohibit raiding parties from embarking upon war (Gearing 1962, pp. 85–119). This argument can be tested if it is formulated into the following hypothesis: *the higher the level of*

Table 7.

Political system	Feuding		
	Frequent or infrequent	Absent	
Centralized	10	13	23
Uncentralized	12	15	27
	22	28	50

$\phi = 0.005$, $\chi^2 = 1$, ns.

Table 8.

Political system	Internal war		
	Continual or frequent	Infrequent	
Centralized	10	3	13
Uncentralized	18	11	29
	28	14	42

$\phi = -0.15$, $\chi^2 = 1$, ns.

political complexity, the less frequently are found both feuding and internal war. The relationship between centralized political systems and feuding is shown in Table 7. The distribution of cases in the contingency table provides no support for the hypothesis since only 50 percent (25 out of 50) of the cases conform to the prediction. The relationship is not significant and the phi coefficient is nearly zero.

The relationship between centralized political systems and internal war is shown in Table 8. As in Table 7, only 50 percent (21 out of 42) of the cases support the hypothesis. In more formal terms, it should be noted that, although the relationship is not significant, it is in the direction opposite of that predicted; that is, the correlation is negative. It should be pointed out that 10 out of 13 centralized political systems engage in continual or frequent internal war; since it appears that nearly all centralized political systems engage in internal war, the presence of fraternal interest groups is irrelevant to or unnecessary for the occurrence of internal war. Thus for neither feuding nor internal war is there any support for the hypothesis that at a higher level of political complexity these two types of armed combat will be less frequent.

At this point in the analysis it can be shown that the influence of the predictive factors or independent variables has a differential effect upon the occurrence of feuding and internal war. In order to examine these effects, it is necessary to deal at one time with three rather than two variables. The technique followed is to control one variable while the relationship between the other two variables is examined: level of political complexity is used as the control variable in this paper. This is accomplished in the tables by placing all uncentralized political systems into a contingency table which appears as the left half of the larger table and by placing all centralized political systems into a contingency table which appears as the right half of the larger table. In other words, these more complex tables are simply composed of two contingency tables; they are interpreted by examining the differences between the phi coefficients of each contingency table. The greater the difference between the phi coefficients, taking into account positive and negative relationships, the greater the influence of level of political complexity upon the relationship between the other variables. There is also a statistical procedure for determining whether this difference between the phi coefficients is significant.

When the relationship between fraternal interest groups, indexed by patrilocal residence, and feuding, is controlled for level of political complexity, no significant difference between uncentralized and centralized political systems occurs. As shown in Table 9, the phi coefficient for the left half of the table is higher than the one for the right half of the table, but the difference between them is not significant.

When the relationship between fraternal interest groups, indexed by polygyny, and feuding is controlled for level of political complexity, once again no significant difference between uncentralized and centralized political systems occurs. As shown in Table 10, the phi coefficients for the two parts of the table are nearly identical. Thus Tables 9 and 10, by demonstrating the absence of a significant difference between phi coefficients, have shown that the type of political system has no influence upon the relationship between fraternal interest groups and feuding.

Table 9.

| | Uncentralized political systems | | | Centralized political systems | | |
| | Feuding | | | Feuding | | |
	Present	Absent		Present	Absent	
Other	3	11	14	4	7	11
Patrilocal	9	4	13	6	6	12
	12	15	27	10	13	23

$\phi = 0.48$, $\chi^2 = 6.24$, $p < 0.02$ (uncentralized); $\phi = 0.14$, $\chi^2 = 0.43$, ns (centralized). Difference between ϕ's not significant.

Table 10.

| | Uncentralized political systems | | | Centralized political systems | | |
| | Feuding | | | Feuding | | |
	Present	Absent		Present	Absent	
Polygyny absent	6	12	18	3	8	11
Polygyny present	6	3	9	7	5	12
	12	15	27	10	13	23

$\phi = 0.32$, $\chi^2 = 2.70$, $p = 0.10$ (uncentralized); $\phi = 0.31$, $\chi^2 = 2.25$, ns (centralized). Difference between ϕ's not significant.

When the relationship between fraternal interest groups, indexed by patrilocal residence, and internal war is controlled for level of political complexity, a large but not significant difference between the phi coefficients occurs, as shown in Table 11. The difference is large because for uncentralized political systems the coefficient is positive (+0.27), while in centralized political systems the relationship is negative (–0.30). When the relationship between fraternal interest groups, indexed by polygyny, and internal war is controlled for level of political complexity, a large and significant difference between the phi coefficients occurs. As is shown in Table 12, the

Table 11.

	Uncentralized political systems			Centralized political systems		
	Internal war			Internal war		
	Continual or frequent	Infrequent		Continual or frequent	Infrequent	
Other	5	6	11	3	0	3
Patrilocal	13	5	18	7	3	10
	18	11	29	10	3	13

$\phi = 0.27$, $\chi^2 = 2.08$, ns (uncentralized); $\phi = -0.30$, $\chi^2 = 1.17$, ns (centralized). Difference between ϕ's not significant.

Table 12.

	Uncentralized political systems			Centralized political systems		
	Internal war			Internal war		
	Continual or frequent	Infrequent		Continual or frequent	Infrequent	
Polygyny absent	6	10	16	7	1	8
Polygyny present	12	1	13	3	2	5
	18	11	29	10	3	13

$\phi = 0.56$, $\chi^2 = 9.15$, $p < 0.01$ (uncentralized); $\phi = -0.32$, $\chi^2 = 1.31$, ns (centralized). Difference between ϕ's is significant at $p < 0.02$.

difference is large because the coefficient is again positive (+0.56) for uncentralized political systems and negative (–0.32) for centralized political systems.

Thus Tables 11 and 12, by demonstrating a large difference between the phi coefficients, have indicated that the type of political system present has a strong influence upon the relationship between fraternal interest groups and internal war. That is, uncentralized political systems which have fraternal interest groups also are likely to be characterized by internal war, while in centralized political systems the relationship between these factors is reversed.

To summarize thus far, in uncentralized political systems fraternal interest groups are a determinant of both feuding and internal war, but in centralized political systems fraternal interest groups are a determinant of feuding but not internal war. Since officials and courts in uncentralized political systems have limited authority and power, it is understandable that officials are unable to prevent fraternal interest groups from engaging in either feuding or internal war; on the other hand, it is difficult to understand why officials in centralized political systems would permit fraternal interest groups to engage in feuding.

Intersocietal Relations

The answer to the above difficulty can be sought in the type of relationship that a political community has with its neighbors. Warfare, the most violent form of intersocietal relationship, should on theoretical grounds be the factor most likely to produce cohesion within the contending societies (Sumner 1906, p. 12). This theory can be tested if it is stated in the form of the following hypothesis: *societies which frequently engage in warfare are less likely to have both feuding and internal war than societies which infrequently engage in warfare.* The relationship between warfare (which would include both internal and external war, since a distinction between these was not made in the feuding study) and feuding is shown in Table 13. The distribution of cases in the contingency table provides no support for the hypothesis, since only 50 percent (25 out of 50) of the cases conform to the prediction. The relationship, of course, is not significant and the phi coefficient is nearly zero.

The relationship between external war, using as a measure being attacked by culturally different political communities, and internal war is shown in Table 14. Although the relationship is in the predicted direction, the phi coefficient is low and the relationship is not significant. Using attacks on culturally different political communities as another measure of external war and correlating it with internal war yields a similar distribution of cases in the contingency table; the phi coefficient is +0.14 and the relationship is not significant (the table is not shown). A third measure of external war can be derived from the first two measures and correlated with internal war. [The method of deriving this measure is described elsewhere (Otterbein 1968).] This correlation yields a phi coefficient of +0.17, but it likewise is not significant (table not shown). Thus there is no

Table 13.

	Feuding		
	Frequent or infrequent	Absent	
Occasional or never	7	10	17
Continual	15	18	33
	22	28	50

$\phi = 0.04$, $\chi^2 = 1$, ns.

Table 14.

Frequency of being attacked	Internal war		
	Continual or frequent	Infrequent	
Continual or frequent	11	8	19
Infrequent	15	6	21
	26	14	40

$\phi = 0.14$, $\chi^2 = 0.80$, ns.

evidence to support the hypothesis that frequent involvement in warfare decreases the frequency of feuding and internal war.

It has been shown above that, if fraternal interest groups are present, feuding and internal war occur in uncentralized political systems and feuding occurs in centralized political systems. It appears that officials in centralized political systems seemingly cannot prevent feuding. Thus far our analysis has not been able to explain this. A possible explanation is that officials in centralized political systems have the authority and power to prevent both feuding and internal war only when their political community is faced with warfare; on the other hand, officials in uncentralized political systems would not have the authority and power under any circumstances to prevent feuding and internal war. Roberts (1965, p. 209) has argued that in societies with "higher political integration" (most of the

Table 15.

War	Uncentralized political systems			Centralized political systems		
	Feuding			Feuding		
	Present	Absent		Present	Absent	
Occasional or never	2	9	11	5	1	6
Continual	10	6	16	5	12	17
	12	15	27	10	13	23

$\phi = 0.44$, $\chi^2 = 5.19$, $p < 0.05$ (uncentralized); $\phi = -0.48$, $\chi^2 = 5.25$, $p < 0.05$ (centralized). Difference between ϕ's is significant at $p < 0.01$.

centralized political systems in the two studies would fall in this category) officials are reluctant to test the limits of their authority except under demanding circumstances. Warfare would be a demanding circumstance.

Although there is no significant relationship between warfare and feuding or internal war, it can be hypothesized on the basis of the above argument that warfare will have a differential effect upon feuding and internal war if the relationship is controlled for level of political complexity. As is shown in Table 15, there is a high positive correlation between war and feuding in uncentralized political systems and an equally strong relationship between war and the absence of feuding in centralized political systems. The correlations run in the opposite directions and the difference between the phi coefficients is significant. Thus in uncentralized political systems warfare and feuding go hand-in-hand, whereas in centralized political systems the presence of continual warfare precludes the existence of feuding. Apparently officials in centralized political systems intervene to prevent the development of feuding only when the society is engaged in war. Thus one part of the hypothesis is confirmed.

When the relationship between external war, using as a measure being attacked, and internal war is controlled for level of political complexity, no significant difference between uncentralized and centralized political systems occurs. As is shown in Table 16, the phi coefficients for each side of the table are identical.

Table 16.

	Uncentralized political systems			Centralized political systems		
	Internal war			Internal war		
Frequency of being attacked	Continual or frequent	Infrequent		Continual or frequent	Infrequent	
Continual or frequent	9	7	16	2	1	3
Infrequent	8	4	12	7	2	9
	17	11	28	9	3	12

$\phi = 0.11$, $\chi^2 = 0.31$, ns (uncentralized); $\phi = 0.11$, $\chi^2 = 0.15$, ns (centralized).

Using attacking as another measure of external war and correlating it with internal war, while controlling for level of political complexity, yields phi coefficients of +0.05 and +0.29; the difference between these is not significant (table not shown). Using the third or derived measure of external war produces phi coefficients of +0.11 and +0.19, which again are not significantly different from each other (table not shown). Thus there is no evidence to support the hypothesis that external war will reduce the frequency of internal war in centralized political systems. In other words, both uncentralized and centralized political systems engage in internal war with the same frequency as they do external war. Apparently officials in centralized political systems do not unite, and thereby eliminate internal war, when engaged in external war. Thus the other part of the hypothesis is not confirmed.

Therefore, it has been shown that warfare (external war in the internal war study) decreases the frequency of feuding, and not that of internal war, in centralized political systems. In the section dealing with political organization, the analysis had difficulty in explaining why, in centralized political systems feuding occurred when fraternal interest groups were present. The analysis in this section has shifted the focus of the problem from an analysis of social and political organization to an analysis of political organization and inter-societal relations. In other words, in attempting to explain one problem, a new variable or factor was introduced, warfare, which changed the problem. The problem now to be explained is why officials in centralized political systems can prevent feuding when engaged in war, but not internal war when engaged in external war.

CONCLUSION

An explanation for the fact that officials in centralized political systems can prevent feuding, but not internal war, when engaged in warfare can be found, I believe, in the difference between the units of analysis focused upon in the study of these two phenomena. In the study of feuding the focus is upon single political communities within a particular cultural unit. The difference corresponds to the distinction made by Bohannan between unicentric and multicentric power systems (1963, pp. 283–284). A political community, by definition, has a single center of power and is therefore a unicentric power system; the degree of power of the political community varies with the type of political system. A grouping of political communities which have relationships with each other constitutes a system with multiple centers of power. (The three political communities diagrammed in Figure 1 constitute a multicentric power system.) Since feuding, by definition, occurs within a political community, it occurs within a unicentric power system, but warfare, which by definition occurs between political communities, is characteristic of multicentric power systems. In a single political community or unicentric power system there is an official who can, if he has sufficient power, and will, if he perceives that the inter-political community situation demands it, intervene between the feuding fraternal interest groups. Since it is only in centralized political systems that officials have sufficient power — power which they may choose to exercise only under demanding circumstances — to control the activities of the military organizations of their political communities, it is only in centralized political systems which are engaged in war that one finds that the feuding of fraternal interest groups is curtailed.

On the other hand, in a grouping of political communities or a multicentric power system there are as many officials as there are political communities. Each official exercises authority only within his political community; he can only control, in centralized political systems, the activities of the military organization(s) of his political community. The only condition, ruling out conquest, under which internal war would cease would be that in which all the officials within the cultural unit form alliances between their political com-

Types of political communities	Power of officials	Armed combat within political community	Armed combat with culturally similar political communities
Uncentralized political systems	Limited under all circum- stances	If fraternal interest groups are present, feuding occurs under all circum- stances	If fraternal interest groups are present, internal war occurs under all circum- stances
Centralized political systems	Limited under some circum- stances, but not limited under demanding circumstances such as war	Feuding occurs if war is absent and if fraternal interest groups are present; feuding does not occur if war is fre- quent, even if fra- ternal interest groups are present	Internal war occurs under all circumstances; since most centralized political systems engage in internal war, fraternal interest groups need not be present for internal war to occur

Figure 2. Paradigm of results.

munities and prevent their military organizations from attacking each other's political communities. Although this could theoretically occur when the political communities are attacked by a culturally different political community, an official's fear that his own political community will become subordinated or incorporated into another political community often prevents alliances from occurring. An official may also fear that he will become politically insignificant or be assassinated by his ally. Rather than form an alliance he may prefer to witness the defeat of a rival but culturally similar political community at the hands of a culturally different political community.

To summarize, the analysis began with an attempt to explain the occurrence of feuding and internal war. The presence of fraternal interest groups was found to be a predictive factor of these two types of armed combat; on the other hand, the type of political system and the nature of intersocietal relations appeared to have no effect on the occurrence of feuding and internal war. If the study had restricted itself to only two-variable analyses, the results would have been that fraternal interest groups produce feuding and internal war irrespective of the level of political complexity and the frequency of warfare. The first hypothesis would have been accepted and the latter two rejected. However, three-variable analysis, in which level of political complexity was used as a control variable, revealed subtle but theoretically important relationships between political systems, fraternal interest groups, feuding, internal war, and external war. (For a four-variable analysis and its interpretation, see Otterbein and Otterbein 1965.) The paradigm in Figure 2 summarizes the results of synthesizing the two cross-cultural studies of armed combat.

Two major conclusions can be drawn from this study. First, in uncentralized political systems, which characterize the political organization of the majority of so-called primitive societies, armed combat both within and between neighboring political communities is caused by fraternal interest groups. These groups form small-scale military organizations which employ ambushing and hit-and-run tactics. Some writers (Malinowski 1941, p. 541; Turney-High 1949, p. 30; Wright 1942, p. 546), in attributing such tactics to peoples at the lowest stages of political development, have inferred that raiding is an unsophisticated form of military operation which does not merit the designation of true warfare. Contemporary warfare, however, has made it blatantly apparent that there is nothing inferior about raiding, or what is currently called guerrilla warfare. Second, centralized political systems which are found among primitive societies and also are characteristic of modern nations, have political organizations whose officials can prevent feuding and presumably other forms of armed combat within the political communities when the political communities are engaged in warfare. In other words, the officials of a modern nation, when their nation is involved in war, will suppress and prevent armed combat and other forms of violence. Presumably, during times of peace the officials will not tax the efficiency of their political organizations by interceding in confrontations between factions within the nation. In times of war, in order to present a united front and to staff the military organization, suppression of armed combat and violence is necessary. On the other hand, the study has provided no evidence that two culturally similar political communities will unite to wage war against political communities which are culturally different, even when one of them has been the victim of an attack. Apparently, the rivalries between officials of different political communities preclude political and military cooperation.

NOTES

1. 1 am indebted to my wife, Charlotte Swanson Otterbein, for advice on statistical procedures and for helpful comments and criticisms on this paper. The results of a cross-cultural study feuding which we conducted jointly are embodied in this presentation.

2. Tables 3, 4, 7, 9, 10, 13, and 15 are based upon the sample used in the feuding study and have appeared in Otterbein and Otterbein (1965). Tables 5, 6, 8, 11, 12, 14, and 16 are based upon the sample used in the internal war study and have appeared in Otterbein (1968).

3. This is Naroll's definition of a territorial team (1964, p. 286). The term political community is preferable because it is difficult to conceptualize large states as teams.

4. The disproportionate distribution of cases for both variables affects the size of the coefficient of correlation and this could be one reason for the lack of significance (cf. Ferguson 1959, pp. 198–199).

REFERENCES

Bohannan, Paul (1963). *Social Anthropology*. New York: Holt, Rinehart & Winston.

Ferguson, George A. (1959). *Statistical Analysis in Psychology and Education*. New York: McGraw-Hill Book Company.

Gearing, Fred (1962). *Priests and Warriors*. American Anthropological Association Memoir 93.

Hoebel, E. Adamson (1954). *The Law of Primitive Man*. Cambridge: Harvard University Press.

Malinowski, Bronislaw (1941). "An Anthropological Analysis of War." *American Journal of Sociology* 46:521–550.

Naroll, Raoul (1964). "On Ethnic Unit Classification." *Current Anthropology* 5:283–312.

Otterbein, Keith F. (1968). "Internal War: A Cross-Cultural Study." *American Anthropologist* 70:277–289.

Otterbein, Keith F., and Charlotte Swanson Otterbein (1965). "An Eye for an Eye, a Tooth for a Tooth: A Cross-Cultural Study of Feuding." *American Anthropologist* 67:1470–1482.

Roberts, John M. (1965). "Oaths, Autonomic Ordeals and Power." *American Anthropologist* 67(6/2):186–212.

Sumner, William (1906). *Folkways*. Boston: Ginn and Company.

Thoden van Velzen, H. U. E., and W. van Wetering (1960). "Residence, Power Groups and Intra-Societal Aggression." *International Archives of Ethnography* 49:169–200.

Turney-High, Harry H. (1949). *Primitive War: Its Practice and Concepts*. Columbia: University of South Carolina Press.

Wright, Quincy (1942). *A Study of War*, Vol. 1. Chicago: University of Chicago Press.

Chapter
SEVEN

A Cross-Cultural
Study of Rape

Rape is often considered a crime and, as such, is subject to punishment. This paper reports a test of a "deterrence theory" of rape
with a cross-cultural study which uses a sample of societies
drawn from the Human Relations Area Files. Fraternal interest
group theory is also tested. This theory argues that the presence of
fraternal interest groups, power groups of related males, predicts
the occurrence of rape in a society. Although the results support
both theories, a composite theory, using both deterrence and fraternal interest group theories, was found to provide a better explanation for the occurrence of rape than either theory alone.

Rape, the act of having sexual intercourse with a woman forcibly and
without her consent, is an ancient social problem which has concerned men and women alike in societies at all levels of social and
political complexity. It is often considered a crime — indeed, most
definitions state that it is a crime (Coughlin 1975, p. 295; Webster

119

1973, p. 1494); and, as a crime, it is frequently subject to punishment. Inherent in the belief system of some cultures, including those in Western civilization, is the notion that the application of punishment will prevent rape. This belief constitutes a "deterrence theory" of rape. This paper reports a cross-cultural study of rape in which this theory is tested using a sample of societies drawn from the Human Relations Area Files. A second theory, fraternal interest group theory, is also tested. Unlike deterrence theory, which sets forth a condition — punishment — for the suppression of rape, fraternal interest group theory sets forth the conditions which give rise to high frequencies of rape. The theory argues that the presence of fraternal interest groups, which are power groups of related males that resort to aggression to defend members' interests, predicts the occurrence of rape in a society.

Coded data for the other variables derive from other sources. The procedures used in indexing fraternal interest groups are identical to those followed in previous studies (Otterbein and Otterbein 1965, p. 1471; Otterbein 1968a, p. 278):

> Two factors which should lead to the formation of fraternal interest groups are a marital residence pattern in which the new family lives with or near the groom's relatives and the presence of polygyny; both indices were derived from the codings given by Murdock in the *Ethnographic Atlas* (1962, pp 117–118). A society was considered to be *patrilocal* if the residence pattern was listed as patrilocal (P),[1] avunculocal (A), virilocal (V), ambilocal, where the majority of couples live with the groom's relative (D), or where a common household is not established but the men of the community either remain in their natal households or live in special men's houses (O). Societies were coded as *other* if the residence pattern was matrilocal (M), uxorilocal (U), neolocal (N), or ambilocal, where the residence was not consistently with the kin of either spouse but was determined by personal circumstances (B, C). The symbols in column 14 of the *Atlas* (1962, p. 116) were used to code for the presence of polygyny (P, Q, R, and S or E, F, and G with either p, q, r, or s following) and its absence (E, F, G, M, N, and O).

Coded data on residence and polygyny came from the *Ethnographic Atlas* (Murdock 1962, 1967).

Codes for the frequency of feuding were taken from Otterbein and Otterbein (1965, p. 1470):

> Feuding ... was defined as blood revenge following a homicide. Ethnographic materials available in the Human Relations Area Files (HRAF) were used for this measure, and were coded on a three-point

scale: frequent, infrequent, or absent. A society was considered to have frequent feuding if, after a homicide, the kin of the deceased was expected to take revenge through killing the offender or any member of his kin group. If the kin of the deceased sometimes would accept compensation in lieu of such revenge, the society was coded as having infrequent feuding. Feuding was considered to be absent in those societies which had formal judicial procedures for punishing the offender, which always settled such matters through compensation, or which were reported to rarely have homicide.

Because this sample differs from the sample having data on rape, the number of societies found both in this sample and the rape sample is small.[2]

METHODOLOGY

Sample

The cross-cultural survey or hologeistic method is used to test the theories. Such a cross-cultural study typically utilizes a large sample of nonliterate societies; often they are drawn from the Human Relations Area Files (HRAF), a massive compilation of indexed but uncoded ethnographic material on nearly 300 societies (Lagace 1974). While several steps are normally followed in conducting a cross-cultural study (Otterbein 1969), the essence of the method is the simultaneous examination, usually by statistical methods, of a set of variables common to the entire sample; thus, the hologeistic method is a way of processing a large number of case studies at once. The sample used in this study was drawn from HRAF by Minturn, Grosse and Haider to demonstrate the "Cultural Patterning of Sexual Beliefs and Behavior" (1969). Included in the study were two variables dealing with rape. Codes for each variable were included. Data on other variables were taken from other sources: one source — the *Ethnographic Atlas* (Murdock 1962, 1967) — contained coded data for most of the societies in the sample, the other source (Otterbein and Otterbein 1965), for only a small number of these societies.

Measures

To test the above theories, data were obtained on the frequency of rape, its punishment, the presence of fraternal interest groups, and the frequency of feuding. Seven-point scales were used by Minturn,

Grosse, and Haider (1969, p. 135) to obtain data on the frequency and punishment of rape:

Frequency of Rape for Men

1. Concept of rape is absent, or rape reportedly never occurs.
2. Rape does not occur but the concept is present.
3. Rape is very rare.
4. Some aggressive seduction is reported.
5. Rape is not uncommon.
6. Rape or aggressive seduction is the preferred form of sexual activity.
7. All sexual relations are viewed as aggressive.

Punishment of Men for Rape

1. Death
2. Exile.
3. Heavy official fines or punishment by government.
4. Fine paid to woman's family or small fine paid to government.
5. Man may or may not be punished, depending upon the sex partner.
6. No official punishment or social stigma; man is ridiculed.
7. No punishment, fine, or social stigma.

RESULTS

Fraternal Interest Group Theory

Nearly twenty years ago, Thoden van Velzen and van Wetering set forth fraternal interest group theory (1960) to explain why some societies were internally peaceful, while others were nonpeaceful. They argued that a fraternal interest group, which is a power group of related males, "resorts to aggression when the interests of one of its members are threatened" (1960, p. 179). The authors set forth their theory in the following manner (1960, p. 180):

(1) In societies with power groups every act of violence elicits a chain reaction and there is danger of any individual deed of aggression

leading to group conflict. Much intrasocietal aggression can be attributed to the existence of power groups. Where they are not present, there will be no struggle for power at group level.

(2) Violence can be more effectively suppressed if the individual concerned is not part of a power group which is ready to support him through thick and thin. Bystanders who separate and restrain combatants can curb a great deal of potential aggression. The individual lacks the psychological assurance of a reliable stronghold behind him.

(3) In societies where there are no power groups, differences in power will merely consist of differences in muscular strength and personality. And violent treatment of the socially weak is also much less frequent.

Cross-cultural support was found for the hypotheses derived from the theory. The theory was elaborated and extended by Otterbein and Otterbein to encompass two forms of intergroup violence — feuding (which occurs between kinship groups within a political community) and internal war (which occurs between political communities within the same culture). In two cross-cultural studies it was shown that the presence of fraternal interest groups predicts feuding and internal war (Otterbein and Otterbein 1965; Otterbein 1968a, 1968b).

The presence of fraternal interest groups was indexed either by patrilocality or polygyny. Patrilocal residence, it was argued, results in a settlement pattern in which related males live close together; when such a condition exists the men will look after each other's interests and welfare. Polygyny produces a similar situation; adult unmarried half-brothers may be living near each other because polygyny frequently delays marital age for young males. The absence of fraternal interest groups was indexed by matrilocality, or some other form of residence, which does not group males locally; the absence of polygyny would have the same effect. If residence practices and marriage rules result in the scattering of related males over a large area, it is difficult for them to support each other's interests.

Fraternal interest group theory, as noted above, has been used to explain high incidences of interpersonal violence within local groups, feuding, and internal war. The theory can be expanded to encompass rape, which is a form of interpersonal violence. Since it has been shown that societies with fraternal interest groups are internally nonpeaceful, and that rape is a violent act, it can be predicted that societies with fraternal interest groups will have high frequencies of rape. Indeed, rape may be directly associated with other forms of violence. Societies with fraternal interest groups are societies which engage in feuding and internal war. It is often noted in the ethnographic literature that rape is a cause of feuding and warfare. On the other hand, one aggressive act of fraternal interest groups may be to attack and rape women. It appears from ethnographic accounts that the motive is often to defile the enemy by violating his women, valued possessions of the enemy. Thus, feuding and internal war can be precipitated by rape or rape may be an aggressive act resulting from feuding or warfare.

Since rape is a violent sexual act of an individual male, fraternal interest group theory as an explanation for rape can be questioned because the theory stresses both group action and group responsibility. Ethnographic accounts, however, indicate that rape is often perpetrated by several males; for example, the Higi of Northeastern Nigeria frequently become embroiled in internal wars due to raids which resulted in abduction or rape (Otterbein 1968c, p. 208). Brownmiller's (1975) comprehensive review provides many examples of gang rape. Furthermore, even if a man acts alone, he has the support of male kin if he is a member of a fraternal interest group. Indeed, it is his awareness of such available support which is a key element in fraternal interest group theory (Thoden van Velzen and van Wetering 1960, p. 180).

From this theory the following hypothesis can be derived: *Societies with fraternal interest groups are more likely to have a high frequency of rape than societies without fraternal interest groups.* The hypothesis was tested by indexing with the presence or absence of patrilocal residence. The relationship between residence and frequency of rape is shown in Table 1. The frequency of rape variable was dichotomized as close to the median as possible: 1–3 = low frequency, 4–7 = high frequency. A moderately strong correlation ($\phi = 0.36$), which is statistically significant ($0.01 < p < 0.02$), is obtained. The hypothesis can also be tested by indexing with the presence or absence of polygyny. The relationship between polygyny and frequency is shown in Table 2. A weak nonsignificant correlation ($\phi = 0.16$) is obtained.[3] It can be cautiously concluded on the basis of these two tests that there is moderate support for the hypothesis.

A second hypothesis can be derived from the theory: *Societies with a high frequency of rape are more likely to have frequent feuding than societies with a low frequency of rape.* The relationship between feuding and frequency is shown in Table 3. A strong correlation ($\tau_c = 0.75$) which is statistically significant ($p < 0.005$) is obtained. However, the

Table 1. Relationship Between Residence
and Frequency of Rape

	Frequency of rape		
Residence	Low	High	Total
Patrilocal	9	16	25
Other	13	5	18
Total	22	21	43

$\phi = 0.36$, $\chi^2 = 5.50$, $0.01 < p < 0.02$.

Table 2. Relationship Between Polygyny and
Frequency of Rape

	Frequency of rape		
Residence	Low	High	Total
Polygyny present	9	12	21
Polygyny absent	13	9	22
Total	22	21	43

$\phi = 0.16$, $\chi^2 = 1.13$, not significant.

small number of cases ($n = 12$) indicates cautious acceptance of the results. (No test was made for the relationship between internal war and frequency because only five cases were available.) Since support has been found for both hypotheses derived from fraternal interest group theory, it can be concluded that there is some support for the theory.

Table 3. Relationship Between Frequency
of Rape and Feuding

Frequency of rape	Frequency of feuding			
	Frequent	Infrequent	Absent	Total
Low	0	4	3	7
High	3	2	0	5
Total	3	6	3	12

$\tau_c = 0.75$, $p < 0.005$, using Fisher's Exact Test. For calculation of Fisher's exact test, the trichotomized variables, in this and each of the following tables, were dichotomized as close to the median as possible.

Deterrence Theory

The notion that certain behavior on the part of individuals or groups can be prevented by prior appropriate actions is know as deterrence theory. Students of military affairs have argued that an efficient military organization will deter would-be aggressors from attacking (Otterbein 1970, pp. 88–92), while students of crime have argued that punishment or the threat of punishment will deter potential criminals from committing crimes (Kadish and Paulsen 1975, pp. 21–33; Packer 1968, pp. 39–48). Deterrence theory as applied to the study of criminal behavior has been delineated as follows (Packer 1968, p. 39):

> The classic theory of prevention is what is usually described as deterrence: the inhibiting effect that punishment, either actual or threatened, will have on the actions of those who are otherwise disposed to commit crimes. Deterrence, in turn, involves a complex of notions. It is sometimes described as having two aspects: after-the-fact inhibition of the person being punished, special deterrence; and inhibition in advance by threat or example, general deterrence.

Forcible rape is considered one of the four most serious crimes in the United States. Along with willful homicide, aggravated assault, and armed robbery, it is viewed as being appropriately subject to the criminal sanction (Packer 1968, pp. 296–301). A major purpose for applying a criminal sanction is to prevent or deter an act. Deterrence theory is found in the literature on rape prevention. Brownmiller's study concludes with a series of recommended changes in sexual assault legislation which are intended to deter rape (1975, pp. 379–389). She states (p. 379):

> I am one of those people who view a prison sentence as a just and lawful societal solution to the problem of criminal activity, the best solution we have at this time, as civilized retribution and as a deterrent against the commission of future crimes.

From this deterrence theory of rape can be derived the following hypothesis: *The greater the punishment for rape, the less likely that rape will occur.* In testing the hypothesis the seven-point scale of punishment of men for rape was trichotomized: 1,2,3 = major punishment, 4,5 = minor punishment, and 6,7 = no punishment. Frequency of rape was measured, as above, with a dichotomous variable. The relationship between punishment and frequency is shown in Table 4. A strong negative correlation (τ_c = –0.68) which is statistically significant ($p < 0.025$) is obtained. This inverse relationship between the severity of punishment and the frequency of rape provides support for the hypothesis and the theory from which it is derived.[4]

Further Analysis

Examination of the hypothesis test results indicates more support for deterrence theory than for fraternal interest group theory. Although the correlations are not directly comparable — the ϕ coefficient is related to the Pearson r while τ_c is not — the magnitude of the difference between a ϕ of 0.36 (see Table 1) and a τ_c of 0.68, ignoring the negative sign (see Table 4), suggests that the latter test result is the stronger. Both the significance levels and visual inspection of the tables support this conclusion. Rather than concluding that there is more support for deterrence theory than for fraternal interest group theory, it is possible — using three-variable analysis — to examine the interaction between fraternal interest groups and punishment and their joint effect upon the frequency of rape in societies. The procedure followed here is to reexamine the results of Table 4 by controlling for the presence and absence of fraternal interest groups, using the two measures of fraternal interest groups — patrilocality and polygyny (see Tables 5 and 6). Since the results of the three-variable analysis, using either index, are nearly identical, Tables 5 and 6 will be discussed simultaneously.

Three important findings emerge from the three-variable analysis: (1) Stronger results are obtained for deterrence theory if fraternal interest groups are absent than if they are present (compare the right

Table 4. Relationship Between Punishment
and Frequency of Rape

Punishment	Frequency of rape		
	Low	High	Total
Major	8	3	11
Minor	3	4	7
None	0	10	10
Total	11	17	28

$\tau_c = -0.68$, $p < 0.025$, using Fisher's Exact Test.

sides of Tables 5 and 6 with the left side of the same tables). Both visual inspection and the larger τ_c's support this finding. (2) The deviant cases in Table 4 (i.e., cases in which major punishment is present and the frequency of rape is high) are explained by the presence of fraternal interest groups. All three of these cases have both polygyny and patrilocal residence, and are to be found on the left sides of Tables 5 and 6. Looked at in another way, when fraternal interest groups are present, major punishment and a high frequency of rape in a society are as likely to occur together as not (about a 50/50 chance); when they are absent, major punishment and a high frequency of rape are not found to occur together. (3) Societies for which there is no punishment for rape have a high frequency of rape whether fraternal interest groups are present or absent (examine the lowest row of both sides of Tables 5 and 6).

These findings can be summarized in a paradigm which shows how the combinations of traits predict the frequency of rape found in a society:

major punishment + no fraternal interest groups → frequency of rape is low

major punishment + fraternal interest groups → frequency of rape may be high or low

no punishment + no fraternal interest groups → frequency of rape is high

no punishment + fraternal interest groups → frequency of rape is high

These findings indicate that while there is more support for deterrence theory than for fraternal interest group theory, neither theory alone gives as complete a picture as does a composite theory based upon the key independent variables in each of the separate theories.

Table 5. Relationship Among Punishment,
Frequency of Rape, and Residence

	Patrilocal			Other		
	Frequency of rape			Frequency of rape		
Punishment	Low	High	Total	Low	High	Total
Major	3	3	6	5	0	5
Minor	1	3	4	2	1	3
None	0	6	6	0	4	4
Total	4	12	16	7	5	12

$\tau_c = -0.42$, not significant; $\tau_c = -0.81$, $p < 0.05$, using Fisher's Exact Test.

Table 6. Relationship Among Punishment,
Frequency of Rape, and Polygyny

	Polygyny present			Polygyny absent		
	Frequency of rape			Frequency of rape		
Punishment	Low	High	Total	Low	High	Total
Major	4	3	7	4	0	4
Minor	2	3	5	1	1	2
None	0	4	4	0	6	6
Total	6	10	16	5	7	12

$\tau_c = -0.42$, not significant; $\tau_c = -0.94$, $p < 0.01$, using Fisher's Exact Test.

CONCLUSION

The results of this cross-cultural study of rape have provided support for both fraternal interest group theory and deterrence theory with stronger supporting evidence for the latter.[5] Further analysis of the data, however, showed the usefulness — indeed, I feel the necessity — of employing the key independent variables in a three-variable analysis. Two conditions appear to be characteristic of societies in which there is no rape — major punishment and the absence of fraternal interest groups. Major punishment alone, however, does appear to act to reduce the frequency of rape in a society. Moreover, it has been found that if there is no punishment the frequency of rape is high. Societies with fraternal interest groups have a high rape frequency if there is no punishment; however, if there is punishment, either major or minor, the frequency of rape may be either high or low. It appears, thus, that the presence of fraternal interest groups may override to some extent the influence of punishment in reducing the frequency of rape in a society. Nevertheless, the results suggest that strong sanctions decrease the frequency of rape, implying that penalties deter rape. It should also be pointed out that, since the frequency of rape is high if punishment is absent and if fraternal interest groups are absent, the presence of fraternal interest groups alone does not predict rape.

From the analysis of the data a composite theory has emerged which combines the two theories which this study set out to test. The above paradigm summarizes the new theory. No encompassing social-science expression, such as deterrence or fraternal interest group theory, is yet available to describe it. However, neither of the two theories initially tested has the explanatory power of the composite theory.

ACKNOWLEDGEMENTS

I am indebted to Charlotte Swanson Otterbein for helpful comments and criticism on this article. My thinking about rape has benefitted from conversations with Gay E. Kang, Doris M. Lemieux, and Julius C. Richardson.

NOTES

1. Capital letters in parentheses are code symbols used in column 16 of the *Ethnographic Atlas*.
2. A major problem confronting any future cross-cultural study of rape is data paucity. In the sample of 135 societies data were found on frequency for 43 societies and on punishment for 32 societies. It has been the awareness of data paucity, brought to my attention first by Donald F. Griffiths who has conducted a cross-cultural study of crime, which has deterred me from drawing my own sample and hiring coders. During the spring of 1977, two students conducting cross-cultural

studies under my direction in HRAF encountered great difficulties in coding due to the lack of sample data on rape for most societies.

3. Bacon, Child, and Barry (1963, p. 294) found that polygynous households were associated with a high frequency of personal crime (by definition rape was considered a personal crime), a result consistent with the hypothesis.

4. Controlling for level of political complexity, using codes from the *Ethnographic Atlas* (Murdock 1967, p. 160), has no measurable influence upon the relationship; that is, the inverse relationship holds for both uncentralized and centralized political communities.

5. Before the testing of the hypotheses, the author had predicted that fraternal interest group theory would receive support as it had in several other studies and that deterrence theory would not receive support for the same reason. The results thus came as a surprise.

REFERENCES

Bacon, M. K., I. L. Child, and H. Barry III (1963). "A Cross-Cultural Study of Correlates of Crime." *Journal of Abnormal and Social Psychology* 66:291–300.

Brownmiller, S. (1975). *Against Our Will: Men, Women and Rape*. New York: Simon and Schuster.

Coughlin, G. G. (1975). *Your Introduction to Law*. New York: Barnes and Noble.

Kadish S. H., and M. G. Paulsen (1975). *Criminal Law and Its Processes: Cases and Materials*, 3rd ed. Boston: Little, Brown and Co.

Lagacé, R. O. (1974). *Nature and Use of the HRAF Files: A Research and Teaching Guide*. New Haven: Human Relations Area Files Inc.

Minturn, L., M. Gross, and S. Haider (1969). "Cultural Patterning of Sexual Beliefs and Behavior." *Ethnology* 8:301–318.

Murdock, G. P. (1962). "Ethnographic Atlas." *Ethnology* 1:113–134, 256–286.

_____ (1967). "Ethnographic Atlas: A Summary." *Ethnology* 6:109–236.

Otterbein, K. F. (1968a). "Internal War: A Cross-Cultural Study." *American Anthropologist* 70:277–289.

_____ (1968b). "Cross-Cultural Studies of Armed Combat." *Studies in International Conflict, Research Monograph No. 1, Buffalo Studies* 4(1):91–109.

_____ (1968c). "Higi Armed Combat." *Southwestern Journal of Anthropology* 24:195–213.

_____ (1969). "Basic Steps in Conducting a Cross-Cultural Study." *Behavoiral Science Notes* 4:221, 236.

_____ (1970). *The Evolution of War: A Cross-Cultural Study.*. New Haven: Human Relations Area Files Press.

Otterbein, K. F., and C. S. Otterbein (1965). "An Eye for an Eye, A Tooth for a Tooth: A Cross-Cultural Study of Feuding," *American Anthropologist* 67: 1470–1482.

Packer, H. L. (1968). *The Limits of the Criminal Sanction*. Stanford: Stanford University Press.

Thoden van Velzen, H. U. E., and W. van Wetering (1960). "Residence, Power Groups and Intrasocietal Aggression." *International Archives of Ethnography* 49:169–200.

Webster, N. (1973). *Webster's New Twentieth-Century Dictionary of the English Language*, 2nd ed. unabridged. Cleveland: World Publishing Company.

Chapter
EIGHT

Feuding: Dispute Resolution or Dispute Continuation?

Review of Boehm, Christopher. *Blood Revenge: The Anthropology of Feuding in Montenegro and Other Tribal Societies*. Lawrence: University Press of Kansas, 1984. xx + 268 pp. including maps, photographs, glossary, index, and bibliography. $25.00 cloth, $9.95 paper.

Blood Revenge is a theoretical treatise on feuding. The potential reader who picks up the volume may think that it is a focused ethnography or an ethnohistorical study. It is neither. It is an analytic study that draws upon fieldwork and historical sources. Although Boehm states that "the main purpose of this book is simply to explain how the Montenegrins' blood feuds work" (p. 11), this is an understatement. It is my view that the main purpose of the book is to explain feuding in tribal societies. The Montenegrins, whom Boehm intensively studied from 1964 to 1966 in the field as well as in the archives, both before and after the fieldwork, are the vehicle which he uses to present his ideas about feuding. *Blood Revenge* thus is a case study of Montenegrin feuding, a case study in the sense that the purpose of the work is not primarily to tell us about Montenegro but to delineate variables and develop hypotheses applicable to any society which feuds. Although each chapter builds on the previous chapters, the book can be viewed as containing two parts: the first part, chapters 1 through 9, presents the case study; the second part, chapters 10 through 14, sets forth Boehm's theory of feuding.[1] This review will focus on Boehm's explanation for feuding.[2] First, however, Montenegrin feuding will be described in detail in its social, political, and environmental context.

MONTENEGRIN FEUDING

The Montenegrins are a European tribal people who in the eighteenth and nineteenth centuries "spent much of their energy in warfare, headhunting, and raiding against external enemies; ... they also carried on vicious blood feuds among themselves" (p. 3). "In the mid 1800s they amazed the Western world by forming a free Christian nation-state right in the midst of a powerful Moslem empire" (p. 5). Today they are a Republic incorporated into the modern nation of Yugoslavia. In recent centuries they have numbered no more than 50,000 (p. 178). For his field study Boehm selected the most isolated large group of people in Montenegro, the Upper Moraca Tribe (p. 8). The members of this tribe of nearly 2,000 people live in eight scattered settlements. Boehm lived in the largest settlement which contained one hundred houses and five hundred people (p. 22). Before living with the tribe for over two years, Boehm learned their language, Serbo-Croatian. What Boehm learned about the Montenegrins gave him insights into the manner in which these people conducted feuding in the nineteenth century.

Traditional Montenegro is described as a "refuge-area warrior society." Such an area maintains its political autonomy by being able to resist the predatory expansion of a kingdom or empire. A combination of five factors seems to be responsible for this type of ecological adaptation: (1) the territory is of marginal economic and strategic value to the predatory power, (2) a highly effective military technology is developed, (3) a segmentary political system enhances military flexibility, (4) the tribesmen must be highly motivated, and (5) they must have some means of supporting themselves when their marginal economy fails — they go raiding (pp. 40–41). Boehm in another book, titled *Montenegrin Social Organization and Values*, describes this adaptation in detail (1983, pp. 130–141).

Montenegro sociopolitical organization is based upon a patrilineal, patrilocal segmentary system composed of households, clans, and tribes. In the mid-1800s the tribes formed a confederation to resist Turkish expansion. I found it useful to develop an outline which I could refer to as I read *Blood Revenge*. (I also found the chart helpful to students who were required to read the book in a course on warfare which I taught fall semester 1984.). The outline shows the levels of sociopolitical organization, the leaders at each level, and the type of armed combat at each level. Also included are the Serbo-Croatian terms for the levels and leaders. Boehm often uses the Serbo-Croatian term in describing Montenegro life. (It is sometimes disconcerting to have Montenegrin terms set in regular type after one italicized usage; the most bothersome example is pop, unitalicized, for local priest.)

Table 1. Outline of Montenegro Sociopolitical Organization

Social/political organization	Leaders	Armed combat
Confederation	Bishop (*vladika*)	Raid (*cetovanje*), war
Tribe (*pleme*)	Chieftain (*vojvoda*) Court of Good men (*sud dobrih ljude*)	Feud, raid, War (*rat*)
Clan (*brastvo*)	Head (*knez*)	Feud (*krvna osveta*)
Close agnates Minimal lineage	(?)	
Household (*kuca*)	Head (*starjesina*)	

The household is a joint family household consisting of brothers and sometimes male cousins; marriage is monogamous, and residence is patrilocal/virilocal. The description of the household is not clear (pp. 47–48): "The members of a kuca owned their winter house and the pastures, fields, and forests around it and operated as a cooperative unit of subsistence involving as many as thirty or forty persons" (p. 48). Boehm's other volume on the Montenegrins provides little additional help (1983, pp. 32–41); one house in the 1930s contained five brothers and thirty people (1983, p. 41). The house that Boehm lived in (pictured on p. 24) appears too small to contain more than two nuclear families, yet it is described as "rather large." Another house pictured (p. 107) is much larger and two-storied; it could contain 30 people. Although no details of settlement pattern are given, I suspect that when a household became large, brothers and cousins would build houses near each other on land owned by the kuca. I have shown on the outline a level between the household and the clan labeled "close agnates/minimal lineage." Although Boehm presents no evidence for such a level, I believe one can correctly conjecture that such a unit existed. (On page 68 Boehm refers to the household as a minimal lineage.) The feuding societies with which I am familiar usually have localized lineages, and the lineages play a more important role in feuding than do the households or clans. If lineages do exist in Montenegro, those within the same clan do not feud with each other, for the clan is the basic unit in the feuding system. The Montenegrin exogamous clans were sometimes localized and sometimes scattered (p. 48). The basic territorial unit was the tribe, which was composed of many *unrelated* clans. Tribes, prior to confederation in 1841, were independent political communities, which not only feuded but raided each other and engaged in warfare in which heads were taken. Although the clans within a tribe were not related to each other, if one clan became involved in a feud with a clan in another tribe, all the clans in both tribes were very likely to become involved. After confederation the new state raided and went to war with the Turks; heads were taken.

The key concept in understanding Montenegrin feuding is *osveta*, vengeance. Boehm had 40 informants respond to a standardized list of 256 cue words. One cue word was *osveta*. About one-half of the informants interpreted *osveta* as *krvna osveta*, or blood revenge, in their responses. (There is no single term for blood-vengeance.) From these data, other field work observations, and historic sources, Boehm concluded that "for a Montenegrin tribesman, the taking of vengeance was a reasonable and eminently moral form of social action" (p. 62). "For their forebears — the tribesmen who lived without any centralized governmental power up to 1840 — blood feud was not merely acceptable and legitimate; for them it was a moral necessity that a man (or a clan) take vengeance, if a decent social status was to be maintained" (p. 66). This concern with appropriate moral behavior was a powerful social control mechanism. Not only might a man feel compelled to seek vengeance, but he might also refrain from committing immoral acts.

At this point in the analysis of Montenegrin feuding, Boehm introduces his explanation for feuding (p. 87). Feuding is "deliberate social engineering." It contains two critical elements of conflict management: "the deliberate limitation of conflict and a deliberate attempt to resolve the conflict." Thus, feuding is seen not as a manifestation or outcome of conflict, but the result of attempts to limit conflict. Feuding is an alternative to uncontrolled fighting between warriors living in close proximity to each other; as Boehm asserts in his closing statement, "feuding was, at one and the same time, socially disruptive but also socially integrative in several very important ways, particularly as a practical alternative to warfare at close quarters" (p. 244). With this theory as background, Boehm describes Montenegrin feuding in detail.

Not all killings lead to feud. Headhunting is not a cause; nor is killing a rapist, an adulterer, or a thief. An unintentional killing would be settled with compensation. Although no reference is made to the game of chess, some of the terminology employed by Boehm is directly taken from analyses of that game. The first homicide is a "major opening move." Causes of the first homicide might be a verbal insult, abduction of a maiden, seduction, adultery, runaway wives, breach of betrothal agreements, as well as disputes over pastures (p. 103). "Early moves in the middle game" deal with the retaliation; the closest kinsmen of the deceased had an obligation to take blood. A small clan might flee if hopelessly outnumbered (p. 108); if they decided not to flee, those seeking vengeance would attack the house of the killer. Houses were constructed of stone with loopholes in all walls through which muskets could be fired. The siege would last only three days. A temporary truce might be arranged. "The long middle game" could last twenty years with as many as twenty deaths on each side. Women were not killed. Assassination through ambush was the usual way that revenge was taken; scorekeeping occurred. A major reason that truces might be arranged was so that military alliances could be formed. "The end game" involved the management of conflict. Three truces would occur before the Court of Good Men would convene to end the feud.

Boehm identifies five predictable points at which individuals or groups were obliged to make critical decisions: (1) whether to insult another warrior, (2) to kill or not to kill, (3) to feud or to accept a truce, (4) whether to end the feud, and (5) judgment by the Court of Good Men. Since feuds were seen by the Montenegrins as highly disruptive to the social order, a backing down or a settlement could occur at any decision point. When a feud involved two clans within the same tribe, the Court of Good Men was motivated to effect a settlement. Intertribal conflicts impaired the ability of the confederation to defend itself against powerful external enemies. Bishops in the eighteenth and early nineteenth centuries used every bit of influence, religious and political, that they had to effect truces and settlements. Not until after 1840 did Bishop Rade Petrovic obtain the power "to punish blood-vengeance killers as they would be punished in a centralized state — by a death penalty" (p. 122).

Boehm's explanation for Montenegrin feuding, introduced before his detailed description of the blood feud, is elaborated upon in a chapter titled "Making Further Sense of the Feud." He next switches to what he calls a "bird's-eye view of Montenegro, focusing upon the total refuge-area adaptation to see how feuding complemented or hindered such a precarious political adaptation" (p. 175). In Boehm's view it aided adaptation in several ways. First, the population of 50,000 remained close to the maximum that subsistence activities plus raiding could sustain. When the population increased, feuding and warfare intensified and the excess male population would be reduced through battle deaths. Some emigration also occurred, helping to reduce the population. Once the population fell below carrying capacity, feuding and warfare would become less frequent. This equilibrium model closely parallels one developed by Vayda to examine the functions of primitive war in maintaining or regulating economic, demographic, and psychological variables (1968, pp. 88–89). Boehm, however, does not place his research in this wider theoretical context.

Not only did feuding reduce population pressure, it served as a latent moral sanction by substituting for coercive authority, "in that the probability of lethal retaliation and a costly feud sharply curtailed certain socially disruptive behaviors" (p. 183). B. Whiting (1950), in a cross-cultural study, called such a process "coordinate control" and contrasted it with "superordinate control."

A third way in which feuding aided adaptation was by inhibiting tribal confederation. Theoretically, this is one of the most interesting sections of the book. Boehm argues that feuding "kept the segmentary system from unifying to a degree that might invite extinction at the hands of the Turks" (p. 185). Yet Turkish attacks did lead to alliances between tribes. These attacks may have created a cohesiveness which itself provoked the Turks to launch an all-out attack upon Montenegro. The Montenegrin "confederation formed and then was shattered nearly half a dozen times before it finally became permanent in the period after 1800. In at least two cases, the entire population of Montenegro came close to genocidal extermination" (p. 185). During the pre-1840 period the bishops aggressively intervened to pacify intertribal feuds; although Boehm does not argue that the Turkish attacks provided the impetus for confederation, such an interpretation is highly consistent with his analysis. The data thus seem to support a conflict-cohesion theory; in societies at war, feuding will be suppressed (Otterbein and Otterbein 1965, pp. 1477–1478). But interestingly, the cohesiveness that was created was actually detrimental to survival. The Montenegrins attempted to deal with their dilemma — to be destroyed as individual tribes or to be destroyed as a confederation — by negotiating limited political submission with the Turks.

A possible reason why the bishops gained increasing power during the eighteenth century may lie in the changes of weaponry that occurred during this period. Boehm does not mention this as a possibility, and there is no evidence for the following interpretation. However, I want to search for an explanation of the means by which the bishops were able to gain such power that by 1840 Montenegro became a despotic state; the origin of the state is a topic that continues to fascinate many anthropologists including myself. Three phases in the development of weapons can be distinguished: (1) a pre-firearm period from early times to about 1700 (probably spears and bows and arrows), (2) a musket period from about 1700 to about 1820 (inaccurate muzzle-loading long guns), and (3) a modern firearms period from about 1820 to the present (accurate rifles which by the late 1800s used cartridges). Montenegrin feuding became fully developed during the pre-firearm period. With the introduction of muskets feuding became more lethal; as muskets improved and rifles began to replace muskets, casualties in feuding greatly increased. These changes in weapons could have produced changes in the sociopolitical organization in the following way. The bishops were probably the first to obtain good muskets and rifles; this would have given them an advantage in conflicts with tribal leaders.[3] Moreover, intertribal feuding would have become so lethal that tribal leaders might have welcomed truces and the settlement of feuds. This latter interpretation is highly consistent with Boehm's theory.

FEUDING IN CROSS-CULTURAL PERSPECTIVE

After completing his analysis of Montenegro feuding, Boehm draws upon other case studies of feuding and also upon cross-cultural studies to develop a theory that he intends to be applicable to all uncentralized political systems. A typology of armed combat is constructed: duel, raid, feud, and war. The typology is used only to orient the reader. Although I find this typology not to be universally applicable, many societies do have these four types of armed combat. (Some have more types, some have fewer.) Of the four types, feud is defined as "deliberately limited and carefully counted killing in revenge for a previous homicide, which takes place between two groups on the basis of specific rules for killing, pacification, and compensation" (p. 194). For Boehm there are two key elements to feuding: (1) retaliatory homicide is a righteous act, and (2) some means is available for stopping the conflict; this usually involves third-party intervention, truces, and material compensation. Ten other distinctive features are identified: rules, scorekeeping, turn taking, need for honor, notions of dominance, notion of controlled retaliation, cross-cutting social ties that retard feuding, a means to avoid warfare, difficulty of resolution, and impossibility of avoidance when population density is high (pp. 218–219). Boehm shows how his findings refute Black-Michaud's analysis of the feuding of Circum-Mediterranean peoples. Black-Michaud, as well as Peters, argues that feuds are "interminable" because resource competition is a persistent condition in the Circum-Mediterranean. Boehm shows convincingly that their analysis is incorrect — data from societies in the region, which include the Montenegrins, do not fit the model which they construct. Research conducted by my wife and me confirms Boehm's conclusion. In a 50-society worldwide sample we found that 14 of 22 societies with feuding had compensation (Otterbein and Otterbein 1965, p. 1473).

Having established that feuds are not interminable, but can be settled by the payment of compensation, Boehm returns to his explanation for feuding: "Thus, I propose the hypothesis that in any society that practices both feuding and warfare, one important function of feuding, as a highly rule-bound activity, will be to control the potential for expression of the warfare pattern within the local group or between closely cooperating groups" (p. 204). War is defined as "active confrontation between hostile groups that are fully mobilized for large-scale combat" (p. 194). The theory is elaborated to include the notion that the warriors themselves deliberately develop feuding in order to prevent warfare. Boehm states (p. 225): "My most radical suggestion is that both parties at feud and also their larger tribal communities realize that their own rules for feuding are what protect them both from intratribal war and from war at such close quarters that the consequences could be disastrous." Boehm recognizes that his "assumption about the avoidance of warfare is inferential" (i.e., he has no data to support this aspect of his theory); however, he believes that "it is susceptible of testing where ethnographic materials are very rich" (p. 204). I suggest that this should be seen as a challenge to any ethnographer who undertakes a field study of feuding and warfare.

Boehm's theory is placed in an even larger context, natural history. He considers the social-dominance behavior of primates, and notes that humans differ from other primates in that human behavior is guided by norms, third-party intervention occurs, and exiting from the group is possible. An "egalitarian ethos" develops which (1) makes it difficult for one man to dominate another and (2) creates consensual decision making. Feuding is part of this system and prevents one group from dominating another.

Boehm's explanation differs from the two major theories of feuding. Both ecological theory and fraternal interest group theory seek the causes of conflict. Feuding is one result. Ecological theory as developed by Peters and Black-Michaud is rejected by Boehm (see above). On the other hand, fraternal interest group theory developed by Thoden van Velzen and van Wetering (1960), Otterbein and Otterbein (1965), and Otterbein (1968, 1979) is accepted (pp. 223–230) and incorporated into Boehm's explanation for feuding. Fraternal interest group theory argues that when fraternal interest groups (i.e., localized groups of related males) are present, the society will have internal conflict, rape, feuding, and internal war. Fraternal interest groups are power groups which support the interests of their members. Any individual deed of aggression may lead to group conflict (Thoden van Velzen and van Wetering 1960, p. 180). Patrilocal/virilocal residence is the most frequently used indicator of the presence of fraternal interest groups. If fraternal interest groups are absent, conflict is at a minimum, rape is rare, feuding is absent, and internal war is infrequent unless the political community is centralized and has a professional military organization. Why does Boehm accept fraternal interest group theory and incorporate it into his theory, when in fact the theories differ? His theory views feuding as a reduction of conflict that otherwise would have occurred; fraternal interest group theory views fraternal interest groups as causing feuding (Otterbein and Otterbein 1965). I believe that Boehm is able to accept fraternal interest group theory because he treats it as an explanation for asocial acts, rather than for feuding; in other words, fraternal interest groups explain conflict, not feuding per se. In effect, Boehm develops a causal chain with the following form (p. 230):

$$fraternal\ interest\ groups \longrightarrow$$
$$homicidal\ retaliation \longrightarrow$$
$$feuding\ with\ compensation$$

Thus, Boehm has combined his theory and fraternal interest group theory. (What he has done is, I believe, a perfectly acceptable way of developing theory.)

One issue that Boehm could have developed, but which he did not, is the relationship of feud to law. He adopts the notion that feud is a functional alternative to law. Since it is not really law, legal anthropologists (as well as members of the "law and society" cross-disciplinary field, which includes legal anthropologists) have given far less attention to feuding than they have to identifiable legal systems (e.g., Bohannan 1963, pp. 284–291). As an alternative to law, feud can be labeled quasi law, but it is not considered law per se. If this approach is accepted, and I believe Boehm would accept it, two categories of societies can be delineated and contrasted: (1) societies with fraternal interest groups have much conflict, feuding, and little or no law, whereas (2) societies without fraternal interest groups have little conflict, no feuding, and much law. Legal anthropologists have focused most of their attention on the latter category. The standard text in legal anthropology, *The Law of Primitive Man* (Hoebel 1954), presents a series of case studies; each case falls in category 2 above. Hoebel selected cases for which there were data on law. Societies with fraternal interest groups, category 1 above, were not selected, presumably because they had little or no law. Since 70 percent of the world's societies are patrilocal (i.e., have fraternal interest groups), the omission of such societies (a group which includes the Nuer, famous for their segmentary lineage system and feuding) from his "sample" led to the production of a book that is heavily biased in favor of those societies with much law. The Montenegrins would not have been included in his text. I believe that Boehm would like to see the Montenegrins, as well as other feuding peoples, given serious scholarly attention by legal anthropologists. I would.

Although Boehm is perhaps not a legal anthropologist in the sense that he has not studied a society with an identifiable legal system, the functional approach which he develops places him squarely in the tradition of legal anthropology. This tradition assumes that (1) disputes are inevitable (the amount of conflict is treated as a constant, not a variable) and (2) order must be maintained (law reduces the amount of conflict). The classic statement of this position is to be found in *The Cheyenne Way* (Llewellyn and Hoebel 1941); this book remains today the centerpiece of legal anthropology. "The law-jobs are in their bare bones fundamental; they are eternal ... what is being said is that to stay a group, you must manage to deal with centrifugal tendencies when they break out, and that you must preventively manage to keep them from breaking out. And that you must effect organization, and that you must keep it effective" (1941, p. 290). If order is not maintained, through law, the society will disintegrate. In the early days of legal anthropology (the 1940s and 1950s) "trouble cases" had to be resolved; today "law and society" people focus on "dispute settlement processing." This set of assumptions and the framework that holds them is functionalism, à la Durkheim and Radcliffe-Brown: A society has needs that must be met, and certain culture traits meet these needs. Law is the culture trait that meets the need of maintaining social order.

The two assumptions of legal anthropology, and the functional approach which embodies them, today comprise the reigning paradigm for studying law. A recent textbook in legal anthropology titled *Order and Dispute* (Roberts 1979, pp. 13–14, 28) explicitly states the assumptions; they are also in *The Behavior of Law* (Black 1976, pp. 6, 107–111). Boehm's theory that feuding prevents internecine warfare is clearly an example of classical functionalism: feuding with compensation resolves conflicts and prevents the society from flying apart.

The two basic assumptions of traditional legal anthropology are incorrect. Fraternal interest group theory and the data which support it provide the evidence that the assumptions no longer stand. First, disputes are not inevitable. Societies without fraternal interest groups have little conflict. When much conflict occurs, it is found to be generated by a particular social structure (i.e., fraternal interest groups created through the practice of patrilocal/virilocal residence). Second, when conflict occurs it is not necessarily resolved. Compensation is not paid in all feuding societies. Conflict may persist at a high level for centuries. The Montenegrins seem to be a case in point. Conflict, and the violence that accompanies it, may escalate. In uncentralized political systems (bands and tribes) multiple deaths and fissioning may occur; in centralized political systems (chiefdoms and states) battle deaths and conquest may occur. Thus, the empirical findings of fraternal interest group theory, by leading to a refutation of the two basic assumptions of legal anthropology, force us to reject the traditional approach.

To recapitulate: Boehm develops a theory of feuding that argues that feuding with compensation terminates many situations of homicidal retaliation in societies with fraternal interest groups. The theory utilizes a functional approach; namely, that feuding is an alternative to law and that social order is maintained through the cultural practice of settling feuds through payment of compensation. However, the first assumption of traditional legal anthropology — that is, the inevitability of disputes — is not accepted by Boehm; rather, he accepts the argument of fraternal interest group theory that such power groups generate asocial acts (if such groups are absent, disputes are rare). The second assumption — that is, order must be maintained — is accepted. Because of my work with fraternal interest group theory and with theories of conflict in general, I believe that both assumptions are empirically incorrect. For this reason, and because Boehm believes that he does not have data to support his theory, I do not accept his functional theory of feuding. I think it is equally plausible that the mounting pressure from the Turks and the obtaining of good firearms by the bishops gave them the ability to force settlements upon reluctant tribal warriors.

NOTES

I am indebted lo my wife Charlotte Swanson Otterbein for innumerable discussions of feuding, discussions which date from our first collaboration — a cross-cultural study of feuding (Otterbein and Otterbein 1965). She has carefully edited this review. I am also indebted to my teaching assistant, Barton McCaul Brown, for several penetrating discussions of *Blood Revenge*. The book was required reading in a course on warfare which I taught during the fall semester of

1984 and again in the spring semester of 1985. He argued convincingly that Boehm's functional theory of feuding was radically different from fraternal interest group theory, the theory which my wife and I had used to explain feuding.

1. The book is a high-quality publication. There are three maps essential for locating Montenegro (distance scales missing); 37 photographs on rag paper (glossies would have been clearer); a useful glossary which is needed (after one italicized usage, Montenegrin words are in regular type). Sometimes there are noticeably more lines on a page (e.g., p. 66). The cloth version has a blood-red cover.

2. In preparing this review I have had the good fortune of having been a reader for the University Press of Kansas, a fact known to the author. Having read a draft of the manuscript two years ago has been both an advantage and disadvantage: an advantage in that I have had two years to think about Montenegro; a disadvantage in that I feel constrained not to raise some specific criticisms which I raised two years ago but which the author and the press apparently chose not to act upon.

3. A critical review of Boehm's other book on Montenegro (1983), which appeared after my book review was completed, points out that Bishop Rade (1830–51) obtained "substantial Russian aid" (i.e., firearms?) which enabled him to create a guard regiment (Grémaux 1984, p. 673).

REFERENCES

Black, Donald (1976). *The Behavior of Law*. New York: Academic Press.

Boehm, Christopher (1983). *Montenegrin Social Organization and Values: Political Ethnography of a Refuge Area Tribal Adaptation*. New York: AMS Press.

Bohannan, Paul (1963). *Social Anthropology*. New York: Holt, Rinehart & Winston.

Grémaux, Rene J. M. (1984). "Politics in 19th-Century Montenegro." *Current Anthropology* 25:673–674.

Hoebel, E. Adamson (1954). *The Law of Primitive Man: A Study in Comparative Legal Dynamics*. Cambridge: Harvard University Press.

Llewellyn, Karl N., and E. Adamson Hoebel (1941). *The Cheyenne Way: Conflict and Case Law in Primitive Jurisprudence*. Norman: University of Oklahoma Press.

Otterbein, Keith F. (1968). "Internal War: A Cross-Cultural Study." *American Anthropologist* 70:277–289.

_____ (1979). "A Cross-Cultural Study of Rape." *Aggressive Behavior* 5:425–435.

Otterbein, Keith F., and Charlotte Swanson Otterbein (1965). "An Eye for an Eye, a Tooth for a Tooth: A Cross-Cultural Study of Feuding." *American Anthropologist* 67:1470–1482.

Roberts, Simon (1979). *Order and Dispute: An Introduction to Legal Anthropology*. Harmondswortb, Middlesex, England: Penguin Books.

Thoden van Velzen, H. U. E., and W. van Wetering (1960). "Residence, Power Groups and Intra-Societal Aggression." *International Archives of Ethnography* 49:169–200.

Vayda, Andrew P. (1968). "Hypotheses About Functions of War." in: *War: The Anthropology of Armed Conflict and Aggression*, eds. M. Fried, M. Harris, and R. Murphy. Garden City, NY: Natural History Press, pp. 85–91.

Whiting, Beatrice B. (1950). *Paiute Sorcery*. New York: Viking Fund Publications in Anthropology No. 15.

Chapter
NINE

The Ultimate
Coercive Sanction:
A Cross-Cultural
Study of Capital
Punishment

Chapter 7: CONFRONTATION THEORY:
CAPITAL PUNISHMENT IN TRIBES

Fraternal Interest Groups in Confrontation

From fraternal interest group theory, developed by H. U. E. Thoden van Velzen and W. van Wetering (1960) and by Keith F. Otterbein and Charlotte Swanson Otterbein (1965), can be devised a "confrontation theory": not only are fraternal interest groups pitted against each other but political leaders also find themselves in confrontation with fraternal interest groups. Fraternal interest group theory was first developed by Thoden van Velzen and van Wetering to explain why the local groups of some cultures are peaceful internally, while others are rife with internal dissension. They argued that a fraternal interest group, which is a power group of related males, resorts to aggression when there is a threat to the interests of one of its members; in societies with power groups, any act of violence will be followed by another act of violence, thereby eliciting a chain reaction. The individual who is a member of a power group acts with the assurance that his group is ready to support him and his interests, "through thick and thin." Thus, any individual act of violence can lead to conflict between fraternal interest groups, and much intrasocietal aggression can be attributed to the power groups and their struggles for power. In contrast there is no such struggle for power in societies without fraternal interest groups, and differences in power consist primarily in differences in "muscular strength and personality." Without the presence of power groups, potential combatants lack psychological support for their acts of aggression; bystanders, instead of supporting violence, may try to avert it (Thoden van Velzen and van Wetering 1960, pp. 179–180). Thus, the difference between peaceful and nonpeaceful local groups was explained by Thoden van Velzen and van Wetering in terms of a single independent variable — fraternal interest groups. Since related males can more easily support each other in conflicts if they reside together, patrilocal residence was employed as an index of the presence of fraternal interest groups. The absence of fraternal interest groups was indexed by matrilocal residence, a social structural condition that usually results in the scattering of related males over a large region, making if difficult for them to support each other's interests. In a cross-cultural study using five measures of peacefulness/nonpeacefulness, including the presence or absence of blood feuds, Thoden van Velzen and van Wetering (1960) demonstrated that the presence of fraternal interest groups is responsible for the conflicts that occur within local groups.

Fraternal interest group theory was elaborated and extended by Otterbein and Otterbein to encompass two forms of intergroup violence — feuding (which occurs between kinship groups within a political community) and internal war (which occurs between political communities within the same culture). In two cross-cultural studies, it was shown that the presence of fraternal interest groups predicts feuding and internal war (Otterbein and Otterbein 1965; Otterbein 1968a, 1968c). These studies showed that polygyny, as well as patrilocal residence, may be employed as an index of the presence of fraternal interest groups, since polygyny usually produces a situation in which men have a number of unmarried sons living with them. The feuding study also demonstrated that the level of political integration of the cultures, considered alone, had no influence on the relationship between fraternal interest groups and feuding.

The original formulation of fraternal interest group theory dealt only with competing fraternal interest groups. However, in the elaboration of the theory by Otterbein and Otterbein, the role of officials or political leaders was also taken into account. The results obtained show that if a political community is centralized, and if it engages in warfare, it is unlikely to have feuding even if fraternal interest groups are present. The explanation is offered that officials in centralized political systems have the authority and power to prevent feuding only when their political communities are faced with warfare; in other words, political leaders are reluctant to test the limits of their authority except under demanding circumstances. Presumably, during times of peace, officials will not tax the efficiency of their "governments" by interceding in confrontations between factions within the political community. In times of war, however, in order to present a united front and to staff the military organization, the suppression of feuding and other forms of violence is necessary. For uncentralized political communities, the results obtained suggest that warfare has no influence in suppressing feuding. Indeed, feuding and warfare were found to go hand-in-hand in uncentralized political communities with fraternal interest groups. The results were interpreted to mean that political leaders in these cultures do not have the authority and power under any circumstances, including warfare, to prevent feuding and other forms of violence within their political communities.

Ethnographic Studies of Confrontation

In a field study of the Higi of Nigeria, Keith Otterbein (1968b) described the manner in which the chief and a council of elders would attempt to prevent feuds between fraternal interest groups. The Higi, a tribal people numbering perhaps 120,000, can be considered a "classic" example of a feuding society; social organization is based on extended family households, patrilineages, and patriclans; polygynous marital groups are the norm, and postmarital residence is patrilocal (1969). Although the Higi chief performs many executive functions (1967, 1968b) too numerous to list here, his authority and power are greatly limited, as the following passage indicates (Otterbein 1968b):

> Blood feuds occur between patrilineages: if a man of one lineage kills a man of another, the dead man's lineage will try to kill the assailant or one of his relatives... When a homicide occurs the chief and elders intervene, and attempt to persuade the victim's relatives to accept compensation. The council meets outside the chief's compound and confers with the relatives of both the killer and the deceased, after which the amount of compensation, usually in sheep and goats, is determined by the council. If the killing was an accident, the deceased's relatives are less likely to demand revenge, and they may accept a smaller amount of compensation. Successful negotiations sometimes are difficult to achieve because many of the elders belong to the feuding lineages and may not want to accept compensation.

Unfortunately, information on what effect warfare might have had upon the ability of the chief and elders to intervene in feuds was not obtained.

Another cross-cultural study conducted by Keith Otterbein (1979) used both fraternal interest group theory and deterrence theory to predict the frequency of rape. The results obtained show that where there is a major punishment for rape, including capital punishment, exile, and heavy official fines, the frequency of rape is almost always low. However, if fraternal interest groups are absent in cultures with major punishments, the frequency of rape is always low; if fraternal interest groups are present, the frequency of rape can be either high or low. The study also shows that feuding and rape are highly correlated. Although the study does not elaborate upon the reasons why a major punishment for rape should be less effective if fraternal interest groups are present, the previous research by Otterbein and Otterbein (1965) suggests that political leaders, who are the ones to administer major punishments, may meet resistance and interference from a fraternal interest group when one of its members is to be punished for rape. In other words, political leaders may find themselves in confrontations with fraternal interest groups.

Two ethnographic studies of the Metá of western Cameroon, both by Richard G. Dillon, deal directly with fraternal interest group theory (Dillon 1980a) and with capital punishment (Dillon 1980b). In precolonial times, the Metá were an uncentralized or egalitarian society of approximately 15,000. Local groups consisted of the residents of villages of several hundred persons, the members of several unrelated lineages. Each village was governed by a council, presided over by the village chief; the council consisted of "lineage head/notables." In addition to the protection of the village from external threats of sorcery, the responsibilities of this council included the settlement of interlineage disputes within the village (Dillon 1980a, p. 661). Dillon argues that although fraternal interest groups are present in Metá society, the presence of "conflicting loyalties" results in an "intermediate level of intrasocietal violence" and the "institutionalization of values favoring intrasocietal peace" (Dillon 1980a, p. 670). In the same study, he points out that dispute settlement sometimes succeeds in uncentralized political systems, even when conflicting loyalties and cross-cutting kinship ties are absent. Dillon mentions two African societies in which members of local groups may execute fellow villagers in order to prevent retaliation from other local groups, and another African society that places a high value on resolving conflicts by negotiation (Dillon 1980a, p. 659). The execution of a kinsman or a fellow villager cannot be explained, according to Dillon, by fraternal interest group theory; the individual who has transgressed against outsiders should, if fraternal interest group theory is correct, be defended by his fellow kinsmen, with whom he resides.

In the companion article, Dillon uses the Metá as a case study of an egalitarian society in which "ultimate coercive authority was a well-integrated part of the legal machinery" (1980b, p. 439). The death penalty was usually reserved for habitual witches and thieves. Secrecy characterized the several steps in the decision-making process: A complaint would be brought — often by individuals who were not kin of the offender — to the chief of the offender's village, who in turn would seek the "unanimous assent of the offender's lineage" (1980b, p. 443) to the execution of the offender. Substantial payments of goats, valuables, and palm wine would be made to the village chief by those bringing the complaint. Once the chief's consent was obtained, the execution could proceed. Usually chosen by the chief for the task would be a member of a lineage recently settled in the area, who would not have kin ties to the offender, i.e., the object of the proposed execution. The executioner, "dressed in a hood of raffia cloth and carrying a soot-blackened club, attempted to surprise the victim, and either kill or subdue him... If the victim had been killed, his corpse was cast into the bush, while if the offender had merely been captured, he was sold by a slave dealer, with the proceeds being turned over to the notables and village chief" (1980b, p. 445).

Fraternal interest groups, however, were an important factor in Metá legal life. They might not give consent for the execution, and, even having given consent, they might renege if the executioners failed to perform the killing secretly from ambush. "Interlineage fighting broke out in one case in which the executioners are said to have gone undisguised to spear their victim in a public market" (1980b, p. 449). Moreover, the "self-help" killing of a thief, or simply the capturing and torturing of the thief, were unusual occurrences: "The fear of violent reprisals by an offender's agnates ordinarily precluded their use" (1980b, p. 446). Nevertheless, Dillon concludes "that many factors worked together to make capital punishment possible within the egalitarian political order of the Metá," including "distributive" authority, secrecy, and the use of stranger-executioners (1980b, p. 450). Dillon concludes that, theoretically, the process of ultimate coercive authority "simultaneously functioned to preserve a precarious balance of power among mutually opposed descent groups in an uncentralized society" (1980b, p. 450). However, the data presented by Dillon can also be interpreted as leading to a different conclusion.

Both of Dillon's studies clearly show the role of political leaders and fraternal interest groups in an uncentralized political system. Not only are the fraternal interest groups seen as being pitted against each other but they are also seen as making use of political leaders to further their own ends. In turn, the political leaders, who are rewarded for their efforts, align themselves periodically with the interests of first one, then another fraternal interest group; thus they may tip the balance in favor of one of the groups. In this manner, political leaders may find themselves in confrontation with fraternal interest groups. Clearly, for the Metá, a strong fraternal interest group can resist the attempt of political leaders to have a member of the group executed. This interpretation differs from Dillon's theoretical conclusion, which views capital punishment as preserving a balance of power in Metá society. Confrontation theory, as set forth below, argues that imbalance may exist and that the entry of political leaders into disputes between fraternal interest groups may create further imbalance, since it is the weaker — not the stronger — fraternal interest group that may be forced to give up a member to the executioner.

In an analysis of legal liability in African tribal societies, Sally Falk Moore (1978) describes the conditions under which a corporate group, such as a fraternal interest group, will either expel or execute one of its own members. The analysis begins with a discussion of group confrontations and the principle of expanding dispute. Simply put, in societies whose legal systems are largely based upon self-help, it is necessary for an individual engaged in a dispute to have the backing of his corporate group; indeed, the dispute does not expand without this backing. Thus, conflicts in these societies are a matter of group, rather than individual, confrontation (Moore 1978, pp. 99–111). Although no mention is made of fraternal interest group theory, Moore's discussion up to this point parallels the theory set forth by Thoden van Velzen and van Wetering (1960). But Moore's theory of legal liability goes further than theirs. Collective obligations exist in situations of self-help that involve expanding disputes: "where every member of a corporate group has the power to commit it in this way to a collective liability a corollary rule always exists whereby the corporation may discipline, expel or yield up to enemies members who abuse this power or whom the corporation does not choose to support in the situation in which he has placed them" (Moore 1978, p. 121, italics in original omitted). In other words, those individuals who endanger the assets or lives of fellow members of their corporate group are likely to be expelled or executed. "Again and again in the literature, where expulsion is mentioned, or execution by one's own group, it is the gross violator or recidivist who is mentioned" (1978, p. 123).

A case study of the Montenegrins of the Balkans elaborates upon Moore's analysis. Like the Higi and the Metá, the Montenegrins are a patrilineal, patrilocal tribal people who engage in blood feuding. In an aptly titled paper, "Execution Within the Clan as an Extreme Form of Ostracism," Christopher Boehm (1985) reports that a Montenegrin clan might not only repudiate a troublesome clansman — thereby denying him clan protection and exonerating the clan from liability for any killings he might perform — but might even execute such a person. Boehm argues that "the execution within the clan ... provides the collectivity a means of eliminating two kinds of threat. One is a threat to its collective reputation, and in feuding societies local groups often are rivalrous in this matter. The other threat is that of a feud which will be very costly in blood, time, wealth and psychological stress" (1985, p. 316). And he argues that "in the case of clan execution ... fear of consequences from other groups spurs the ostracizers to the extreme of homicidal sanctioning" (1985, p. 318).

Moore's analysis, as well as Boehm's case study, could go further, however. Two important factors are omitted: First, the relative strength or weakness of the corporate groups is not considered. Dillon's studies of the Metá make it clear that the relative strength or weakness of a fraternal interest group influences whether the group executes or turns over to political leaders or a rival kinship group one of its members. A weak fraternal interest group will be forced to give up a member, while a strong group will not. Here seems to lie the reason why fraternal interest groups do not always defend a fellow kinsman. Second, the role of political leaders in group confrontations is not considered. Again Dillon's study of the Metá shows the role of the chief in carrying out executions. In performing this task, the chief is likely to become involved in confrontations with fraternal interest groups.

The following example, taken from the now famous warring Yanomamö of Venezuela, illustrates what can occur when the fraternal interest groups in a village are matched in size, and dual political leadership exists (Chagnon 1979, p. 394):

> The dissolution of a marriage where both spouses represent major political factions of the village has more political consequences than the dissolution of marriage where only one spouse comes from a politically significant group. An example illustrates the point. Several years ago in Village 18, the wife of one of the village headmen began having a sexual affair with another man. She came from the other large lineage in the village, and her brother, also one of the village headmen, attempted to persuade her to stop the affair. The two headmen were brothers-in-law and had exchanged sisters in marriage. The woman in question refused to follow her brother's advice, so he killed her with an ax. The recalcitrant woman's brother acted in such a way as to demonstrate to his brother-in-law that he considered the marriage alliance between them and their respective groups of kin to be more important than the life of his sister. The two men were the most important leaders in the village and the fount of the village's solidarity and cohesion and there was, therefore, considerable political pressure on them to keep these bonds strong.

Although a variation on the "typical" situation in which confrontation theory is usually seen to operate, this example clearly supports confrontation theory. The headmen — husband and brother of the woman — were in agreement that she must die for her sexual offense. And the reason is clear: the political stability of the village was threatened.[1]

Political Leaders in Confrontation

Confrontation theory posits that a political leader will be on occasion in conflict with segments of the political community. The conflict arises through the attempts of the political leader and his aides and supporters to control those persons who have committed crimes that threaten the structure of the political community, particularly violent crimes, such as homicide, and sexual offenses. As described above, if a conflict develops between individuals who are members of different fraternal interest groups, group confrontation arises. Since the source of the conflict is often an act that most members of the political community deem to be a crime, the political leader has a reason for becoming involved. If a party to the conflict can be identified as the culprit, the political leader is likely to seek the punishment of this individual. He may also wish to prevent the conflict from being escalated by the contending fraternal interest groups. The political leader and his aides and supporters, in attempting either to prevent the conflict from escalating or to apprehend the culprit, are themselves drawn into the conflict. They may choose to intervene, or they may be requested to do so by one of the contending interest groups, as was the case with the Metá.

When a political leader becomes involved in confrontations with fraternal interest groups, therefore, a three-party situation develops, with the political leader aligning with one of the fraternal interest groups. (In another conflict situation, at a different time, the political leader may align with the other fraternal interest group.) The intercession of the political leader may tip the balance, if a balance has ever existed, in favor of one of the fraternal interest groups. This may force a termination of the conflict or lead to the punishment of the culprit. It also may not do either. A strong fraternal interest group may be able to resist the united forces of the political leader and the rival fraternal interest group. In such a case, the strong fraternal interest group may be asked to deal with its own member; if it does not exile or execute the culprit, the political leader can do nothing more. A weak fraternal interest group may be pressured to turn the culprit over to the political leader or to the aggrieved party for punishment, which often means execution.

The presence of a council of elders, probably representing rival fraternal interest groups if such groups are found within the political community, gives formal institutional backing for the decisions of the political leader. A council may be a major source of supporters for the political leader. The presence on the council of representatives from rival interest groups may make it difficult for the council to reach a consensus, but if a consensus is reached, then it is likely that the conflict can be terminated or the culprit punished. Thus councils make the task of governing easier for political leaders. If there are no fraternal interest groups, and hence little likelihood of feuding, a political leader and a council of elders do not have as many serious disputes to settle, nor is it as difficult for them to punish wrongdoers.[2] On the other hand, if fraternal interest groups and feuding are present, the tasks of political leader and council are rendered more difficult.[3]

NOTES

1. The Yanomamö (Yanoama) are a sample society that was classified as "Feud, no council." Becher (1960), not Chagnon, was the author of the ethnography in the PSF. (Chagnon uses the spelling Yanomamö; the HRAF Files, following Becher, use the spelling Yanoama for the same group.) The Chagnon example was found after coding and data analysis had been completed. When Chagnon's description was coded and compared with the codes derived from Becher's data, additional codes relating to this study of capital punishment were found. From the Chagnon example, the codes are: sexual offense, no judicial torture, political leader decides, political leader executes, no *supplice*, weapons used, and reason — disposal of wrongdoer. From Becher's data, the sexual offense was incest, not adultery.

2. The Huron Indians of North America, a matrilineal people without fraternal interest groups but with councils of chiefs at the village, tribe, and confederacy levels of sociopolitical organization, illustrate the greater ease with which political leaders can punish wrongdoers in such societies. The Huron are culturally very similar to one of the sample societies — the Iroquois. Among the Huron, clan segments, villages, and tribes were responsible for the behavior of their members. Thus they brought pressure to bear on an individual to behave properly. If social pressure failed, the wrongdoer might be killed. "One woman is reported to have been killed by her brother because she was an incorrigible thief" (Trigger 1969, p. 80). Expulsion from their long-houses was another possible punishment among the Huron (Trigger 1969, pp. 80–81). If the offense was witchcraft or treason, Huron chiefs were likely to meet in secret, and, if the culprit was judged guilty, an "executioner was appointed to kill him without warning." On occasion, however, a trial took place. Torture was sometimes used to make the witch reveal the names of accomplices. Then followed further torturing with fire. The head was split open and the body burned. A specific case is described in primary materials from the early 1600s (Thwaites 1896–1901, Vol. 14, pp. 37–39). Witches were so feared that anyone had the right to kill a witch; however, most people refrained from doing so, in order to avoid being accused of murdering an innocent person. Thus, the task of disposing of witches was normally left to the chiefs (Trigger 1969, pp. 88–89).

3. The only monograph-length treatment of fraternal interest group theory is to be found in a cross-cultural study of reproductive rituals by Paige and Paige (1981). Their major hypothesis is that uncentralized political systems with fraternal interest groups are more likely to have reproductive rituals than political systems without fraternal interest groups. The political behavior of such groups is responsible for the rituals. Considerable support can be found for this theory. (For a lengthy review of the study, see McElroy 1982.) The sample societies used in the study are bands and tribes, which do not have central governments with independent military organizations. These societies are classified as having either strong or weak fraternal interest groups. The theory set forth by Paige and Paige takes a different view of tribal society than does confrontation theory; for the former theory, tribes have no government, and fraternal interest groups are either strong or weak. Confrontation theory, on the other hand, posits the existence of government (e.g., political leaders and/or councils) in tribal society and considers the relative strength of competing fraternal interest groups within these societies.

REFERENCES

Becher, Hans (1960). *Die Surára und Pakidai: Zwei Yanonami-Stamme in Nord-west-brasilien* (HRAF translation). Hamburg: Museum fur Volkerkunde, Mittheilungen, Vol. 26, pp. 1–133.

Boehm, Christopher (1985). "Execution Within the Clan as an Extreme Form of Ostracism." *Science Information* 24(2):309–321.

Chagnon, Napoleon A. (1979). "Is Reproductive Success Equal in Egalitarian Societies?" in: *Evolutionary Biology and Human Social Behavior: An Anthropological Perspective*, ed. N. A. Chagnon and William Irons. North Scituate, MA: Duxbury Press, pp. 374–401.

Dillon, Richard G. (1980a). "Violent Conflict in Metá Society." *American Ethnologist* 7:658–673.

_____ (1980b). "Capital Punishment in Egalitarian Society: The Metá Case." *Journal of Anthropological Research* 36:437–452.

McElroy, Ann (1982). "Ritual as Puffery/Empiricism as Defense." *Reviews in Anthropology* 9:251–267.

Moore, Sally Falk (1978). *Law as Process: An Anthropological Approach*. London, Routledge and Kegan Paul.

Otterbein, Keith F. (1967). "Mortuary Practices in Northeastern Nigeria." *Bulletin of the Cultural Research Institute, Government of India* 6(1/2):10–19.

_____ (1968a). "Cross-Cultural Studies of Armed Combat." *Studies in International Conflict, Research Monograph No. 1, Buffalo Studies* 4(1):91–109.

_____ (1968b). "Higi Armed Combat." *Southwestern Journal of Anthropology* 24:195–213.

_____ (1968c). "Internal War: A Cross-Cultural Study." *American Anthropologist* 70:277–289.

_____ (1969). "Higi Marriage System." *Bulletin of the Cultural Research Institute, Government of India* 8(1/2):16–20.

_____ (1979). "A Cross-Cultural Study of Rape." *Aggressive Behavior* 5:425–435.

Otterbein, Keith F., and Charlotte Swanson Otterbein (1965). "An Eye for an Eye, A Tooth for a Tooth: A Cross-Cultural Study of Feuding." *American Anthropologist* 67:1470–1482.

Paige, Karen Ericksen, and Jeffrey M. Paige (1981). *The Politics of Reproductive Ritual*. Berkeley: University of California Press.

Thoden van Velzen, H. U. E., and W. van Wetering (1960). "Residence, Power Groups and Intrasocietal Aggression." *International Archives of Ethnography* 49:169–200.

Thwaites, Reuben G. (Ed.) (1896–1901). *The Jesuit Relations and Allied Documents*, 73 vols. Cleveland: Burrows.

Trigger, Bruce G. (1969). *The Huron: Farmers of the North*. New York: Holt, Rinehart & Winston.

Chapter
TEN

The Anthropology
of War

While many anthropologists have devoted attention to phenomena variously designated as warfare, feuding, armed conflict, or armed combat, they seldom attempt to define what they are describing. Warfare is defined by Malinowski (1941, p. 522) as "an armed contest between two independent political units, by means of organized military force, in the pursuit of a tribal or national policy." A year earlier Mead (1940, p. 402) had defined warfare as a recognized conflict between two groups *as groups*, in which each group puts an army (even if the army is only fifteen pygmies) into the field to fight and kill, if possible, some of the members of the army of the other group."

Recently Mead (1968, p. 215) stated: "Warfare exists if the conflict is organized and socially sanctioned, and the killing is not regarded as murder." Her criteria for this definition (1968, pp. 215–216) are "organization for the purpose of a combat involving the intention to kill and the willingness to die, social sanction for this behavior, which distinguishes it from murder of members of its own group, and the agreement between the groups involved on the legitimacy of the fighting with intent to kill."

Other anthropologists are concerned with the distinction between warfare and feuding. Naroll (1964, p. 286) defines warfare as "public lethal group combat between territorial teams. (N.B. Thus blood feuds between nonterritorially defined kin groups are not considered warfare.)" A territorial team is "a group of people whose membership is defined in terms of occupancy of a common territory and who have an official with the special function of announcing group decisions — a function exercised at least once a year." My own distinction between warfare and feuding is based upon Naroll's definition of a territorial team. In my definitions the term "political community" has the same meaning as Naroll's "territorial team." Warfare is "armed combat between political communities," while feuding is "a type of armed combat occurring within a political community, in which if a homicide occurs, the kin of the deceased take revenge through killing the offender or any member of his kin group" (Otterbein 1968b, p. 93). Armed combat is fighting with weapons. The fighting is performed by military organizations (Otterbein 1970, pp. 3–5).

Schneider (1950, p. 777), a sociologist, is critical of those anthropologists who consider "fighting which occurs among primitives who live in exogamous clans or local residence groups" as warfare. For Schneider, such fighting is a "matter of crime and punishment within populations where systems of public justice are undeveloped." Although he does not explicitly say so, Schneider seems to imply that fighting between exogamous kinship groups is feuding. In a review article on feuding, Pospisil (1968) takes issue with Schneider. Pospisil's definition (1968, p. 392)

> sets feud apart from war and external self-redress because the last two terms refer to acts of violence committed by members of politically unrelated groups: in war both combat groups act as units in the organized fighting; in external self-redress members of two subgroups only, each belonging to a different politically unrelated group, participate in the hostilities.

Feud itself consists of a series of acts of violence — injury, revenge, and counterrevenge — "usually involving killings, committed by members of two groups related to each other by superimposed political-structural features ... and acting on the basis of group solidarity."

From three basic concepts — warfare, political community, and cultural unit — I have derived three types of warfare (Otterbein 1968a, 1970). The first two concepts have been defined above; the third is derived from Malinowski (1941). "A cultural unit is composed of contiguous political communities that are culturally similar" (Otterbein 1968a, p. 277). Internal war is "warfare between political communities within the same cultural unit." External war is "warfare between culturally different political communities, i.e., political communities which are not members of the same cultural unit." I distinguish two types of external war (Otterbein 1968a, p. 277; 1970, pp.84–92): offensive external war (external war — attacking) and defensive external war (external war — being attacked). The two types of external war can be combined to produce a third measure of external war (Otterbein 1968a, pp. 286–287). Ember and Ember (1971) make a similar distinction between internal and external war.

WARFARE IN ANTHROPOLOGICAL LITERATURE

Although many ethnographies contain brief but adequate descriptions of warfare, there are actually few anthropological books and articles that are devoted primarily to the analysis of warfare. There are adequate ethnographies for comparative research (Otterbein 1970, p. 11). In order to have a fifty-society probability sample for a cross-cultural study, I needed to peruse the sources for seventy-four societies. Thus two thirds of the randomly chosen ethnographic accounts examined had sufficient information on warfare to be included in the study. On the other hand, the theoretical anthropological literature dealing with warfare is scant compared to the thousands of books and articles devoted to such topics as kinship, religion, and technology. The list of references at the end of this article, which attempts to be comprehensive, includes fewer than 250 items, and not all the items listed are written by anthropologists or discuss warfare. [Many items in the original reference list are not included since only the introductory sections are reprinted here.] A few books are included, primarily those noted for their sections on warfare (e.g., Barton 1919; Berndt 1962; Evans-Pritchard 1940; Karsten 1923; Keiser 1969; Mariner 1820; M. E. Opler 1938; and Warner 1958). A substantial number of articles are included which deal solely with warfare, but from a descriptive point of view (e.g., Beemer 1937; Bell 1935; Fortune 1939, 1947, 1960; Glasse 1959;

Goldschmidt, Foster, and Essene 1939; Grinnell 1910; Hasluck 1967; Hill 1936; Hocart 1931; Jeffreys 1956; Kroeber 1928; Landes 1959; M. K. Opler 1939; Padden 1957; Skinner 1911; Slobodin 1960; Stewart 1947; Van der Kroef 1952; Warner 1931; and Zegwaard 1959). Several historical and ethnohistorical studies are listed (e.g., Adcock 1962; Ajayi and Smith 1964; Bram 1941; Follett 1932; Oman 1960; Peckham 1961; Russel 1957; Wales 1952; Wintringham 1943; Wolf 1959; Woolley 1965; and Yamada 1916). Recently Divale (1971) has compiled a comprehensive bibliography on warfare which lists many descriptive studies not cited above.

There are few review articles on war. Regional reviews cover Oceania (Wedgewood 1930), highland New Guinea (Berndt 1964), and the northeastern woodlands of the United States (Hadlock 1947). Vayda and Leeds (1961) present a brief introduction to three articles that appear in one issue of the journal *Anthropologica*. Two review articles dealing with the anthropology of conflict scarcely touch upon the subject of warfare (Siegel and Beals 1960; LeVine 1961). Pope (1962) describes a series of experiments with the bow and arrow and draws a number of conclusions concerning the efficiency of various weapons, and Klopsteg (1963) discusses various types of bows and arrows used in the New World. Carneiro (1970, pp. 865–866), who is undertaking cross-cultural studies of cultural evolution, has recently published his comprehensive trait list: 57 out of 618 traits deal exclusively with warfare. The evidence for warfare and "intrahuman killing" in the Pleistocene is surveyed by Roper, who concludes (1969, p. 448) that "although there seems to be sound evidence for sporadic intrahuman killing, the known data is not sufficient to document warfare."

Collections of papers and readings include only a limited number of selections by anthropologists dealing with primitive warfare. One volume titled *War: Studies from Psychology, Sociology, Anthropology* (Bramson and Goethals, eds., 1964) contains twenty-one selections, only two by anthropologists — Malinowski (1941) and Mead (1940). Three other selections, by McDougall (1964), Sumner (1911), and Schneider (1950), deal with primitive war. (The revised edition includes an article by a third anthropologist, Vayda [1968].) A reader titled *Law and Warfare: Studies in the Anthropology of Conflict* (Bohannan 1967) contains twenty-three selections; only six are case studies of primitive war. At the 1967 annual meetings of the American Anthropological Association a symposium devoted solely to warfare was held. While all but two of the sixteen papers are by anthropologists, nine of the contributions scarcely deal with primitive war. (Twelve of the items are listed in the bibliography to this article.) This group of papers has since been published (Fried, Harris, and Murphy, eds., 1968). Reviews of the collection have not been favorable (Fürer-Haimendorf 1968; Fox 1969). Fox's review (1969, p. 315) in the *American Anthropologist* concludes: "Somehow I don't think this is the book on WAR that the world has been waiting for."

Few textbooks in anthropology make more than passing mention of warfare. A perusal of many anthropological textbooks reveals only five that include sections or chapters on warfare. Keesing (1958, pp. 295–297) has a brief chapter. The second edition of Hoebel's (1958, pp. 508–522) textbook contains a substantial chapter. Honigmann (1959, pp. 504–507) provides a brief section. Bohannan (1963, pp. 301–306) has a section on diplomacy and warfare. And Turney-High, who is the author of a book on primitive war (1949), devotes part of a chapter of his *Man and System* (1968, pp. 381–388) to warfare. I include three sections on warfare and one on feuding in my textbook (Otterbein 1972).

Why have anthropologists been so little concerned with the study of warfare? Only a tentative answer can be given. If one is willing to accept the assumption that most of the major problems and research areas in anthropology have been set forth and delineated by great anthropologists, an answer is available. A scanning of the references listed at the end of this article reveals few articles and no books written by the major figures in anthropology. Not one important anthropologist has devoted more than a small fraction of his professional life to the study of warfare. This is still, however, not a satisfactory answer to our initial question. It raises a further question: Why were the great anthropologists not interested in studying warfare? There are several possible answers: (1) The peoples studied by most anthropologists, even in the nineteenth century, had ceased to engage in war long before the anthropologists arrived on the scene; hence warfare was not an ongoing phenomenon while they were conducting their fieldwork. (2) Many anthropologists have been morally opposed to war. Two of the founding fathers, Tylor, a Quaker, and Boas, a German expatriate, were pacifists. Currently many anthropologists oppose specifically the war in southeast Asia. In most instances this opposition, for reasons that seem sufficient to them, precludes their studying war in general. Those who participated in the 1967 symposium are notable exceptions. (3) Early anthropologists failed to appreciate the important role that warfare can play in the affairs of primitive societies. Although these anthropologists were omnivorous readers, many of them focused their attention upon the humanities rather than upon the writings of historians and political scientists. Thus they were more likely to "discover" the importance of, for example, folklore and mythology among primitive peoples than military organization and warfare.

The situation is changing today. In the past decade or two a number of anthropologists have begun to turn their attention to the study of war. In 1964 the profession was treated to a film that shows actual battle scenes taken among the Dani of highland New Guinea (Gardner 1964). A book version of the film (Gardner and Heider 1968), a popular account (Matthiessen 1962), and an ethnographic account of the Dani (Heider 1970) are available. And one anthropologist (Wolf 1969) has recently turned his attention to the study of peasant wars. Many of the publications reviewed in this paper have been written in the last fifteen years. Since many of these publications are not well known, more space will be devoted to these contributions than to better known works published in the first half of this century.

APPROACHES TO WARFARE

Warfare, when it has been analyzed by anthropologists, has been treated as a topic, not a theoretical approach. That is, it is a topic to be studied in the sense that kinship, religion, or technology is a topic, rather than a theoretical approach such as evolutionism, functionalism, or structuralism. Many studies of warfare, as we have seen, are purely descriptive; many other studies are primarily descriptive, but have theoretical approaches injected into them. As a rule, these studies reflect the theoretical interests of the period at which they were written. Thus in the nineteenth century warfare was viewed from an evolutionary perspective and now it is seen from an ecological perspective. Hence it seems appropriate to review the literature dealing with primitive war according to the theoretical approach employed, since warfare is a topic rather than a theory per se.

Sixteen approaches are used to classify the various studies of primitive warfare. Since half of the approaches treat war as a dependent variable (i.e., as a phenomenon to be explained by independent variables) and the other half treat war as an independent variable (i.e., as a phenomenon that explains certain dependent variables), the theories can be grouped into two major categories: (1) causes of war and (2) effects of war. However, rather than first discuss the eight approaches that purport to explain the causes of war and then the eight approaches that purport to describe the effects of war, it is possible to pair the approaches and discuss first a cause-of-war approach and then an effect-of-war approach, then another cause-of-war approach and another effect-of-war approach, and so on until all eight pairs of approaches have been described. The paired theoretical approaches are these:

Causes of war (Dependent variable)	Effects of war (Independent variable)
Innate aggression	On species
Frustration-aggression	Ethnocentrism
Diffusion	Acculturation
Physical environment	Ecological adaptation
Goals of war	Patterns and themes
Social structure	On social organization
Military preparedness	Survival value
Cultural evolution	Origin of the state

The logic behind pairing the approaches is simple. For each pair, the variable that is responsible for warfare (first column) is essentially the same variable that is affected by warfare (second column). For example, the "innate aggression" approach finds in biological man the cause of war, while the "effects on species" approach examines the effects of war upon man viewed biologically. The following variables appear to be common to each pair of remaining approaches: hatred of enemy, spread of invention, natural environment, values of men, social groupings, efficient military organization, and level of sociopolitical complexity. There is no inherent logic to the order in which the pairs are presented. "Cultural evolution" and "origin of the state" could just as well be the first pair as the last.

REFERENCES

Adcock, F. E. (1962). *The Greek and Macedonian Art of War*. Berkeley: University of California Press.

Ajayi, J. F. Ade, and Robert S. Smith (1964). *Yoruba Warfare in the Nineteenth Century*. New York and London: Cambridge University Press in association with the Institute of African Studies, University of Ibadan.

Barton, Roy. F. (1919). *Ifugao Law*. University of California Publications in American Archaeology and Ethnology, No. 15.

Beemer, Hilda (1937). "The Development of the Military Organization in Swaziland." *Africa* 10:55–74, 176–205.

Bell, F. L. S. (1935). "Warfare Among the Tanga." *Oceania* 5:253–279.

Berndt, Ronald M. (1962). *Excess and Restraint: Social Control Among a New Guinea Mountain People*. Chicago: University of Chicago Press.

_____ (1964). "Warfare in the New Guinea Highlands." *American Anthropologist* 66(4/2):183–203.

Bohannan, Paul (1963). *Social Anthropology*. New York: Holt, Rinehart & Winston.

_____ (Ed.) (1967). *Law and Warfare*. Garden City: Natural History Press.

Bram, Joseph (1941). *An Analysis of Inca Militarism*. American Ethnological Society Monograph No. 4.

Bramson, Leon, and George W. Goethals (Eds.) (1964). *War: Studies from Psychology, Sociology, Anthropology*. New York: Basic Books (Rev. ed. 1968).

Carneiro, Robert (1970). "Analysis, Evolutionary Sequences, and the Rating of Cultures." in: *A Handbook of Method in Cultural Anthropology*, eds. R. Naroll and R. Cohen. Garden City: Natural History Press, pp. 834–871.

Divale, William T. (1971). *Warfare in Primitive Societies: A Selected Bibliography*. Los Angeles: California State College, Center for the Study of Armament and Disarmament.

Ember, Melvin, and Carol. R. Ember (1971). "The Conditions Favoring Matrilocal Versus Patrilocal Residence." *American Anthropologist* 73:571–594.

Evans-Pritchard, E. E. (1940). *The Nuer*. Oxford: Clarendon Press.

Follett, Prescott H. (1932). "War and Weapons of the Maya." *Middle American Research Series* 4:373–410.

Fortune, Reo F. (1939). "Arapesh Warfare." *American Anthropologist* 41:22–41.

_____ (1947). "The Rules of Relationship Behaviour in One Variety of Primitive Warfare." *Man* 47:108–110.

_____ (1960). "New Guinea Warfare: Correction of a Mistake Previously Published." *Man* 60:108.

Fox, Robin (1969). "Review of *War: The Anthropology of Armed Conflict and Aggression*, eds. M. Fried, M. Harris, and R. Murphy." *American Anthropologist* 71:314–315.

Fried, Morton H., Marvin Harris, and Robert Murphy (Eds.) (1968). *War: The Anthropology of Armed Conflict and Aggression*. Garden City: Natural History Press.

Fürer-Haimendorf, Christoph von (1968). "Review of *War: The Anthropology of Armed Conflict and Aggression,* eds. M. Fried, M. Harris, and R. Murphy." *Saturday Review* June 1, pp. 27–29.

Gardner, Robert (1964). *Dead Birds* (16-mm film, 83 min). Cambridge: Peabody Museum, Harvard University.

Gardner, Robert, and Karl G. Heider (1968). *Gardens of War: Life and Death in the New Guinea Stone Age.* New York: Random House.

Glasse, Robert M. (1959). "Revenge and Redress Among the Huli: A Preliminary Account." *Mankind* 5:273–289.

Goldschmidt, Walter, George Foster, and Frank Essene (1939). "War Stories from Two Enemy Tribes." *Journal of American Folk-Lore* 52:141–154.

Grinnell, George B. (1910). "Coup and Scalp Among the Plains Indians." *American Anthropologist* 12:296–310.

Hadlock, Wendell S. (1947). "War Among the Northeastern Woodland Indians." *American Anthropologist* 49:204–221.

Hasluck, Margaret (1967). "The Albanian Blood Feud." in: *Law and Warfare,* ed. P. Bohannan. Garden City: Natural History Press, pp. 381–408.

Heider, Karl G. (1970). *The Dugum Dani: A Papuan Culture in the Highlands of West New Guinea.* Chicago: Aldine.

Hill, William W. (1936). *Navajo Warfare.* Yale University Publications in Anthropology, No. 5.

Hocart, A. M. (1931). "Warfare in Eddystone of the Solomon Islands." *Journal of the Royal Anthropological Institute of Great Britain and Ireland* 61:301–324.

Hoebel, E. Adamson (1958). *Man in the Primitive World: An Introduction to Anthropology.* New York: McGraw-Hill.

Honigmann, John J. (1959). *The World of Man.* New York: Harper & Row.

Jeffreys, M. D. W. (1956). "Ibo Warfare." *Man* 56:77–79.

Karsten, Rafael (1923). *Blood Revenge, War, and Victory Feasts Among the Jibaro Indians of Eastern Ecuador.* Bureau of American Ethnology Bulletin No. 79. Washington, DC: Smithsonian Institution.

Keesing, Felix M. (1958). *Cultural Anthropology: The Science of Custom.* New York: Holt, Rinehart & Winston.

Keiser, R. Lincoln (1969). *The Vice Lords: Warriors of the Streets.* New York: Holt, Rinehart & Winston.

Klopsteg, Paul E. (1963). "Bows and Arrows: A Chapter in the Evolution of Archery in America." in: *The Smithsonian Report for 1962.* Washington, DC: Smithsonian Institution, pp. 567–592.

Kroeber, Alfred L. (1928). "A Kato War." in: *Festschrift d'hommage offerte à P. W. Schmidt,* ed. W. Koppers. Vienna: Mechitharisten-Congregations-Buchdruckerie, pp. 394–400.

Landes, Ruth (1959). "Dakota Warfare." *Southwestern Journal of Anthropology* 15:43–52.

LeVine, Robert A. (1961). "Anthropology and the Study of Conflict: An Introduction." *Journal of Conflict Resolution* 5:3–15.

Malinowski, Bronislaw (1941). "An Anthropological Analysis of War." *American Journal of Sociology* 46:521–550.

McDougall, William (1964). "The Instinct of Pugnacity." in: *War: Studies from Psychology, Sociology, Anthropology*, eds. L. Bramson and G. W. Goethals. New York: Basic Books, pp. 33–43.

Mariner, William (1820). *An Account of the Natives of the Tonga Island in the South Pacific Ocean*. Boston: Charles Ewer.

Matthiessen, Peter (1962). *Under the Mountain Wall*. New York: Viking Press.

Mead, Margaret (1940). "Warfare is Only an Invention — Not a Biological Necessity." *Asia* 40:402–405.

_____ (1968). "Alternatives to War." in: *War: The Anthropology of Armed Conflict and Aggression*, eds. M. Fried, M. Harris, and R. Murphy. Garden City: Natural History Press, pp. 215–228.

Naroll, Raoul (1964). "On Ethnic Unit Classification." *Current Anthropology* 5:283–312.

Oman, C. W. C. (1960). *The Art of War in the Middle Ages*. Ithaca: Cornell University Press.

Opler, Marvin K. (1939). "The Ute Indian War of 1879." *El Palacio* 46:255–262.

Opler, Morris E. (1938). *Dirty Boy: A Jicarilla Tale of Raid and War*. American Anthropological Association Memoir No. 52.

Otterbein, Keith F. (1968a). "Internal War: A Cross-Cultural Study." *American Anthropologist* 70:277–289.

_____ (1968b). "Cross-Cultural Studies of Armed Combat." *Studies in International Conflict, Research Monograph No. 1, Buffalo Studies* 4(1):91–109.

_____ (1970). *The Evolution of War*. New Haven: Human Relations Area Files Press.

_____ (1972). *Comparative Cultural Analysis: An Introduction to Anthropology*. New York: Holt, Rinehart & Winston.

Padden, Richard C. (1957). "Cultural Change and Military Resistance in Araucanian Chile, 1550–1730." *Southwestern Journal of Anthropology* 13:103–121.

Peckham, Howard H. (1961). *Pontiac and the Indian Uprising*. Chicago: University of Chicago Press.

Pope, Saxton T. (1962). *Bows and Arrows*. Berkeley: University of California Press.

Pospisil, Leopold (1968). "Feud." in: *International Encyclopedia of the Social Sciences*, ed. D. L. Sills, Vol. 16, pp. 389–393.

Roper, Marilyn Keyes (1969). "A Survey of the Evidence for Intrahuman Killing in the Pleistocene." *Current Anthropology* 10:427–459.

Russell, Carl P. (1957). *Guns on the Early Frontiers*. Berkeley: University of California Press.

Schneider, Joseph (1950). "Primitive Warfare: A Methodological Note." *American Sociological Review* 15:772–777.

Siegel, Bernard J., and Alan R. Beals (1960). "Conflict and Factionalist Dispute." *Journal of the Royal Anthropological Institute of Great Britain and Ireland* 90:107–117.

Skinner, Alanson (1911). "War Customs of the Menomini Indians." *American Anthropologist* 13:229–312.

Slobodin, Richard (1960). "Eastern Kutchin Warfare." *Anthropologica* 2:76–94.

Stewart, Kenneth M. (1947). "Mohave Warfare." *Southwestern Journal of Anthropology* 3:257–378.

Sumner, William G. (1911). *War, and Other Essays.* New Haven: Yale University Press.

Turney-High, Harry H. (1949). *Primitive War: Its Practice and Concepts.* Columbia: University of South Carolina Press.

_____ (1968). *Man and System: Foundations for the Study of Human Relations.* New York: Appleton-Century-Crofts.

Van der Kroef, Justus M. (1952). "Head-Hunting Traditions of Southern New Guinea." *American Anthropologist* 54:221–235.

Vayda, Andrew P. (1968). "Primitive War." in: *International Encyclopedia of the Social Sciences,* ed. D. L. Sills, Vol. 16, pp. 468–472.

Vayda, Andrew P., and Anthony Leeds (1961). "Anthropology and the Study of War." *Anthropologica* 3:131–133.

Wales, Horace G. Q. (1952). *Ancient South-east Asian Warfare.* London: B. Quaritch.

Warner, W. Lloyd (1931). "Murngin Warfare." *Oceania* 1:457–494.

_____ (1958). *A Black Civilization: A Study of an Australian Tribe.* New York: Harper & Row.

Wedgewood, Camilla H. (1930). "Some Aspects of Warfare in Melanesia." *Oceania* 1:5–33.

Wintringham, Tom (1943). *The Story of Weapons and Tactics: From Troy to Stalingrad.* Boston: Houghton Mifflin Company.

Wolf, Eric. R. (1959). *Sons of the Shaking Earth.* Chicago: University of Chicago Press.

_____ (1969). *Peasant Wars of the Twentieth Century.* New York: Harper & Row.

Woolley, C. Leonard (1965). *The Sumerians.* New York: Norton.

Yamada, Nakaba (1916). *Ghenkô: The Mongol Invasion of Japan.* New York: Dutton.

Zegwaard, Gerald A. (1959). "Headhunting Practices of the Asmat of Netherlands New Guinea." *American Anthropologist* 61:1020–1041.

Chapter
ELEVEN

Convergence in
the Anthropological
Study of Warfare

Today, all the major writers on the anthropology of war
— I can think of no exceptions — employ models that contain three
components: material causes, efficient causes, and consequences.
(These consequences are likely to include, to use Robert Merton's
[1968] term, latent functions. Merton's manifest functions are approximately the same as efficient causes.) The distinction between
material and efficient causes is drawn from Aristotle (1984, pp. 149–
155; Bunge 1959, pp. 31–33). Material causes include the instability
which arises when a shift occurs in the size of kinship groups, social
classes, ethnic groups, ruling elites, and military organizations. Efficient causes include the feelings and motives of those who go to war.
Twenty years ago theoretical models or approaches proliferated.
Throughout the 1960s, as anthropologists became aware of the importance of studying war, one approach after another appeared,
many of which, of course, had their roots in the past. I became aware

of the great diversity of theories when John Honigmann commissioned me to write a review article on "The Anthropology of War" for his *Handbook* (1973). My sorting of publications for the article led to the delineation of sixteen theoretical approaches.[1] The only order I could bring to this burgeoning literature was to pair the theories: one theory in each pair dealt with "causes of war," the other "effects of war." (See pp. 164–165 above.)

While the literature on the anthropology of war has continued to increase since 1970, the number of distinct theories has diminished, diminished in the sense that many of the theories are no longer advanced and new distinct theories have not appeared. See Figure 1 for the list of current theories grouped according to the three components. Those theories that are currently advocated have been amalgamated into composite theoretical models that contain at least the above mentioned three components. When new theoretical models have appeared they are similar to existent theoretical models in that they likewise contain the three components. Furthermore, some of the scholars writing on warfare for many years have changed their formulations in a direction that makes them similar to existent theoretical models. This has been done by incorporating into their theoretical models, which already contained two components, the remaining third component. I have in mind specifically Napoleon Chagnon and Andrew Vayda.

This phenomenon whereby there is a decrease in disparity of theories, structural forms, or body plans followed by an increase in diversity within the few surviving theories, forms, or plans, has been described for social evolution by Hallpike (1987, cf. Otterbein, 1988) and for paleontology by Gould (1989, p. 49). Gould has gone far to elucidate this process. "I have struggled over a proper name for this phenomenon of massive elimination from an initial set of forms, with concentration of all future history into a few surviving lineages. For many years, I thought of this pattern as 'winnowing,' but must now reject this metaphor because all meanings of winnowing refer to separation of the good from the bad" (1989, p. 47). He now prefers to speak of diversification and decimation as occurring at an early stage. Eventually "life settles down to generating endless variants upon a few surviving models" (1989, p. 47). This is exactly what has happened in the anthropological study of warfare: A single model has emerged which has seemingly endless variants. A few of these variants will be described.

This paper will focus on the recent writings of nine writers on the anthropology of war: Andrew Vayda, Keith Otterbein, William

---

Theories of warfare being advocated, grouped according to the three-component theoretical model:

Material causes
  Physical environment (CSR)
  Social structure

Efficient causes
  Goals of war
  Military preparation

Consequences
  Effects on social organization
  Survival value
  Origin of the state

Theories no longer being advocated strongly:

Causes
  Innate aggression
  Frustration-aggression
  Diffusion
  Cultural evolution

Effects
  Effect on species
  Ethnocentrism
  Acculturation
  Ecological adaptation
  Patterns and themes

Figure 1. Contemporary theories of warfare.

Divale and Marvin Harris, Napoleon Chagnon, Robert Carneiro, Ronald Cohen, Raymond Kelly, and Brian Ferguson. Comprehensive evaluation of theories by others or myself will not be given. They are being reviewed to simply show they contain at least the three components. The writings of other anthropologists could be included. Lastly, I will summarize how the theories discussed have converged upon a single theoretical model.

The impetus to this study grew from two feelings. More and more, in recent years, my reaction to what I read on warfare caused me to say to myself either: "I have read this before" or "I wrote that a number of years ago." In two cases authors, I felt, changed their theories to more closely correspond to my approach. Then I began to realize that my own writings have recently incorporated a materialist perspective (cf. 1989).

Andrew Vayda has been the primary proponent of ecological theories of warfare, his first publication on the subject appearing in 1961. He argues that a culture suffering from overpopulation will expand into unoccupied lands or will occupy land of militarily weaker neighbors. Warfare, then, is adaptive because it results in the spacing out of populations, the greater utilization of natural resources, and the more equitable distribution of resources.[2] Remarkably, Vayda (1989) has recently criticized his own theory. The major section of an article on Maring warfare is headed "Recantation." Vayda now argues that it is important to focus on the "context-relatedness of purposeful human behavior" (1989, p. 173); in other words, efficient causes. In earlier publications he argued that such reasons, which he called proximate causes, were of less importance than material causes (1971, pp. 4–6). The scarcity of resources should still be studied, as well as the consequences of war, according to Vayda.

My own research focuses upon the three components. Fraternal interest group theory argues that the causes of rape (1979), feuding (1965) and internal war (1968) lie in social structure (material causes). The efficient causes of war are to be sought in the "goals of war," an approach that "assumes that wars are caused by the decisions of men as members of organizations, whether they are military organizations or governing bodies" (1970, pp. 63–64). Economic reasons, including land and plunder, are nearly universal goals (1970, pp. 65–66). Emphasis was also placed on the "outcomes of war," which included frequencies of different kinds of war, casualty rates, and territorial expansion or contraction (1970, pp. 81–103). In my 1973 review article, discussed above, I sorted anthropological theories of war into those that dealt with "causes of war" and those that focused on the "effects of war." Recently, I have brought together the three approaches which I have used and other approaches into what, for want of a better expression, I have called "a unified theory of feuding and warfare" (1989). (See Chapter 13 below.)

William Divale's theory of population control in primitive society incorporates a number of elements (Divale, Chambers, and Gangloff 1976). Before describing these elements, it should be noted that Marvin Harris has explicitly subsumed his protein theory under Divale's population control theory (1984a; 1984b is 1984a plus appendixes). The warring groups are patrilocal and polygynous (i.e., fraternal interest groups are present). A war will begin if a man is killed in a dispute, or if a man's wife is stolen (efficient causes). If resources are scarce (material causes), infanticide is likely; if adult males are needed for war, female infants rather than male infants are likely to be neglected or killed. The shortage of women that results leads to fighting and warfare as men forcibly seek wives from other groups. Villages that have more warriors (where there is a bias against rearing females) will defeat groups without this bias; that is, warring villages with large male populations will be selected (Harris 1984b, pp. 132–133). The consequence of warfare and female infanticide is population control (a latent function). (My criticism of the theory focuses on the alleged need to control population, which is said to explain the presence of the complex [Otterbein 1977, p. 701]. Consequences, I contend, are confused with causes.)

The key to understanding Napoleon Chagnon's theory of warfare is to examine the changes that have taken place in his writings over the past 20 years (see Figure 2). In early publications he views political sovereignty as the reason for Yanomamö warfare; the underlying theory comes from international relations approaches (1968, pp. 158–159). By the third edition of Yanomamö (1983), in order to argue more effectively against the protein scarcity hypothesis, Chagnon argues that fighting over women is the major reason for Yanomamö warfare (1983, p. 86). Inclusive fitness theory underlies this formulation (1983, p. 140). Chagnon's recent article in Science (1988) departs from his previous views. Revenge now takes center stage as the major reason for Yanomamö warfare; this change stems from a new analysis that argues that kin groups, not sovereign villages, are the units that fight (1988, p. 987). The underlying theory examines individual motivation: grief and anger are the psychological states that lead to aggression (1988, p. 986); the use of a goals of war approach or decision-making model is explicitly acknowledged (1988, p. 985) (efficient causes). Chagnon, furthermore, is explicit that revenge arises from competition for material (e.g., food, water, and territory) and reproductive (i.e., mates) resources (1988, p. 985). Several consequences, in particular increased settlement size and villages located great distances from each other, are attributed to warfare. Villages at war also have larger plazas for entertaining visiting allies. The fourth edition of Yanomamö (1992) contains a new view of their warfare based upon field research in villages in the highlands, which he believes is a refuge area. The reason now for warfare is to obtain a place in the resource-rich lowlands. Ecological theory guides the new interpretation.

Robert Carneiro's theory of the evolution of chiefdoms and states has from its inception employed the three components (1970).

Reason for war	Underlying theory	Reason for change
1. Political sovereignty (1968, pp. 158–159)	International relations theory (1974, p. xi)	To more effectively argue against materialists, particularly protein scarcity hypothesis.
2. Fighting over women (1983, p. 86)	Inclusive fitness theory (1983, p. 140)	Kin group, not village, unit that fights (1988, p. 987)
3. Revenge (1988, p. 986)	Individual motivation: grief and anger lead to aggression (1988, p. 986). Inclusive fitness becomes effect — it is no longer cause (1988, p. 985).	Field research on highland villages (1992, p. 81)
4. To reside in the resource-rich lowlands (1992, p. 83)	Ecological theory: adaptation to lowland and highland environments. Highlands a refuge area (1992, p. 87)	

Figure 2. Chagnon's changing views of the Yanomamö.

Population increase in conjunction with environmental circumscription (or resource concentration and social circumscription), which are material causes, lead to fighting for land (rather than revenge) and for subjugation, both efficient causes. The outcome was first the rise of chiefdoms, then states (1981). Consequences were a decrease in the number of political communities and an increase in their size (1978, p. 206).

The three components emerge in the writings of Ronald Cohen, who explicitly states that "theories of warfare must therefore develop at least three differing and related models of political process: (1) a model of conditions leading to war, (2) a model explaining the conduct of war and its relation to society, and (3) an explanation and predictive set of statements about the consequences of wars" (1984, p. 353). Specifically, in his theory of state formation, he has viewed competition over scarce resources (CSR), circumscription, and the presence of third-party mediation as material causes. Efficient causes include going to war to obtain "access to new resources or control of new trade routes, markets, and productive capacities" (1984, p. 352). Among latent functions are higher central government exactions (1984, p. 352).

Raymond Kelly's theory of Nuer expansion at the expense of the Dinka contains several variables which group themselves under the three components. Kelly (1985) argues that the Nuer have a larger bride price requirement than the Dinka and hence keep more cattle on wet season sites (material causes). Dry season grazing shortages, referred to by Kelly as a proximate cause (1985, p. 242), lead to large-scale raids for cattle, raids in which Dinka women were also obtained (efficient causes). The Nuer had an organizational advantage that enabled them to mobilize larger raiding parties; they defeated the Dinka which resulted in territorial expansion (consequences). Recently de Wolf (1990) has argued that the data now available do not support Kelly's model.

Brian Ferguson (1989a, pp. 142–143; 1990, pp. 27–31) has developed a model that contains what he calls three premises: a materialist orientation, motivations of those who decide on war, and war as a mechanism of selection. These three premises are the same as the three components. Ferguson, moreover, has subjected the ecology approach to meticulous scrutiny and concluded that game scarcity is insufficient, in itself, to explain war (1989c) and that war does not produce a better relationship between people and their natural environment (1989b).

I have shown that the models or theories now being employed to study warfare contain the same three components, and that these models are, thus, variants of a single paradigm. Viewed schematically the theoretical model can be depicted as follows:

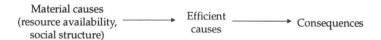

Material causes influence the goals that men fight for. The fighting itself has consequences, including latent functions. Feedback from consequences to material causes and efficient causes can occur: the consequences of war may be perceived by warriors and alter the reasons they wage war; these consequences may also effect changes in social structure and alter resource availability.

Assuming my observations are correct, so what? First, we have seen how one small specialty in anthropology has "evolved" over two plus decades. The process identified — namely, that a decrease in disparity of theories followed by an increase in diversity within a paradigm which has emerged from several surviving theories — may be found in other specialties within anthropology and other social sciences. I believe it is valuable to know how research results either accumulate or replace each other. This paper suggests it is neither one nor the other, but rather a process that involves both attrition and combination. Thus, this "finding" may be a contribution to the history of science. Second, we who study warfare can proceed to do a variety of case and comparative studies in the full knowledge that we are operating within a shared paradigm. Instead of viewing each study as a rival to all others, I believe it is more fruitful to view them as compatible and supportive.

ACKNOWLEDGMENTS

This paper was read at the November 1990 American Anthropological Association meeting held in New Orleans. It was part of a symposium organized by S. P. Reyna and R. E. Downs titled "New Directions in the Analysis of Warfare."

I am indebted to S. P. Reyna for helpful suggestions in revising the paper for publication. I am also indebted to Paul Diesing, a philosopher who has specialized in the social sciences (1991), for his advice on the terminology to use to describe the components of the model. And, as always, I am indebted to Charlotte Swanson Otterbein for helpful comments and criticisms on this paper.

NOTES

1. The list could have even been longer. Missing from the original list are psychoanalytic theories. None existent, however, dealt explicitly with primitive war. For a review of the literature see Fornari (1974). Freud, however, was briefly considered under "innate aggression" theories.
2. For a more thorough review of Vayda's theories see Otterbein (1977, pp. 695–696).

REFERENCES

Aristotle (1984). *The Politics*. Translated by Carnes Lord. Chicago: University of Chicago Press.

Bunge, Mario (1959). *Causality: The Place of the Causal Principle in Modern Science*. Cambridge: Harvard University Press.

Carneiro, Robert (1970). "A Theory of the Origin of the State." *Science* 169: 733–738.

_____ (1978). "Political Expansion as an Expression of the Principle of Competitive Exclusion." in: *Origins of the State: The Anthropology of Political Evolution*. eds. Ronald Cohen and Elman R. Service. Philadelphia: Institute for the Study of Human Issues, pp. 205–223.

_____ (1981). "The Chiefdom: Precursor of the State." in: *The Transition to Statehood in the New World*, eds. Grant D. Jones and Robert R. Kautz. Cambridge: Cambridge University Press, pp. 37–79.

Chagnon, Napoleon (1968). "Yanomamö Social Organization and Warfare." in: *War: The Anthropology of Armed Conflict and Aggression*. eds. Morton Fried, Marvin Harris, and Robert Murphy. Garden City, NY: Natural History Press, pp. 109–159.

_____ (1974). *Studying the Yanomamö*. New York: Holt, Rinehart & Winston.

_____ (1983). *Yanomamö: The Fierce People*, 3rd ed. New York: Holt, Rinehart & Winston.

_____ (1988). "Life Histories, Blood Revenge, and Warfare in a Tribal Population." *Science* 239:985–992.

_____ 1992 *Yanomamö*, 4th ed. Fort Worth, TX: Harcourt Brace Jovanovich College Publishers.

Cohen, Ronald (1984). "Warfare and State Formation: Wars Make States and States Make Wars." in: *Warfare, Culture, and Environment*, ed. Brian R. Ferguson. Orlando, FL: Academic Press, pp. 329–358.

de Wolf, Van V. (1990). "Ecology and Conquest: Critical Notes on Kelley's Model of Nuer Expansion." *Ethnology* 29:341–373.

Diesing, Paul (1991). *How Does Social Science Work?* Pittsburgh: University of Pittsburgh Press.

Divale, William T., F. Chambers, and D. Gangloff (1976). "War, Peace, and Marital Residence in Pre-Industrial Societies." *Journal of Conflict Resolution* 20:57–78.

Ferguson, R. Brian (1989a). "Anthropology and War: Theory, Politics, Ethics." in: *The Anthropology of War and Peace*. eds. Paul R. Turner, David Pitt, and Contributors. Granby, MA: Bergin & Garvey, pp. 141–159.

_____ (1989b). "Ecological Consequences of Amazonian Warfare." *Ethnology* 28:249–264.

_____ (1989c). "Game Wars: Ecology and Conflict in Amazonia." *Journal of Anthropological Research* 45:179–206.

_____ (1990). "Explaining War." in: *The Anthropology of War*, ed. Jonathan Haas. Cambridge: Cambridge University Press, pp. 26–55.

Fornari, Franco (1974). *The Psychoanalysis of War*. Garden City, NY: Anchor Books (Translated from the Italian by Alenka Pfeifer).

Gould, Stephen Jay (1989). *Wonderful Life: The Burgess Shale and the Nature of History*. New York: W. W. Norton.

Hallpike, C. R. (1987). *The Principles of Social Evolution*. New York: Clarendon/Oxford University Press.

Harris, Marvin (1984a). "Animal Capture and Yanomamö Warfare: Retrospect and New Evidence." *Journal of Anthropological Research* 40:183–201.

_____ (1984b). "A Cultural Materialist Theory of Band and Village Warfare: The Yanomamö Test." in: *Warfare, Culture, and Environment*, ed. Brian R. Ferguson. Orlando, FL: Academic Press, pp. 111–140.

Kelly, Raymond C. (1985). *The Nuer Conquest: The Structure and Development of an Expansionist System*. Ann Arbor: The University of Michigan Press.

Merton, Robert K. (1968). "Manifest and Latent Functions." in: *Social Theory and Social Structure*. New York: The Free Press, pp. 73–138.

Otterbein, Keith F. (1968). "Internal War: A Cross-Cultural Study." *American Anthropologist* 70:277–289.

_____ (1970). *The Evolution of War: A Cross-Cultural Study*. New Haven: Human Relations Area Files Press.

_____ (1973). "The Anthropology of War." in: *Handbook of Social and Cultural Anthropology*. ed. John J. Honigmann. New York: Rand McNally and Company, pp. 923–958.

_____ (1977). "Warfare: A Hitherto Unrecognized Critical Variable." *American Behavioral Scientist* 20:693–709.

_____ (1979). "A Cross-Cultural Study of Rape." *Aggressive Behavior* 5:425–435.

_____ (1988). "Review: *The Principles of Social Evolution*, by C. R. Hallpike." *American Anthropologist* 90:444–445.

_____ (1989). "A Unified Theory of Warfare." Appendix F in: Keith F. Otterbein, *The Evolution of War: A Cross-Cultural Study*, 3rd ed. New Haven: Human Relations Area Files Press, pp. 167–172.

Otterbein, Keith F. and Charlotte Swanson Otterbein (1965). "An Eye For an Eye, a Tooth For a Tooth: A Cross-Cultural Study of Feuding." *American Anthropologist* 67:1470–1482.

Vayda, Andrew P. (1961). "Expansion and Warfare Among Swidden Agriculturalists." *American Anthropologist* 63:346–358.

_____ (1971). "Phases of the Process of War and Peace Among the Marings of New Guinea." *Oceania* 44:1–24.

_____ (1989). "Explaining Why Marings Fought." *Journal of Anthropological Research* 45:159–177.

Chapter
TWELVE

The Dilemma
of Disarming

Proposals to disarm nations and individuals are intended to benefit all by reducing levels of violent conflict between and within nations. Since arms races are seen as a cause of war, just as the possession of guns is seen as a contribution to high homicide rates, these alleged causes of violent conflict would be reduced in importance or eliminated by disarming nations and the citizens of those nations. Such proposals have been almost universally resisted by those possessing arms. The reason for rejecting such proposals is inherent in the use to which such arms are put — they are used to protect one's nation or one's person. The efficiency of weapons, particularly firearms, is so great that if an opponent is armed and one is not, the opponent is the certain winner. Thus, the very survival of a nation or of an individual may depend upon their being adequately armed. While the possession of armies and weapons may prevent the annihilation of a nation and give gun owners the means to kill assailants, it also gives them the ability to carry out, for reasons of aggrandizement (and sometimes just to test the weapons), attacks upon other nations and individuals. Not only may they be tempted to use the arms in non-self-defense situations, but their mere possession may provoke others to attack because they either fear being attacked or desire to take the weapons for their own use. Hereupon lies the dilemma of disarming: Weapons are needed for survival, yet their possession is likely to involve their owners in the very armed conflicts which the weapons were intended to prevent. Ironically, it is the basic need for self-preservation — as a nation or as an individual — which is both the reason for arms possession and the cause of the killing which the weapons were intended to prevent.

I first became aware of the dilemma of disarming in my research on warfare. Although I have always seen war as a type of armed combat, only recently have I seriously expanded my research interests to include internal violence. Homicide and gun control are two topics I have focused upon. The dilemma of disarming is as relevant to analyzing gun usage within a nation as it is to studying warfare. In this essay I will first describe the dilemma of disarming as it applies to warfare and relate my empirical findings from my warfare research to the dilemma; second, I will describe the dilemma of disarming as it applies to firearms ownership and discuss gun usage, primarily within the United States; and, finally, I will draw parallels between warfare (and disarmament proposals) and gun usage (and gun control legislation), showing that the dilemma of disarming pertains to both. I will conclude by making recommendations both for nations and for individuals, which may make them more secure and yet reduce the escalating levels of violence between and within nations.

The dilemma of disarming, as it applies to the study of warfare, can be described as follows: Nations build strong military organizations to defend themselves from attack. But merely having an excellent military organization is not usually seen as sufficient by political and military leaders. They reason that their nation must be stronger than any likely enemy or combination of enemies. This felt need to be stronger than one's potential adversaries arises both from the desire to prevent an attack and, if an attack occurs, to defeat the enemy. Military readiness prevents an attack by a potential aggressor by creating in the minds of its political and military leaders the belief that if they were to attack, their military would be defeated. This mode of reasoning by defense planners is, of course, known as deterrence theory. Briefly, deterrence theory argues that military readiness, by deterring potential aggressors, decreases the likelihood that a nation will become involved in war. It is today the official position of the major world powers. However, if the leaders of each nation attempt to make their nation the strongest militarily, then each nation will continue to build and improve its military organization. The consequence of such continuous and expanding military preparation is an "arms race." Arms races, as often noted, frequently lead to war (Richardson 1960; Beer 1981, pp. 231–39, 269–73).[1]

Military preparedness can itself be considered a cause of war; that is, if a nation is well prepared militarily, it is more likely to become involved in wars than nations that are not so well prepared. Two reasons seem to account for the relationship (Otterbein 1973, p. 942): first, the possession of an efficient military organization may tempt leaders of the nation or of the military organization to attack countries that they believe are militarily less well prepared.[2] A study of twentieth-century warfare which focuses upon "conventional deterrence" (i.e., non-nuclear deterrence) shows that those nations which have developed a military armament program based on the concept of the blitzkrieg ("lightning war"), rather than pursuing programs based on the concepts of attrition or limited aims, are more likely to attack their neighbors — and they are usually successful in their use of the blitzkrieg (Mearsheimer 1983, pp. 203–206). Second, an efficient military organization that is in readiness for operations, but not actually engaged in war, may provoke an attack by a neighboring nation, since the neighbor fears it may be suddenly attacked and wishes to have surprise on its side.[3] Again, the study of twentieth-century warfare shows that a blitzkrieg strategy may be developed in order to launch a preemptive attack (Mearsheimer 1983, pp. 35–43).

Since military preparedness and arms races can be a cause of war, a finding which no one seems to dispute, many thoughtful individuals have proposed disarmament. Disarmament proposals are intended to reduce the likelihood of war by preventing arms races. These proposals call upon all nations involved either to stop increasing the strength of their military organizations or to reduce the magnitude of the strength (Myrdal 1982; Schell 1984). Such proposals are seldom adopted.[4] This is true even when negotiators for both sides have reached a tentative agreement. Political leaders from both nations may reject the agreement (Fallows 1984, pp. 138, 140). The reason for rejecting disarmament proposals lies, in most instances, in the fear that political and military leaders have that, if they disarm to the extent that their nation is less prepared militarily than their potential adversary, they may be attacked, and, if attacked, they will be defeated. Thus, the dilemma of disarming. Strong military organizations are needed for survival, yet military preparedness leads to arms races and wars. Ironically, the basic need for self-preservation is both the reason for building a strong military organization and the cause of war which it was intended to prevent.

In a cross-cultural study of warfare, using a sample of fifty societies ranging in size from hunting and gathering bands to large states (Otterbein 1985), I developed a scale of military sophistication which measures the fighting ability of political communities, a technical term for a maximal political unit. The scale score for a political community reflected eleven efficient military practices, including both weaponry and characteristics of the military organization. The hypothesis tested stated that the higher the scale score the more likely that the political community would defeat its enemies and survive in intersocietal struggles. It was found that political communities with high scale scores were likely to have territorial boundaries expanding, while political communities with low scale scores were likely to have constant or contracting territorial boundaries, a clear indication that being well-armed contributed to societal survival (1985, pp. 92–108). Moreover, more than two-thirds of the political communities with high scale scores were found to attack neighboring societies continually or frequently; the less well armed the political community, the more likely it was to attack neighbors only infrequently. And, the data provided no evidence that possession of a strong military organization deterred enemies from attacking (1985, pp. 87–92).[5] Only four societies out of the sample did not have military organizations and warfare. There are indications that the members of all four of these societies were driven from other areas and forced to seek refuge in isolated locations such as islands, Arctic wastelands, or mountaintops. Protected by their isolation, they have found it unnecessary to maintain military organizations (1985, pp. 20–21).

The dilemma for political leaders: They must create a strong military organization if their political community is to survive or have a chance to survive, yet the possession of a strong military organization may involve the political community, both as attacker and as defender, in warfare. Faced with the realization that societal survival depends upon maintaining a strong military organization, political leaders are unlikely to seriously consider disarmament for their political communities. With these results in front of me, I drafted a dedication to my book which was intended to highlight the dilemma: "To all those who have died in defense of their political communities" (1985, p. vii). Students have frequently either been mystified by the dedication or felt it to be an expression of a pro-military attitude. The parent of one student, an academic economist who had not read the study, was disturbed that his son was required to read the book (in an advanced course in political anthropology); he conjectured that I had guns hanging on the walls of my home.[6]

The dilemma of disarming, as it applies to the study of firearms ownership, can be described as follows: Many individuals purchase and practice with firearms in order to have a means of defending themselves from attack. Body armor may even be worn. In addition, they may secure their homes with quality locks, alarm systems, and watch dogs. In many parts of the world houses are surrounded by walls, and bars are placed over windows. Sometimes glass or barbed wire is embedded in the tops of walls. The most affluent may hire bodyguards or maintain private security forces. Generally the wealthier or the more important politically the person is, the more likely the use of fortress architecture.[7] The reason for firearms ownership and other defensive measures is the felt need to be stronger than those who would harm or steal.

These measures are taken to dissuade potential criminals from attacking oneself or one's home or, if an attack occurs, to prevent its success by thwarting or killing the assailant.[8] Firearms ownership and other defensive measures prevent attack by creating in the minds of potential criminals the belief that they will be unsuccessful; lack of success can range from inability to enter the property to the apprehension or death of the attacker. The deterrence of crime is a major concern of security planners. Briefly, criminal deterrence argues that firearms ownership and other defensive measures, by deterring potential criminals, decreases the likelihood that the "law abiding" will be robbed, injured, or killed. Criminals, however, may go to great efforts — if what they want to steal is of immense value or the person they wish to kill is politically important — to achieve their ends by using weapons that can penetrate defenses (including body armor) or by devising means of defeating security systems. Indeed, it appears often that those seeking greater security and those seeking to defeat that security are involved in a domestic "arms race."

The possession of firearms gives individuals, whether they are homeowners or security personnel, the ability to kill. They may at times use their weapons in non-self-defense situations, either in anger or in furthering their own self-interest. Also, the possession of weapons may provoke an attack by criminals, either out of fear that the weapons may be used upon them or to take the weapons.

Since firearms ownership has been seen by many as a cause of violent crime and homicide in the United States, gun control legislation has often been proposed (Clark 1970, pp. 101–114; Newton and Zimring 1969). Such legislation is intended to reduce the number of weapons in private hands, thereby lowering the homicide rate, a result which will occur because fewer firearms will be used in the commission of crimes[9] and guns will not be available to those involved in domestic quarrels. Such proposals, at least in the United States, have been vigorously fought by legitimate gun owners (Kennett and Anderson 1975, pp. 165–256). The reason for rejecting such legislation lies in the fear that gun owners have that "if guns are outlawed only outlaws will have guns."[10] Thus, the dilemma of disarming. Firearms are needed for self-defense, yet their possession may involve their owners in armed confrontations. Ironically, the basic need for self-preservation is both the reason for gun ownership and the cause of the homicides which the weapons were intended to prevent.

Gun ownership in the United States is extensive; one national survey indicates that guns (long guns — rifles and shot guns; handguns — revolvers and pistols) are possessed by about half of the households in America, with nearly half of these households possessing a handgun (Davis et al. 1981, p. 233). The long guns are owned primarily for hunting and target shooting, with self-defense being a secondary purpose. Handguns are owned primarily for self-defense, although many owners use handguns for hunting and target shooting.[11] Some research shows that handguns are being bought by citizens not to commit crimes, but out of fear that crimes will be perpetrated upon them (Lizotte and Bordua 1980). Policemen and other security personnel carry handguns, likewise, for protection.[12] Practicing with handguns for self-defense, by both police and non-police, is on the increase; "combat shooting," in contrast to traditional target shooting, stresses practice with larger-caliber handguns rapidly fired at human-like silhouettes. New magazines devoted to combat shooting are appearing on newsstands. The possession of handguns and the skills to use them increase the likelihood that citizens and police will kill those threatening them.[13] Indeed, law enforcement agencies are concerned with this problem — the term "deadly force" is used to refer to police self-defense (Lindgren 1981). Although it is not legally classified as murder, such deaths contribute to the homicide rate. The availability of handguns in homes and on the police provides criminals, who cannot legally purchase handguns, a source of weapons.[14] Whenever the police make an arrest there is the possibility that their handguns may be snatched from their holsters; and being shot without warning is a constant possibility.

The dilemma to citizens and police: they feel they must arm themselves, as well as devise other defensive measures, in order to avoid becoming victims, yet the possession of firearms is apt to involve them in self-defense homicides. And, believing that their personal survival may depend upon being armed, neither gun owners nor police are likely to consider seriously legal restrictions.

The dilemma of disarming emerges as a central issue both in the study of warfare and in the study of gun usage. Four striking parallels emerge: (1) The need for self-preservation compels nations to build military organizations and citizens to purchase guns (and police to carry handguns). Not to do so puts both nations and citizens in jeopardy of their lives. The only apparent alternative is for the nation to hide itself (an impossibility) or the citizen to move to a less threatening neighborhood (an impossibility if he does not have the financial means). (2) The possession of arms, intended for self-defense, is likely to involve the nation in war and the citizen and police in shootings. On the other hand, nations may build military organizations in order to go to war and criminals may steal guns (or obtain them from other criminals) in order to commit armed robbery. (3) The possession of arms may provoke an attack. The armed forces of a militarily strong nation may become the target of a "preemptive attack." Homes may be robbed and policemen may be assaulted for their weapons. (4) Disarmament proposals and gun control legislation, while aimed at reducing levels of violent conflict between and within nations, are strongly resisted by both nations and citizens who feel the need for self-defense. When the proposals are presented in a manner which would make them binding, as is the case with federal gun control legislation in the United States, well-financed organized resistance emerges. Disarmament and gun control are viewed by those who are to be disarmed as a threat to their safety. Moreover, it appears that the proponents of such proposals and legislation often exclude themselves from the group to be disarmed or prevented from arming. For example, at the international level, proposals to prevent the proliferation of nuclear weapons are sponsored in part by nations possessing nuclear power; at the national level, legislation to control handguns is backed by politicians who have private or government bodyguards.[15]

I believe there is a solution to the dilemma, both as it pertains to well-armed nations and to citizens within nations. The solution takes a slightly different form, depending upon whether the focus is upon nations or upon citizens, but the reasoning is the same. The solution is to be well prepared, but not so well prepared that it provokes potential adversaries.

For the individual the safest posture to take is to be well protected, but not to appear overly so. The open carrying of firearms and the use of security measures may suggest to criminals that the individual is carrying large sums of money or that his home contains objects of great value, such as silver, coins, or firearms. In order to prevent the criminal from imagining, correctly or incorrectly, that valuables are being protected, firearms should be carried concealed and the features of security systems should not be obvious.[16] The first line of defense is to avoid becoming a target of an attack, but if an attack comes, the individual needs appropriate defensive measures as outlined earlier. This would, when deemed necessary, include the carrying of firearms.[17]

For nations the safest posture to take is probably to be nearly as strong as the potential aggressor and to be perceived that way. Perception is all important. If one is weak, it is desirable to be perceived as strong; but if one is very strong, it may be desirable to be perceived as slightly less strong. The latter statement is contrary to deterrence theory. The purpose in appearing not too strong is to avoid provoking the potential adversary into an attack. The appearance of overwhelmingly superior strength invites preemptive attack. It would be better not to advertize such superiority. This military posture is likely, or so I hope, to create in the minds of the political and military leaders of the other nation the belief that they could win. However, they will probably not attack for two reasons: (1) The leaders do not fear an attack — they perceive their potential adversary as not strong enough militarily to attack and win; and (2) The leaders realize that victory, which they probably could achieve, would be gained only at great expense to their military forces. Indeed, this latter situation could leave them vulnerable to attack form other well-armed nations.[18]

The diagram on the following page illustrates what I believe is the preferable level of military preparedness. The preferred level of military preparedness for Nation A is marked by two arrows. It falls just below the level of military preparedness of Nation B.

If one or more nations were to adopt the above solution (I wish I had a fine-sounding term for it), several beneficial results would take place. First, the nation with the strongest military organization would no longer need to continue defense spending. If this occurred,

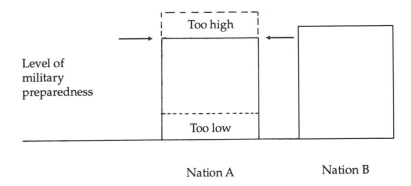

Nation A   Nation B

there would be no arms race. That alone would contribute to a lessening of the possibility of war. Second, if the leaders of the strongest nation came to believe that their high level of military preparedness might provoke other nations into attacking them, they might subscribe to the solution. The effect of this would be that they would reduce the size and strength of their military organizations. Such an act would create deescalation, or an arms race in reverse. Third, arms reduction talks would no longer need to be a competition in which each negotiator tries to get the "best deal," that is, tries to get the other to give up more in the way of armaments than he himself gives up. Ideally, negotiators would compete to see who could give up the most in military preparedness.

NOTES

I am indebted to Barton Brown, Barbara Howe, Charlotte Swanson Otterbein, and A. T. Steegmann for helpful comments and criticism on this essay. A shorter version of this chapter appeared in the *Newsletter of the Association for Political and Legal Anthropology* 4(2):7–10 (October 1980).

1. Shaw (1985) states: "The future looks bleak, if only because the nuclear powers are embroiled in the advanced stages of yet another classical arms race. In keeping with the most widely used arms race model, the 'Richardson model,' there is every reason to anticipate the outbreak of the Third World War because we are now entering a critical final stage called 'fatigue'... Crucial features of this stage are that (1) the nations involved in the arms race are approaching a position in which one is

not clearly superior to the other, (2) the nations involved begin to exhaust their resources to maintain their military power balance, and (3) awareness of this exhaustion says, in effect, 'it may be better to attack now while there is still a chance of winning.' In other words, the USSR and the U.S. threatening parity in military power, with speculation that the USSR, if not the U.S. is in a state of exhaustion due to domestic economic troubles, and with the U.S. announcing plans for a massive military buildup by 1987 war might well break out soon" (pp. 159, 177).

2. Although it is obvious that President Harry S. Truman cannot be accused of starting World War II, he became an enthusiastic proponent of the atomic bomb when he learned of its first successful detonation. It gave him increased confidence in negotiating with the Soviets and an opportunity to take revenge on the Japanese (Wyden 1984, pp. 223–226). When the first atomic bomb was dropped on Hiroshima, President Truman exclaimed, "This is the greatest thing in history" (Truman 1955, p. 421).

3. Even articles that argue — as well as demonstrate — that some United States policy makers hope to outspend the Soviets, thereby forcing them to continue massive spending that will eventually break them, are provocative. An example of such an article is one by N. Lemann in the October 1984 issue of *The Atlantic*.

4. *The United Nations Disarmament Yearbook* for 1983 states that "no objective observer of the international stage can help but be struck by ... the apparent contradiction between the quest of States for international security and well-being and their reluctance to promote those purposes by restricting their armaments" (Department for Disarmament Affairs 1984, p. 1). I do not see it as a "contradiction," but as a dilemma, a dilemma which I attempt to explain in this chapter.

5. Two other comparative studies of deterrence, one a cross-cultural study (Naroll 1966) and the other a cross-historical study (Naroll, Bullough, and Naroll 1974) obtained the same result.

6. At the time I had no guns hanging on the wall. Today I have three BB guns on a gun rack that belonged to my father.

7. This is my term for such elaborate defensive measures. Domestic forts could be another term. Fortress architecture contrasts with a concept known as defensible space (Newman 1972).

8. Criminal law, with its penal sanctions (including incarceration and capital punishment), is another measure developed by all political communities for coping with those who steal and kill (Otterbein 1986).

9. A recent review of the literature by Wright, Rossi, and Daly (1983, pp. 273–308) argues that evidence that gun control will reduce violent crime is not conclusive.

10. From a bumper sticker in the author's collection of progun, antigun memorabilia.

11. In the Niagara Frontier region (Erie and Niagara Counties of Western New York) where I live, holders of pistol permits usually first purchase a handgun for hunting or target shooting. A subsequent purchase is likely to be a small, concealable pistol; in New York State handguns, if carried on one's person, must be carried concealed.

12. For the nineteenth century development of this practice in the United States see Kennett and Anderson (1975, pp. 148–151). They describe how urban police were forced to carry weapons for self-defense.

13. For many years the *American Rifleman* has published a one-page feature titled "The Armed Citizen." Each month the feature reprints excerpts from approximately ten to twenty news reports that show how armed citizens have defended themselves with firearms. Often the assailant is killed. From 2 to 6 percent of American adults have actually fired a weapon in self-defense (Wright, Rossi, and Daly 1983, pp. 145, 148).

14. It is estimated that as many as 275,000 handguns are stolen annually in the United States from legitimate handgun owners. Most thefts would, however, be from homes (Wright, Rossi, and Daly 1983, pp. 177–188).

15. On January 9, 1986, Senator Edward Kennedy's private bodyguard was arrested at the Senate Office Building for carrying two submachine guns and a pistol. The bodyguard was charged with three counts of District of Columbia gun law violations. Senator Kennedy has been an advocate of gun control legislation (*American Rifleman* March 1986, p. 40).

16. The trend in the installation of burglar alarm systems is toward concealing wires, contacts, bells or sirens, and control panels. Over ten years ago the display of these items was thought to have a deterrent effect. Today installers of alarm systems do not want potential burglars to know the extent and nature of the system; if the burglar has this information, it is easier for him to defeat the alarm system.

17. Christians should not find this position unacceptable. Even Jesus's disciples, when accompanying him, carried weapons: "[Jesus said] ... and he that hath no sword, let him sell his garment, and buy one... And they said, Lord, behold, here are two swords. And he said unto them, It is enough" (St. Luke 22:36, 38, King James Version).

18. A similar proposal, which focuses solely upon the nuclear confrontation between the United States and the Soviet Union, has been advanced by Narveson (1985, pp. 226–227): "My proposal, in effect, is that it [a state] make clear its defensive stance by limiting itself to a force that could not plausibly be employed to serve basically aggressive purposes. My proposal calls for A opposing B with a force that is clearly quantitatively inferior to that of B by any reasonable measure...

What is the rationale for the present proposal? Two different considerations converge to support it. In the first place, it is assumed that nothing is really lost in the way of defensive security by inferiority as compared with parity or even superiority. Thus the state following my policy will not expose itself to greater risk than is faced by anyone exposed to attack by nuclear missiles. And in the second, this stance offers a clear inducement to the opponent to reduce, and certainly not to increase, his arms establishment."

REFERENCES

Beer, Francis A. (1981). *Peace Against War*. San Francisco: W. H. Freeman and Company.

Clark, Ramsey (1970). *Crime in America: Observations on Its Nature, Causes, Prevention and Control*. New York: Simon and Schuster.

Department for Disarmament Affairs (1984). *The United Nations Disarmament Yearbook*, Vol. 8: *1983*. New York: United Nations Press.

Davis, James A., Tom W. Smith, and C. Bruce Stephenson (1981). *General Social Survey Cumulative File, 1972–80*, James A. Davis, Principal Investigator. IGPSR ed. Ann Arbor, MI: Inter-University Consortium for Political and Social Research.

Fallows, James (1984). "What Good is Arms Control?" *The Atlantic* 244(6):136–140.

Kennett, Lee and James LaVerne Anderson (1975). *The Gun in America: The Origins of a National Dilemma*. Westport, CT: Greenwood Press.

Lemann, Nicholas (1984). "Peacetime War." *The Atlantic* 254(4):71–94.

Lindgren, James (1981). "Organizational and Other Constraints on Controlling the Use of Deadly Force by Police." *Annals of the American Academy of Political and Social Science* 455:110–119.

Lizotte, A. J. and D. J. Bordua (1980). "Firearms Ownership for Sport and Protection." *American Sociological Review* 45:229–244.

Mearsheimer, John J. (1983). *Conventional Deterrence*. Ithaca: Cornell University Press.

Myrdal, Alva (1982). *The Game of Disarmament: How the United States and Russia Run the Arms Race* (revised and updated edition). New York: Pantheon Books.

Naroll, Raoul (1966). "Does Military Deterrence Deter?" *Transaction* 3:14–20. Reprinted in *Sociological Realities*, eds. I. L. Horowitz and Mary Strong. New York: Harper & Row, pp. 402–408, 1971.

Naroll, Raoul, Vern L. Bullough, and Frada Naroll (1974). *Military Deterrence in History: A Pilot Cross-Historical Survey*. Albany: State University of New York Press.

Narveson, Jan (1985). "Getting on the Road to Peace: A Modest Proposal." in: *Nuclear Deterrence: Ethics and Strategy*, eds. Russell Hardin, John J. Mearsheimer, Gerald Dworkin, and Robert E. Goodin. Chicago: University of Chicago Press.

National Rifle Association (1986). "'Glitch' in D.C. Gun Law Snares Kennedy Bodyguard." *American Rifleman* (NRA Official Journal) 134(3):40.

Newton, George D., and Zimring, Franklin E. (1969). *Firearms and Violence in American Life: A Staff Report to the National Commission on the Causes and Prevention of Violence*. Washington, DC: US Government Printing Office.

Newman, Oscar (1972). *Defensible Space: People and Design in the Violent City*. New York: Macmillan.

Otterbein, Keith F. (1973). "The Anthropology of War." in: *Handbook of Social and Cultural Anthropology*. ed. John J. Honigmann. New York: Rand McNally and Company, pp. 923–958.

_____ (1985). *The Evolution of War: A Cross-Cultural Study*. New Haven: Human Relations Area Files Press (originally published 1970).

_____ (1986). The Ultimate Coercive Sanction: A Cross-Cultural Study of Capital Punishment. New Haven: Human Relations Area Files Press.

Richardson, Lewis F. (1960). *Arms and Insecurity*. London: Stevens and Sons.

St. Luke (1614). "The Gospel According to St. Luke." in: *Holy Bible* (King James Version).

Schell, Jonathan (1984). "Reflections: The Abolition. I — Defining the Great Predicament. II — A Deliberate Policy." *The New Yorker*, January 2, pp. 36–75; January 9, pp. 43–94.

Shaw, R. Paul (1985). "Humanity's Propensity for Warfare: A Sociobiological Perspective." *Canadian Review of Sociology and Anthropology* 22:158–183.

Truman, Harry S. (1955). *Memoirs by Harry S. Truman: Year of Decisions*, Vol. 1. Garden City: Doubleday and Company, Inc.

Wright, James D., Peter H. Rossi, and Kathleen Daly (1983). *Under the Gun: Weapons, Crime, and Violence in America*. New York: Aldine Publishing Company.

Wyden, Peter (1984). *Day One: Before Hiroshima and After*. New York: Simon and Schuster.

Chapter
THIRTEEN

A Unified Theory of Feuding and Warfare

The following "unified theory of feuding and warfare" attempts to combine various empirical results and theoretical approaches into a comprehensive scheme (see Fig. 1). Two causal chains are developed and related to each other through the "goals of war" approach developed in *The Evolution of War* (1970, pp. 4–5; see also Otterbein 1973, pp. 935–938). The unified theory is one way of schematically showing the interrelationships among several of the major findings concerning the causes of warfare. Specifically, it attempts to reconcile the structural and ecological approaches, two approaches that have sometimes been treated as rival alternatives. A recent study of South American aboriginal warfare attempts to do

Figure 1. A unified theory of feuding and warfare.

this for a single region (Ferguson 1988). Here the attempt is to develop a scheme that can be applied to any region.

The appropriate starting point for the first causal chain is with fraternal interest groups. The great majority of nonliterate peoples known to anthropologists are patrilocal (70 percent); these societies are usually also patrilineal and polygynous (Divale 1983, pp. 13–14). Such societies have fraternal interest groups, which I consider to be the basic cause of feuding and internal war.[1] Thus, a social structure characterized by fraternal interest groups, feuding, and internal war is a "natural system," natural in the sense that it has its roots in our primate past (Service 1962, pp. 107–108). Service argues that the patrilocal band is found in all major physical environments — "the patrilocal band is early; it seems almost an inevitable kind of or- ganization" (p. 108). This system is found in many different physical environments and with many different subsistence technologies. However, it is mostly likely to be found in societies with one resource procurement strategy — or at most two or three strategies.[2] When a single subsistence resource prevails in a region, the culturally similar kinship groups and political communities compete for the resource.

That resource — whether it be hunting territories, fishing sites, agricultural land, or herd animals — becomes a goal of war. If the warring fraternal interest groups are militarily equipped in the same way — as they are likely to be, since they are from the same culture — then the warriors of the larger groups will be victorious. The winner gains access to the single, scarce resource that is the goal of the warfare (Vayda 1974, 1976).[3]

Differential shortages within a region may be the precipitating reason for a larger group to attack a smaller one. Shortages can arise in two ways. First, natural disasters can cause immediate shortages in some areas of a region. A group with shortages will consider attacking other groups that did not suffer severe shortages. If the group has a sufficient number of warriors, it will attack. A recent study by Ember and Ember (1992) found that disasters caused by weather or pests are associated with frequent feuding and internal war. Second, differential population growth of the groups in a region can also lead to shortages for the groups that have experienced the greatest growth. Again, the larger group will attack.[4] If a group is successful, resources will be reallocated in its favor (Boehm 1984, pp. 175–227). In both situations, if the larger group achieves victory, resource reallocation will occur. The formation of alliances between political communities is one means by which smaller groups can prevent defeat by larger groups (Otterbein 1985, pp. xx–xxi). Real-location of scarce resources to the larger victorious groups, be they fraternal interest groups, political communities, or alliances, is a mode of ecological adaptation for the culture that inhabits the region.

The second causal chain begins with a high level of military sophistication. Through centuries of feuding and internal war, the warriors of a culture will develop skill in conducting raids and battles. Means of socializing young males into the military organizations will be refined (Otterbein 1989). If the skills that are developed are combined with the invention or introduction to the region of new weapons and other efficient military practices, the military sophistication of the organizations will increase. The military personnel will become professionals as the society increases in population (Carter 1977). With an increase in the military sophistication of some of the political communities within the region, a process may be set in motion whereby the superior political communities destroy the weaker, thus reducing the number of political communities within the region. If the conditions are present for centralization to occur (Otterbein 1985, pp. xxiii–xxiv), the political communities with the greater military sophistication will conquer the others, not just destroy them, further reducing the number of political communities (Carneiro 1978). These several processes are illustrated by the evolution of Zulu warfare (Otterbein 1967): new weapons are invented and military practices increase in efficiency; warriors become professional military personnel; and there is a reduction of the number of political communities within a region (Otterbein 1970, pp. 45–46, 82).

Once the military organizations rise to a level of military sophistication that is higher than that of the military organizations of neighboring political communities in other cultures, they are likely to attack those culturally different political communities, thus engaging in offensive external war. This military preparedness theory is supported by the finding that high military sophistication is related to offensive external war (Otterbein 1970, pp. 87–89). Engagement in war with an enemy in a different region may lead to new goals of war. If the military organizations are now professional, their major reasons for going to war are likely to be plunder and subjugation (Otterbein 1989, p. 161). The reasons for internal war may continue — defense, revenge, trophies/honors, and land.) If military organizations have attacked other military organizations that are militarily less efficient, they are likely to be successful. Not only will their goals of war be achieved but their political communities will probably expand territorially, even if land was not a goal of war. High military sophistication scale scores are related to territorial expansion (Otterbein 1970, pp. 92–108). Such expansion will permit population growth. Thus, the possession of efficient military organizations has a survival value for the victorious political communities within the culture; the goals of war are obtained, territorial size enlarges, and the population increases.

ACKNOWLEDGMENT

My wife, Charlotte Swanson Otterbein, has collaborated with me on much of the research leading to this statement. She has also done the typing and editing of the manuscript.

NOTES

1. Both feuding and internal war are forms of armed combat; feuding occurs within a political community, internal war between culturally similar political communities (Otterbein 1977, pp. 137–148).

2. A recent study by Fleising and Goldenberg (1987) found that patrilocal societies characteristically have only one, two, or three subsistence modes. This same study, through cross-cultural research, also demonstrates that sociological variables (e.g., fraternal interest groups) provide a better explanation for feuding than do ecological variables.

3. Vayda has argued that "proximate causes" (e.g., revenge for murder) may lead to an initial phase of war, consisting of raids or battles. He states further that the existence of "perturbations" (i.e., disparities) is not necessarily the cause of war, but that if warfare escalates to a final phase, land redistribution will counteract the perturbations.

4. Ember (1982) has also noted that in highland New Guinea, a region characterized by fraternal interest groups, victorious groups are likely to occupy vacated land after a war among peoples in areas of high population density (where, presumably, resources are scarce).

REFERENCES

Boehm, Christopher (1984). *Blood Revenge: The Anthropology of Feuding in Montenegro and Other Tribal Societies.* Lawrence: University Press of Kansas.

Carneiro, Robert L. (1978). "Political Expansion as an Expression of the Principle of Competitive Exclusion." in: *Origins of the State: The Anthropology of Political Evolution.* eds. Ronald Cohen and Elman R. Service. Philadelphia: Institute for the Study of Human Issues.

Carter Jr., Harold (1977). Military Organization as a Response to Residence and Size of Population: A Cross-Cultural Study. *Behavior Science Research* 12:271–290.

Divale, William T. (1983). *Matrilocal Residence in Pre-Literate Society.* Ann Arbor: UMI Research Press.

Ember, Carol. R., and Melvin Ember (1992). "Resource Unpredictability, Mistrust, and War: A Cross-Cultural Study." *Journal of Conflict Resolution* 36:242–262.

Ember, Melvin (1982). "Statistical Evidence for an Ecological Explanation of Warfare." *American Anthropologist* 84:645–649.

Ferguson, R. Brian (1988). "War and the Sexes in Amazonia." in: *Dialectics and Gender: Anthropological Approaches*, eds. Richard R. Randolph, David M. Schneider, and May N. Diaz, Boulder, CO: Westview Press, pp. 136–154.

Fleising, Usher, and Sheldon Goldenberg (1987). "Ecology, Social Structure, and Blood Feud." *Behavior Science Research* 21:160–181.

Otterbein, Keith F. (1967). "The Evolution of Zulu Warfare." in: *Law and Warfare*, ed. Paul Bohannan. Garden City: Natural History Press, pp. 351–357.

_____ (1970). *The Evolution of War.* New Haven: Human Relations Area Files Press.

_____ (1973). "The Anthropology of War." in: *Handbook of Social and Cultural Anthropology.* ed. John J. Honigmann. New York: Rand McNally and Company, pp. 923–958.

_____ (1977). *Comparative Cultural Analysis: An Introduction to Anthropology,* 2nd ed. New York: Holt, Rinehart & Winston.

_____ (1985). *The Evolution of War,* 2nd ed. New Haven: Human Relations Area Files Press.

_____ (1989). "Socialization for War." in: *The Evolution of War,* 3rd ed. New Haven: Human Relations Area Files Press, pp. 156–166.

Service, Elman (1962). *Primitive Social Organization: An Evolutionary Perspective.* New York: Random House.

Vayda, Andrew P. (1974). "Warfare in Ecological Perspective." *Annual Review of Ecology and Systematics* 5:183–198.

_____ (1976). *War in Ecological Perspective: Persistence, Change, and Adaptive Processes in Three Oceanian Societies.* New York: Plenum Press.

Index

197; ownership (USA), 182, 185, 186, 191; and police, 191; and self-preservation, 181–182

Guns on the Early Frontiers (Russell), 5

H

Haider, S., 122

Hallpike, C. R., 172

Handbook of Social and Cultural Anthropology, xxix, 172

Harkins, Arthur 31

Harris, Marvin, 162–163, 173, 174–175

Hawaiians, 41, 51, 54, 56, 57, 59, 62, 65, 66, 67, 99

headhunting, 136, 137

Heidenreich, Conrad, 10

Higi, xxiv, xxvi–xxvii, xxviii; and battle, 90–93; and capital punishment, xxix, 149–150; and council, 95; and duels, 80–81; and external conflict, 89–93; and feuding, 84, 94, 149–150; and internal conflict, 80–84; and maps, 77, 79; and military organization, 86–88; and patrilocal residence, 78; and rape, 123; and secondary marriage, 79, 84–86; social organization of, 94; and staff fights, 81–84, 94–95; and tactics, 82–83, 91–92; and weapons, 86–88; *see also* Mwecika Higi

Hobhouse, Leonard T., 35

Hoebel, E. Adamson, 142, 143, 163

homicide, 80, 82, 83, 142, 182

Honigmann, John J., xxix, 163, 172

Howe, Barbara, 189

Human Relation Area Files (HRAF), 120, 122

Hunt, George T., 2, 10

Huron, xxv, 4, 156; and casualties, 14, 17–18; and conflict with Iroquois (1649), 9, 11–21; defeat of, 18–19; and military organization, 18–19; and political leaders, 156; and reasons for combat, 93; and social organization, 156; and tactics, 2–5, 6, 11–21

Huronia (Heidenreich), 10

I

Iban, 99

Ifugao, 99

Ila, 41, 51, 54, 56, 57, 59, 62, 65, 66, 67, 99

Inca, 50

Ingassana, 41, 51, 56, 57, 59, 62, 65, 66, 67, 99

initiation of war, 42, 48

innate aggression, cause of war, 165

intergroup relations approach: feuding and warfare, xix–xx, xxviii

internal war, xv, 53–54, 174; defined, 37, 100, 148, 161, 198; and armed combat, 98, 101, 104–109; and culturally similar political communities, 198; and external war, 80–84; and fraternal interest groups, 55, 104, 108, 109; and homicide, 80; and Higi, 80–84; and land, 80; and military sophistication, 55, 58; and natural system, 196; and patrilocal residence, 103, 104, 108; and political centralization, 55; and political systems, 105; and

Yukaghir, 41, 51, 56, 57, 59, 62, 65, 66, 67, 99

Z

Zulu, xxii; army's size, 28; and casualties, 28, 53; and evolution of warfare, xxv–xxvi, 198; and tactics, 30; and territory's size, 28; and types of wars, 29–31; and weapons, 25–30; *see also* Shaka Zulu

Zwide, 27